CONTRACT FARMING
IN INDIA

CONTRACT FARMING
IN INDIA

Dr. V.B. Khandare
N.V. Kole

ABD PUBLISHERS
Jaipur ■ New Delhi

ABD PUBLISHERS

Regd. Off. "Bony Residency", Gate No. 2
Opp. Tilak Public School, Vishweswariya Nagar,
Gopalpura Road, Jaipur - 302018, India
Ph: 0141 - 2761280, Telefax: 2761381
Email: abdpublishersjpr@gmail.com

Delhi Office: 102, 1st Floor, Satyam House,
4327/3, Ansari Road, Darya Ganj,
New Delhi - 110002, India
Ph: 011-45652440

visit us: www.oxfordbookcompany.com

Distributed By
KEYA INTERNATIONAL PRESS LLP
E-mail: keyainternationalpressllp@gmail.com

Published in India, 2025

ISBN: 9788183764384

Price : ₹1995/-

Typeset by Shivangi Computer, Jaipur

Printed and bound in India by Thomson Press Ltd.,
New Delhi

CONTENTS

PREFACE

The important of agriculture in the economic development of any country rich or poor, is borne but by the fact that it is the primary sector of the economy which provides the basic ingredients necessary for the existence of mankind and also provides most of the raw materials which when transformed in to finished product serve as basic necessities of the human race. In a preponderantly agrarian economy, agriculture plays a most strategic role from several points of view. At a minimum farm production must be increased rapidly enough to keep pace with population growth however, in a speedily industrializing economy this is not enough. Industrialization necessarily brings with it urbanization and a rapid expansion of the industrial labour force. This may be than expected to bring with it a rising per capita demand for food, based on higher urban incomes.

In an age of market liberalization, globalization and expanding agribusiness, there is a danger that small farmer will find difficulty in fully participating in the market economy. In many countries such farmers could become increasingly necessary for a profitable operation. A consequence of this will be a continuation of the drift of population to urban areas that is being witnessed almost everywhere.

Contract farming system has old historical resonances, such as the infamous contracts enforced by indigo planters in eastern India during the early colonial period. But recent pattern of contract farming has been developed especially in the United States where corporate penetration of agriculture is probably the most advanced. Agricultural trade globally is dominated by transnational corporations like Cargill, Archer Daniels Midland

and Monsanto, which are increasingly involved at each stage of the agriculture system. These corporations achieve domination over the market through a combination of horizontal and vertical integration. This has increased the margins for the procuring and processing firms while at the same time reducing farm incomes and increasing the prices for the consumers. This explains the rising spread between retail prices and the prices received by farmers the farmers really gain from agribusinesses which provide them huge and increased profits.

The main focus of the study is on evaluating the impact of contract farming on agricultural production. It also studies the performance of contract farming in India and Maharashtra, the cropping pattern of selected farmers participated in contract farming, impact of contract farming on economic development of farmers, effect of contract farming on agricultural production of selected farmers and to study the changes in processing industries due to contract farming.

Many project evaluation type studies helped contracting farmers become better farmers, gave more reliable income generated in employment especially for women, and provided new skills of farming, this way with patron client relationship between large and small producers. So the present topic is chosen to study the helpfulness of contract farming is solving the problem of input supplies, marketing of produce income increasing product price etc. This book has discussed some important policy implications.

This work has been completed at Shri Asaramji Bhandwaldar Arts, Commerce and Science College, Deogaon (R.) Dist. Aurangabad. I am thankful to Dr. Prakash Bhandwaldar, President Shri Ganesh Education Society, Shri Karbhari Bhandwadar, Secretary, Shri Ganesh Education Society, Deogaon (R.). I also thank to Principal, Dr. U. B. Pathre, Librarian, S.P. Chavan, Shri Asaramji Bhandwaldar College, Deogaon (R.). I am also thankful to Dr. V.B. Bhise, Professor, Department of Economics, Dr. Babasaheb Ambedkar Marathwada University, Aurangabad.

Dr. V.B. Khandare

N.V. Kole

1

INTRODUCTION

1.1 Introduction

The words agricultural economics are made up of words, vis., agriculture and economics. Before define agricultural economics as whole, it would be appropriate to define agriculture and economics separately. The word agriculture, since long, has been associated with the industry of basic food production, known as farming. Agriculture and farming were synonymous till farming was not commercialized and was done more or less on a subsistence basis. But after the commercialization of the agricultural sector, production of food and fiber (farming) has become only one part of scientific agriculture. Modern agriculture has much wider scope today and it includes the farm supply industries as well as the product processing industries and distribution industries. The industries closely related to farming are known as agriculturally related industries or agri-businesses. The scope of modern agriculture has been depicted in Fig. No. 1.1.

Agriculture thus, may be defined as the production, processing, marketing and distribution of crops and livestock. These four activities were previously all farm centred. However, with improvement in technology, transport and communication had been developed and specialized of labour.

Some of these activities have moved away from farm into certain strategic control point. Modern agriculture also includes the farm supporting as well as product processing and distribution industries.

Economics, on the other hand is the science of analysing the use of limited resources to achieve desired ends. It is a social science which studies now man satisfies wants through the allocation of scarce resources. The English word 'Economics' is derived from the Greek word 'Oekonomous' which means 'housekeeping' and one of the tasks of the housewife is of making most effective use of the resources that are available. Prof. Lionel Robbins has defined economics as "the science which studies human behavior as a relationship between ends and scarce means which have alternative uses." [1]

Fig. No. 1.1

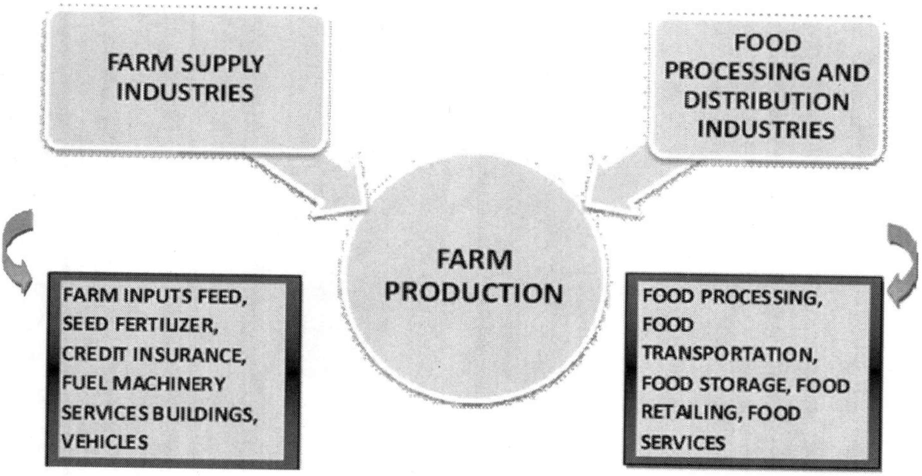

1.2 Agricultural Economics

In a very simple language agricultural economics may be defined as an applied phase of economics in which attention is given to all aspects of problems related to agriculture. It helps the farmer in deciding about what kind of food should be product, which crop should be raised to maximize his profits and at what level should be price his product. As such, it is a social science concerned with the allocation of scarce resources among the uses associated with producing processing and consuming the farm product,

According to Prof. Gray, "Agriculture economics may be defined as the science in which the principles and methods of economics are applied to the conditions of agricultural industry."

According to A.W. Ash by, "agricultural economics is an applied science that is, it is a methodical pursuit of knowledge of economics process and organization in agricultural and of their results, for the purpose of stabilizing, adopting or modifying it when necessary, of changing their results."

In short we can define agricultural economics as an applied science which is mainly concerned with economic problems that are associated with farmer's effort to make a living. Their problems as we know are numerous and varied in character but can be grouped under three main heads: i) Production ii) Marketing and iii) Financing. Thus, agricultural economics is concerned with the evolving of appropriate principles that govern the amount of land, labour and capital, which a farmer should use to farm most efficiently agricultural economics is equally concerned with the forces that affect the prices of the things he buys sells or in other words, the relation between agriculture and the rest of the economy.[2]

1.3 Role of Agriculture in Economic Development

The importantance of agriculture in the economic development of any country rich or poor, is borne out by the fact that it is the primary sector of the economy which provides the basic ingredients necessary for the existence of mankind and also provides most of the raw materials which when transformed into finished product serve as basic necessities of the human race. In a preponderantly agrarian economy, agriculture plays a most strategic role from several points of view. At a minimum farm production must be increased rapidly enough to keep pace with population growth. However, in a speedily industrializing economy this is not enough. Industrialization necessarily brings with it urbanization and a rapid expansion of the industrial labour force. This may be than expected to bring with it a rising per capita demand for food, based on higher urban incomes.

In addition to supplying food, agriculture must provide many of the raw materials for industry. Therefore, the pace of advance in a wide range of consumer goods manufactures will be eventually affected by the pace of agricultural development.

In addition, agriculture must generate export surpluses in order to earn the foreign exchange with which to finance the import of capital goods and certain kinds of industrial raw materials.

However agriculture is not only a supplier of goods for domestic and export need but is also a supplier of production factor such as capital and labour. A rapidly expanding industrial sector necessarily drowse some of its labour force from the rural areas. Moreover, in one form agriculture is called upon to save and finance a significant part of the investment for an expansion of industrial part, transport and other sector as well.

The ideas which called the intellectual and emotional basis of agricultural fundamentalism have deep roots in human history. For a mankind throughout most of its existence has been either postural or earning livelihood directly from early. The shift to industrialism and urban living is of recent origin almost a current development when consider in the current historical respective.

1.4 Role of Agriculture in India

Agriculture is the backbone of Indian economic. More than 65 per cent of the population is dependent on agriculture.

Indian farm is distinct from other nation's farm but it cannot provide the grains as per the need of population. The performance of the agricultural sector influences the growth of Indian economy. Agriculture (including allied activities) accounted for 14.4 per cent of the Gross Domestic Product (GDP at constant 2004-05 base year prices) in 2010-11 as compared to 16.4 per cent in 2007-08. Notwithstanding the fact that the share of this sector in GDP has been declining over the years. Its role remains critical as it accountance for about 57 per cent of the employment in the country. Apart from being the provider of food and fodder, its important also stems from the raw materials that it provides to industry. The prosperity of the rural economy is wholly dependent on agriculture. Agriculture sector contributed 10.59 per cent of national exports in 2010-11.The rural sector (including agriculture) is being increasingly seen as potential source of domestic; a reorganization, that is shaping. The marketing strategy of entrepreneurs wishing to has been widening demand for goods and services.

Further, good crops implying large purchasing power with the farmers lead to greater demand for manufactures and therefore better prices. In other words prosperity of the farmers is also the prosperity of industries likewise bad crops lead to a depression in business. Generally, it is failure in the agriculture that has lead to failure of economic planning in a particular periods.[3]

Agricultural growth has direct impact on poverty eradication. It is also an important factor in containing inflation arising agricultural wages and for employing generation. It is a therefore clear that agriculture had been the backbone of the Indian economy. The rural area is the biggest market for low priced and middle priced consumer goods, including consumer durables. Besides, rural domestic saving is an important source of resource mobilization.

According to Datt and Sundram, only change in the agriculture sector positive or negative have been a multiplier on the entire economy since 2002-03. Indian agricultural sector is almost since going through various crises such as huge food grain surplus wiped out large import of wheat benign planned and farmer suicides more frequent all over the country. A nation of more than a billion people cannot be dependent on imports for basic items like food grains and edible oils. The Tenth Plan asserts emphatically that the agricultural sector acts as a bulwark in maintaining food security and in the process national security as well.

Besides, the allied sector like horticulture, animal husbandry dairy and fisheries have the important roles in improving the overall economic conditions and health and nutrition of the rural masses. To maintain the ecological balance, there is need for sustainable and balanced development of both the agriculture and the allied sector. To conclude the Indian economic development it occupies a central place in the national economy.[4]

1.5 Types and System of Farming in Agriculture

The classification of farming is based on the similarity in a) crops and livestock rising and (b) Economic and social functioning. Types of farming refer to the nature and degree of product or a combination of product being produced at the farm and methods and practices adopted for production. Systems of farming generally concerned with the organizational set up under which the farm is being run. It mainly involves the questions like who is the owner of land, whether the resources are pooled or used individually and who makes the managerial decisions.[5]

1.5.1 Types of farming

In India farming is classified into the following five types based on the enterprises and income.[6]

1. Specialized farming
2. Diversified farming
3. Mixed farming

4. Dry and Irrigated farming
5. Ranching farming

1.5.2 Systems of farming

The term system of farming is generally referred to the methods of agriculture. Thus the system of farming which are based on different organizational set up (on the basis of economic and social functioning), may be classified into six broad categories.[7]

1. Peasant farming
2. State farming
3. Capitalistic farming
4. Collective farming
5. Cooperative farming
6. Contract farming

There are various problems in the above five farming systems. Contract farming is a suitable method because it helps in overcoming the problems in the existing farming systems in India. Contract farming helps small farmers to participate in the production of high value crops.

1.6 Contract Farming

In an age of market liberalization, globalization and expanding agribusiness, there is a danger that small farmer will find difficulty in fully participating in the market economy. In many countries such farmers could become increasingly necessary for a profitable operation. A consequence of this will be a continuation of the drift of population to urban areas that is being witnessed almost everywhere.

Attempts by governments and development agencies to arrest this drift have tended to emphasize the identification of 'income generation' activities for rural people. Unfortunately there is relatively little evidence that such attempts have borne fruit. This is largely because the necessary backward and forward market linkages are rarely in place .i.e. rural farmer and small scale entrepreneurs lack both reliable and cost-efficient inputs such as extension advice, mechanization services, seeds, fertilizers and credit, and guaranteed and profitable market for their output. Well organized contract farming does however, provides such linkages, and would appear to puffer an important way in which smaller producer can farm in a commercial manner. Similarly, it also provides investors with the opportunity to guarantee a reliable source of supply from the perspectives of both quality and quantity. In the era of globalization the concept of contract farming is an effective way to coordinate and promote production and marketing in agriculture.[8]

1.7 Definition of Contract Farming

Contract farming facilitates farmers in getting inputs and technical advice on time and firms involved in contracts earn profit from, agriculture production either by lifting the production and supplying to the agro-processing companies or by exporting the product after processing by its own. In the first case the firms act as a facilitator alone but in the letter they enjoy the profits of exports.[9]

Various authors have tried to explain contract farming and they give their own definitions on various aspects and situations. According to Sukhpal Singh[10] "As a system for the production and supply of agricultural and horticultural produce by farmers / primary producers under advance contract, the essence of such arrangements being a commitment to provide agricultural commodity of a type, at a specified time, price, and in specified quantity to a known buyer."

According to Charles Raton and Andrew W. Shepherd[11], "An agreement between farmers and processing and/ or marketing firm for the production and supply of agricultural product under forward agreements frequently at predetermined prices; the agreements also invariably involve the purchaser in providing a degree of inputs and the provision of technical advice; the basis of such commodity in quantities and at quality standards determined by the purchaser and commitment on the company to support the farmer production and to purchase the commodity."

Ray[12] defines, "contract farming as those contractual arrangements between farmers and companies whether oral or written specifying one or more conditions of production and / or marketing of an agricultural product"

As per Nigel key and James MacDonald; [13]

(a) Agreement between farmers and the commodity buyer.

(b) Firms govern the terms under which product are transferred from the farm.

(c) Firms specify the date of delivery product price and required production practices.

The intensity of the contractual agreement varies according to the depth and complexity of the provision in each of the following three areas:

1. **Marketing Provision :** The grower and buyers agree to terms and conditions for the future sale and purchase of a crop or livestock product;
2. **Resources Provision :** In conjunction with the marketing arrangements the buyer agrees to supply selected inputs, including on land preparation and technical advice;
3. **Management Specifications:** The grower agrees to follow recommended production methods, inputs regimes, and cultivation and harvesting specifications.

With effective management, contract farming cab is a means to develop markets and to bring about the transfer of technical skills in a way that is profitable for both the sponsors and farmers. The approach is widely used, not only for tree and other cash crop but increasingly, for fruits and vegetables, poultry, pigs, dairy produce and even prawns and fish. Indeed, contract farming is characterized by its 'enormous diversity' not only with regard to the products contracted but also in relation to the many different ways in the contract farming system should be seen as a partnership between agribusiness and farmers. To be successful it requires a long term commitment from both parties. Exploitative arrangements by manager are likely to have only a limited duration and can jeopardize agribusiness investments. Similarly, farmers need to consider that honouring contractual arrangements is likely to be their long term benefit.

Fig. No. 1.2: A Contract Farming Framework

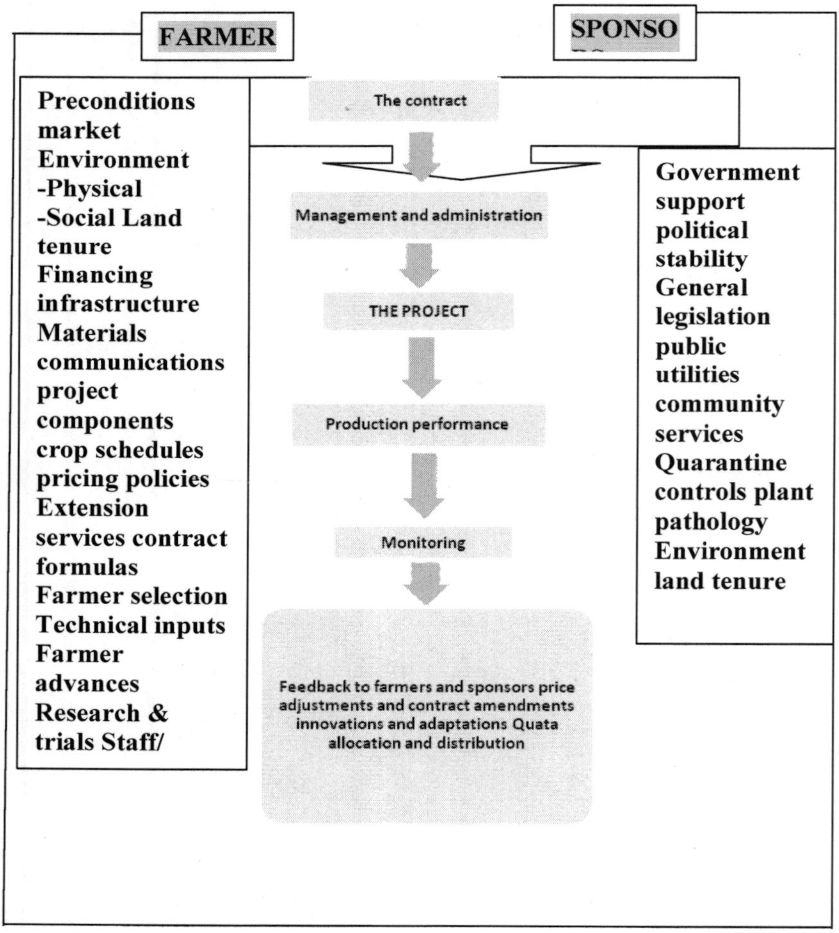

Source: Eaton and Shepherd (2001)

Contract farming is becoming an increasingly important aspect of agribusiness, whether the product are purchased by multinationals, smaller companies, government agencies, farmer co-operatives or individual entrepreneur.

1.8 Types and Models of Contract Farming

Multinational corporations, smaller private companies, parastatals, individual entrepreneurs and in some cases, farmer co-operatives can all act as sponsors and are also responsible for management of the venture.

Contract farming can be structured in a variety of ways depending on the crop, the objectives and resources of the sponsor and the experience of the farmers. Contracting out production is a commercial decision to facilitate on adequate supply within a designated period and at an economic price. Any crop or livestock product can theoretically be contracted out using any of the models; however certain product favour specific approaches .Various authors have tried to explain types and models of contract farming.

1.9 Joy Harwood[14]

Classified contracts into two forms, namely, production contracts and marketing contract. They discuss these forms of contracts in following words:-

1.9.1 Production Contracts

Firms have a huge say in production contracts by providing them more control over the production process. The processing firm specifies the quality standards and the technology to be used in the production process for getting desired quality the firm decides.This production contract is further classified as: i) Production management contract and ii) Resource providing contracts.

1.9.2 Marketing Contracts

Market specified contracts are the predetermined agreements prior to the harvest season or harvest of the produce. Generally such type of contract are signed in the initial stage of the crop i.e. seeding or planting with a binding that the farmer sells the produce to the firm in particular set of conditions like pricing quality and price. Here the buyer firm assures a market for the farmer produce. In such contracts the farmers controls over production process alone but the firm holds full control over all the marketing process.

1.10 T. P. Rajmanohar, K.S. Kumaravel[15]

Contracting arrangements broadly can also be classified into two groups according to nature of relationship between firm and a farmer – private or commercial contracts, and economic or out grower schemes.

1.10.1 Commercial or Private Contracts

Commercial or private contracts is some form of contractual arrangement either written or oral between a group of small scale farmers and an agribusiness partner in order to undergo commercial activities like purchasing, processing selling and marketing of the crop produced. It is a co-operative venture between the farmer-producer and private firms on commercial motives in order to market the firm so as to take advantage of private sector infrastructure delivery and service management's skills and the firm gets profits by procuring the farm produce in a specified quality and in a specified price.

1.10.2 Economic or out Grower Schemes

Outgrower schemes are those schemes that provide production and marketing services to farmers on their own land. Outgrower schemes generally cannot a government schemes with a public enterprise, purchasing crops from farmers, either on its own or as a joint venture with a private firm. When a firm, estate, or a factory established in a particular area and farmer of the vicinity grow crops on their land and sell to the factory for processing then this type is called Nucleus Estate out grower schemes.

1.11 Singh and Bhagat[16]

There are three types of contract farming arrangement emerging in the Indian agricultural scenario based on the nature of relationship between the farmer and the company. They explain these three types of contract farming as below:

1.11.1 Market Specification Contracts

Market specification contract is a pre-harvest agreement that binds the firm and the grower to particular set of conditions governing the sale of the crop. The conditions specify price, quality and pricing. These represent an agreement by the buyer to provide a market for the seller of agricultural produce. The buyer may assume some risk and the right to make decisions about the time of marketing and the farmer retains control over production practices.

1.11.2 Resource Providing Contracts

Resource providing contracts oblige the processor to supply seeds, extension or credit in exchange for a marketing agreement or resource provision. These represent the greatest level of control for buyer, who provide market outlet, supervise production practices and supply key inputs. In proportion of the risk they may even retain ownership of the product.

1.11.3 Production Management Contracts

Production management contracts bind the farmer to follow a particular production method and input management usually in exchange for a marketing agreement or resource provision. They allow the buyer to specify or monitor production practices, input usages, etc.

1.12 Eaton and Shepherd (2001)[17]

Broadly classify five different types of contract farming agreements depending on the crops, objectives, and resources of the sponsors and the experience of the farmers as centralized model, Nucleus Estate Model, Informal Model, Multipartite Model, and Intermediary model. The above mentioned types of contract arrangements i.e. production management contracts and resource providing contracts fit into one of these models.

1.12.1 The Centralized Model

Centralized Model is a vertically co-ordinate model where the sponsor purchases the crop from framers and processes or packages and markets the product except in a limited number of cases farmer quotas are normally distributed at the beginning of each growing season and quality is tightly controlled. A sponsor may purchase from tens of thousands of small scale farmers within a single project. The centralized scheme is generally associated with tobacco, cotton, sugarcane and bananas and with tree crops such as coffee, tea, cocoa and rubber, but can also be used for poultry, pork and dairy production. The level of involvement of the sponsor in production can vary from a minimum where perhaps, only the correct type of seed is provided to the opposite extreme where the company provides the land preparation, seedlings, agrochemicals and even harvesting services.

1.12.2 The Nucleus Estate Model

Nucleus estate model is a variation of the centralized model. In this case the sponsor of the project also owns and manages an estate plantation, which is usually close to the processing plant. The estate is often fairly large in order to provide some guarantee of throughput for the plant, but on occasion it can be relatively small, primarily serving as a trial and demonstration farm. A common approach is for the sponsor to commence with a pilot estate then, after a trial period, introduction to farmer (sometimes called 'satellite' growers) the technology and management techniques of the particular crop. Nucleus estates have often been used in connection with resettlement or transmigration schemes, such as in Indonesia and Papua New Guinea, for oil palm and other crops. While mainly used for tree crops, in Indonesia this is primarily used for the rearing of 'parent stock', vertical coordination in this model varies.

1.12.3 Multipartite Model

Under the multipartite model a joint venture between a statutory body and a private company contracts with farmers. Also public or private providers of credit, extension services, and inputs may be port of the arrangement. As part of the liberalization process in the 1980s and 1990s, many governments in developing countries actively invested in contract farming through joint ventures with private companies. Multipartite structures are common in China where government departments as well as township committees have set up joint ventures with domestic and foreign investors to establish a processing unit and to enter a contract farming arrangement with local farmer. When the joint venture has sufficient discretion to control its transactions with the farmers, vertical coordination will be intense. Given the involvement of a public partner in the joint venture, the farmer contractor relationship may be affected by the political interests of this partner.

1.12.4 Informal Model

The informal model is characterized by individual entrepreneurs or small companies contracting informal with farmers on a seasonal basis, particularly for crops such as fresh fruits and vegetables. Crops usually require only a minimal amount of processing, such as sorting, grading and packaging. Emphasize that the success of the informal initiative depends on the availability of supporting services, which, in most cases, are likely to be provided by government agencies. For example, while contractors following the centralized model will probably employ their own extension staff, small individual traders usually have to depend on government extension services. An informal contractual relationship provides fewer options for vertical coordination than a more formal relationship.

1.12.5 Intermediary Model

In the intermediary model there are at least three parties to the contract farming arrangement; a processor or major trader formally contracts with middlemen who then informally contracts with a number of farmers. This model, which can be considered as a combination of the centralized and informal models, is common practice throughout Southeast Asia. As there is no direct link between contractor and farmers, this model has several disadvantages for vertical coordination and for providing paper incentives.

All the above models are very much adopted by different sponsors for different commodities. The National Institute of Agricultural Marketing (NIAM). in its recent study (2004) on contract farming covering Karnataka, Madhya Pradesh, Punjab, Tamil Nadu and Maharashtra has identified four types of contract. The various types of contracts are:[18]

Type-I: involving none other than the contracted farmers and the sponsoring firms mainly providing the planting materials to the farmers. The extension wing of the procuring wing of the company takes care of the registration and other issues of pre-production and production. As there is no credit facility given by the sponsor, there is the risk of the farmers running into the hands of money-lenders. Some of the companies following this model are Nikker Agro (Tomato and Chilly in Punjab), Tinna Oils (Soyabean in Maharashtra), SNC Oil (for Dhavana in Karnataka), Himalayan Drugs Private Ltd (Ashwagandha, Karnataka), PepsiCo (Basmati, Punjab) etc.

Type-II: This is a three tier model involving the sponsor, the farmers and an implementing agency which could be a public or a private body or a local NGO. The implementing agency conducts contract farming with the set of quality specifications and guidelines set by the corporate which is the ultimate buyer. The implementing agency coveys the contracted price as agreed by the purchaser of the commodity under contract to the farmers. The implementing agency may charge some minor share of the value of the produce from the buyer and from the farmers as an extension charge. "Ion Exchange Enviro Farms" is following this model in Maharashtra for contract farming of organic produce.

Type-III: The model is similar to type-II as it has three tiers and the middle tier is replaced by a traditional channel member like arthiya. These channel member help the corporate in indentify the farmers, arranging for the cleaning and grading of the produce and also procuring the produce. At the same time the company is in direct contact with the farmers for provision of extension services. The model provides transparency but provides ample scope for the arthiyas to cut corners for their benefits. The companies that adopt this model are United Breweries Limited (Barley, Punjab), ITC-ISD (Soyabean, wheat, Madhya Pradesh) etc.

Type –IV: This model is the most elaborate model, under which all the services are provided under a single umbrella. The implementing agency in this model, which could be an independent corporate or an arm of the buying company, coordinates with all the agencies such as seed companies, input providers, banks and insurance providers for providing a plethora of services under the same roof. The implementing agency renders its services for a nominal fee from the farmers for extension services and a meagre share of 0.5 percent to 1 percent share on the interest received by the bank and the value of the produce purchased by the buyer. The companies adopting this model are Mahindra Subhlabh Services Ltd. (Basmati, Non-basmati, maize, Punjab, Tamil Nadu), Escorts Machinery Group (Basmati, Punjab), Super Spinning Mills (cotton, Tamil Nadu), Cargill India Pvt. Ltd. (Soyabean, wheat, maize, Madhya Pradesh and U.P.), Appachi Cotton India (Cotton, Tamil Nadu), Gherkin exporters (Gherkin, Karnataka, Tamil Nadu, Andhra Pradesh).

1.13 Specifications of Contract Farming

This point reviews the legal framework of contracts, the basis for the agreement (the formula), the format or way the contract is presented and the detailed specifications that must be included for formalizing and operationalizing contracts for contract farming. Agreements, in the form of a written contract or a verbal understanding, usually endorse the responsibilities and obligations of each party, the manner in which the agreement can be enforced and the remedies to be taken if the contract breaks down interimly/ prematurely. The type of contract used depends on a number of factors such as the nature of the product, the primary processing required, if any, and the demand of the market in terms of supply reliability. The nature of the agreement is also influenced by quality incentives, terms of payment arrangements, the level of control the sponsor wants to have over the production process, and the extent to which the parties tie-up capital in the contract. The farmers and their representatives must be given the opportunity to contribute to the drafting of the agreement and assist in the wording of specifications which farmers are able to understand. Contract should represent a mutual understanding between the contracting parties. Management must, therefore, ensure that agreements are fully understood by all farmers. The terms and conditions entered into must be written down for independent examination and copies be given to the farmers' representatives. Copies should also be made available to relevant government agencies. Four following aspects need to be considered when drafting contracts:[19]

1.13.1 The Legal Framework

All countries have basic laws that govern contracts.

Farming contracts, whether written or oral, should comply with the minimum legal requirements that apply in a particular country. At the same time, it is equally important to take into account the prevailing practices and societal attitudes towards contractual obligations, because, in almost all societies, these factors can produce an outcome that differs from the formal letter of law. Local practice may also influence the decision as to how detailed a contract should be, or whether, it should be a formal contract or a mere simple registration.

In majority of the cases, as in the present study, it is highly unlikely that a sponsor does not take any legal action against a small holder for a breach of contract. Very often, it so happens that the costs involved tends to be far in excess of the amount claimed, and as a consequence thereof legal action threatens the relationship between the sponsor and the beneficiary farmers: not just those against whom action is being taken. Action by a farmer against a sponsor is similarly improbable. However, the improbability that a contract or agreements should not be entered into, since such contracts can benefit both the parties by clearly spelling out the rules of the relationship. As neither side is likely to seek a legal remedy through the courts, it is important that ways of resolving probable disputes are identified in the agreement. A body representing the sponsor, farmers and other interested parties could be established in some cases, while in others, a government agency might be the most appropriate institutional arrangement. It is preferable that the contract farming industry regulates itself in order to offer a measure, which is system based for protection of all participants. Participation of political nominees in such bodies should generally be avoided. Agreements between contract firms/ sponsors and contracted farmers are essentially voluntary undertakings (as observed in the study area) and the two parties should exercise control over their own contract formulas and specifications.

1.13.2 The Formula

The contract farming models can operate under a variety of institutional arrangements. Each contract is designed to suit specific situation, the formula of which may be based on one, or a combination of the following.

(i) **Market Specifications:** Under a market specification contract, only quality standards are specified. The sponsors / contractor normally provides only minimal material and technological inputs e.g. Jain Irrigation System Ltd. in Jalgaon for onion and Mahyco in Jalna for cotton seed production insist only quality criteria/ specifications with no input supply.

(ii) **Resource Specifications**: In this type of contract, key components are stipulated (viz. male and female lines supplied by Mahyco for F1 hybrid-seed production of cotton in Jalna district) and the condition under which the crop is purchased. Normally few material advances are provided under resource specification formulas.

(iii) **Management and Income Specifications:** This contract specifications strictly regulate product standards. They are basically a combination of the market and resource specification formulas, but, in addition, sponsors may establish predetermined pricing structures and make firm commitments in the form of farm inputs advances, technical inputs and managerial control (viz. for Potato production by PepsiCo in Pune, guidance is provided by the PepsiCo firm to the member farmers).

(iv) **Land Ownership and Land Tenure Specifications:** This type of contract is an extension of the management and income model, with additional clauses relating to land tenure. Wherever private companies or government agencies lease land to farmers for contract farming, formal crop-land tenancy contracts on a long-term basis is necessary. For such a contract there should be a legal binding and this should, inter alia, contain clauses relating to both crop and land husbandry.

1.13.3 The Format

The various formats that a contract may take shape of are :

(i) **Formal Agreements**: Explicit, legally endorsed contract formats, which closely detail the conditions and obligations of each party, are particularly common in project that involve heavy investment in capital infrastructure, as also where sponsors lease land to farmers specifically to grow crops under contract.

(ii) **Simple Registration**: The term "Registration" usually refers to a signed confirmation from the farmer that he /she wishes the sponsor to reserve a contract for him/ her. Simple registrations are based on so-called informal associations of trust and patronage that bypass formal legalities. Normally, the registration of farmers for the ensuing season commences immediately after the last harvest. In well-established project, (like all sample firms under the study) registration for many farmers is only a formality or, perhaps, involves just a change of name of a family member. Following registration, field staff approves the land/ site on which the crop/ production activity is to be taken.

(iii) **Verbal Agreements**: Unwritten or verbal agreements are commonly used by informal individual developers and sometimes by corporate sponsors. A major problem of verbal agreements is the interpretation and fixing of responsibilities and specifications. Confusion and misunderstanding can easily creep in if the agreements are not clearly explained by the management to the farmers and / or their representatives. Equally, the manager's field extension staff must also have a clear understanding of the terms of the agreement.

1.13.4 The Specifications

Contracts should stipulate to specify some or all the following aspects of the sponsor-farmers agreement.

(i) **Contract Duration**: The duration of agreements depends on the nature and life-span of the entity. Contracts for short-term entity such as onion production and hybrid seed production of cotton are normally issued and meant to be renegotiated on a seasonal basis, whereas entities like onion and cotton seed require long-term contracts, which can be further amended periodically.

(ii) **Quality Standards**: Product quality, or more precisely, the absence of quality, can have far-reaching consequences in terms of market acceptance and future expansion. Most contracts contain detailed quality specifications so that produce that does not conform to the pre-agreed quality standards can be rejected. It is important that farmers fully understand the rationale for developing such standards; along with the consequences in case of non-compliance. Quality specifications may specify the size, shape, weight, genetically purity etc. A major problem generally encountered with quality standards is they are frequently vague and not so clearly understood, like in potato and onion seeds; and hence become open to interpretation and vulnerable for corruption.

(iii) **Production Quotas:** Both insufficient and excessive production can have serious business ramifications. Overproduction can entail unpopular quota reduction and costly stockpiles. Conversely, under-production results in a project becoming insolvent, as processing costs per tonne could rise to unacceptable levels, besides also being unable to meet pre-arranged marketing contracts, which may lead to reduction or cancellation of future orders. Quotas are generally incorporated into contracts in order to achieve the following objectives.

(a) ***Optimization of Capacities:*** Failure to purchase any part of a farmer's production that meets the specifications of the contract will cause serious discontent. This could occur through poor calculation of the sponsor's capacity to handle, process, store and market the production. Sponsors need to limit their contractual commitment to buy from farmers only the quantities they can process (in total and, depending on the product, on any one working day) and market. Processing is also often restricted by the capacities of the sponsors and farmers warehouses.

(b) ***Guaranteed Markets for all Farmers:*** Failure to purchase any part of a framer's produce, meeting the specifications of the contract, will cause serious discontentment. Sponsors, therefore, need to tie-up their buy-backs with processing, storage and marketing capacities in a synchronous, sequential and harmonized manner.

(c) ***Ensure Quality Control:*** Quotas can sometimes be used to control the quality of the raw / final product. For some crops, like hybrid-seed production of cotton area allotted to each farmer, was only 1 acre.

(d) ***Monitor Farmer's Performance:*** As a means of monitoring farmer's production, quotas are used as benchmark by which to analyse crop/entity yields. Through the efficient monitoring of crop/ entity development, extension officers can usually make realistic yield forecasts. The use of quotas also permits the sponsor to monitor as to whether farmers are actually selling crops/entities outside the purview of the contract (i.e. extra-contractual marketing) or supplementing their other farmers (in violation of contract).

Where there are alternative markets for crops; and in the absence of quotas several buyers being in active competition, such as onion seed and cotton seed in case of present study, farmers are tempted to sell outside the contract, especially when the sponsors purchase only the amount they require, leaving the farmers with no option but to sell surpluses in the open market at a relatively reduced price. Under these circumstances, the farmers must have much greater bargaining power. Farmers of hybrid-seed of cotton as well as potato producers were much responsive, reassuring and loyal despite the fact that the respective buyers did not purchase the entire lot of farm produce at a time to honour their terms of contracts with the farmers.

(iv) **Cultivation Practices**: When sponsors provide seeds (e.g. male and female lines of cotton by Mahyco), they have the right to expect that those inputs will be used in correct quantities in accordance with the recommended cultivation/ farming practices. Of particular concern (in seed farming) in this case, however, is the possibility that farmers may apply unauthorized or prohibitive agrochemicals, which can result in toxic residues. It is therefore essential that managers and their extension staff must make every effort to explain to member farmers why the specifications and input recommendations must be followed in practice in totality.

(v) **Crop/Entity Delivery Arrangements:** Arrangement for collection of products or delivery by the farmers vary widely. Some ventures such as Jain Irrigation System Pvt. Ltd., Jalgaon and Mahyco in Jalna stipulate that farmers should deliver harvested outputs to processing plants or at the collection centre on given dates. While the others may arrange sponsor's transport to collect harvested crops as happened in cases of Bejo Sheetal Seed Pvt. Ltd. in Aurangabad and PepsiCo India Holdings Pvt. Ltd. in Pune.

(vi) **Pricing Arrangements:** Pricing and payment arrangements are the most debated and challenging components of all farming contracts. The choice in regard to which crop/ entity pricing structure to be used is influenced by whether the crop/entity is for the local or export market, seasonal in nature of production, the degree of competition in the marketing system etc. The application of transparent pricing formula is crucial together with the drafting of a clear pricing structure and the organization of a practical method of payment with a view to be able to build confidence and goodwill amongst all partners. There are several ways in which prices offered to farmers can be computed, including the following.

(a) ***Fixed Prices:*** The practice is usually to offer farmers a predetermined price at the beginning of each season such as Rs. 500/Kg. of cotton seeds by Mahyco in Jalna. Generally, the fixed prices are related to observance of quality specifications. Fixed price formulas are usually ideal for the sponsor for budgeting and marketing purpose.

(b) ***Flexible Prices:*** This structure applies to prices calculated on a formula related to changing global and local market trends. Farmers are paid on the basis of a formula which takes into account agreed processing and other costs of the sponsor as well as world/domestic market prices over a particular period. In some cases, farmers and sponsors share price increases and costs proportionately. In Pune district, for example, under contract Potato farming system, contract specify that final payment will be made to the member farmers as per the potato obtained after duly deducting the costs of inputs provided by the sponsor. In partial breach of this contract, member-farmers were subjected to the vagaries of market price against the pre-decided price of potato by the sponsors.

(c) ***Prices Calculated on Spot-Market Values***: Payment based on spot-market prices can be very complex and often lead to undesirable misunderstanding and disputes. Such an arrangement removes the built-in provision of income guarantees for farmers. Contract prices offered by Bejo Sheetal seed for onion seed 10 percent above the local market price and Mahyco for cotton seed 20 percent above the prevailing local market price falls under this category.

(d) ***Prices on a Consignment Basis:*** Prices calculated after the produce has been marketed and sold may be considered under another form of spot-market pricing system. This form of payment is normally termed as on-consignment. Such pricing arrangements are rarely found and preferably be avoided. The growing importance of supermarkets suggests that more and more fresh produce will be delivered at predetermined prices rather than on a consignment basis, especially under a volatile market ambience.

(e) ***Split Pricing:*** Under this system, an agreed base price is paid out at the time of purchase or at the end of the harvesting season. The final price is calculated once the sponsor has sold the commodity, depending on the prevailing market price.

(vii) **Payment Procedures:** For all farmers, the most convenient and acceptable method of payment is usually by way of cash-in-hand immediately, following delivery of any part of their harvested produce. However, this is not always possible for the sponsors. In case of present study payment was made through cheques within 2 weeks after delivery of the produce. Any material and cash advances given to farmers during the season were deducted from the committed final payment.

(viii) **Insurance Arrangements:** Agricultural investments always involve risk. The five most likely reasons for investment failure are: poor crop management, climatic calamities, pest epidemics, market collapse and price fluctuations. The standard agri-business approach to indemnify against quantity shortfalls is crop insurance. The government-run crop-insurance schemes have since proved to be unsatisfactory/inadequate. It was found that not a single entity under the study was properly insured by the respective sponsors. As the farming involved in a contract arrangement becomes technologically more advanced, the range and nature of risks to which it is exposed generally becomes more critical. In the given scenario, the government and banking sector can play a crucial role and safe deal under the thrust area of agricultural finance/refinance.

1.14 Monitoring Performance

All farming ventures need reliable records to provide monitoring, evaluation and diagnostic functions of the key activities that determine the product's performance. Managers need to accumulate, analyse and distribute information not only for the maintenance of project and farmer records but also to evaluate production performance and calculate yield indicators. Such monitoring is particularly necessary in large ventures that involve thousands of farmers, where it is difficult for management to have close interaction with individual farmers.[20]

The basic elements of monitoring, or process control, are essentially the same in all industrial or agricultural activities: management should identify each component, measure its performance, compare the results to a benchmark and, if necessary, take action to rectify any problem at an early stage. A routine analysis should be carried out to ensure that current and future production remains within the quality and quantity parameters required. Deterioration of quality can have serious and far-reaching consequences for any business venture. Quality controls are especially critical for high-value crops such as exotic fresh fruits and many varieties of vegetables. Quantity shortfalls can reduce processing efficiency and jeopardize markets. How a project's extension staff can monitor quality and quantity is discussed below.

1.14.1 Quality Controls

Each venture must develop quality control and monitoring systems suitable for its particular operation. Management must prioritize monitoring procedures and decide how often they should be carried out, in what locations and who should be inspected and assessed. Checking product quality can take place before, during and immediately after harvesting as well as at the time farmers grade their own production and when the products reach the company's processing or packaging facilities.

Quality controls may start as specifications in a written contract or as verbal explanations of quality standards given in both pre-season and pre-harvest farmer-management meetings. Perhaps the most practical method is for management to demonstrate by visual presentation the quality criteria that must be met, either for the entire production or, where appropriate, for different grades. When extension staff at the farmgate or buyers at processing stations purchase crops they should explain to the farmers the reasons why they are grading the crop as they are. Where farmers have mixed their grades they should, if practical, be given the opportunity to regard.

1.14.2 Yield Estimations

Yield forecasting has become increasingly important in agriculture for processing, marketing and budgeting as well as for monitoring of production. Where production is limited to a target quantity, any major shortfall can cause serious embarrassment for the sponsor as a result of inability to meet forward orders. Overproduction will result in expenditure above budgets, unnecessary and expensive stockpiles and quota reductions in following seasons. This will result in income loss for many farmers. The aim of all contract farming ventures is to maximize economic returns. It should be borne in mind that with some crops the highest yield does not necessarily mean the highest income as high yields may only be achieved at the expense of quality or through the uneconomic use of inputs.

1.14.3 Calculated Yield Indicators

A number of methods can be used for forecasting crop yields. These include a top-down model using a hierarchy of variables to the point where optimum performance cannot be improved further, as well as the Baysian model using categorical variables based on experience. Another model for crop forecasting is through the Monte Carlo simulation method based on soil and management parameters. In many cases, however, visual methods based on the knowledge of experienced field staff should suffice to estimate yields.

Higher than expected production justified an investigation to identify those villages introducing produce from outside the contract. The wide variation between actual and calculated yields discovered in this example reinforced the belief that extra-contractual production had been infiltrated into the project. Indicator models provide information for management to identify farmers who circumvent buying procedures. The modelling of a calculated yield indictor is, however, dependent on reliable data and the ability of the assessors to interpret it.

1.14.4 Production Matrices

Simulated modelling of crop production on a scientific basis is a highly complex, ever-expanding and normally efficient discipline. Analytical decision models, such as a production-marketing consumption (PMC) matrix, are useful in agricultural projects to evaluate managerial, agronomic and infrastructural factors necessary for the success of the crop. The model was first introduced in California in 1979 to structure the production and marketing requirements of a new commercial crop, jojoba. The basic concept of the production matrix, a subsystem of the total PMC matrix, is to formally identify all the key components that influence production in terms of their significance, responsibility and performance. The information on which to base the performance assessment can be extracted from production statistics, farmer records and field observations.

1.14.5 Monitoring Human Resources

Managing, motivating and monitoring human resources involves the recruiting, training and deployment of employees as well as an appraisal of their work. The production performance of each farmer also needs to be recorded and assessed so as to determine the need for quota changes and on occasion, the cancellation of contracts. To support the decisions that managers must make, which can affect the livelihoods of thousands of individuals, there must be detailed monitoring procedures. The two human resource areas that managers of ventures are directly responsible for are:

- appraising employees; and
- reviewing farmer performance.

1.14.5.1 Appraising Employees

Employees who have been successful in an agribusiness context that does not involve contract farming may not easily make the transition to a contract farming environment. This can apply to senior management as well as to junior staff.

Some highly competent and qualified staff members have proved unsatisfactory when required to work with farmers. In projects with only a small number of employees, staff appraisals are relatively simple as the interactions between managers and their staff members are almost on a daily basis.

1.14.5.2 Reviewing Farmer Performance

Formal monitoring of the crop at all stages of its development may lead to the identification of factors that could cause poor production. For instance, the failure of farmers to notice the early signs of disease may delay the application of fungicides, thus endangering both quality and yield. Extension staff must therefore carry out routine inspections of all the farms they supervise. For some crops, such as sugar cane and fruit, inspections may be on a weekly or fortnightly basis. For vegetable crops, several visits a week may be required. Simple report cards should be kept indicating each farmer's code, locality, quota, land unit, the estimate of production and the inputs advanced. The extension officers must document the dates of showing, transplanting, irrigation, harvesting and any other major activity carried out, such as fertilizer application and chemical use. Comments on climatic conditions, standards achieved and advice given on the farmer should also be recorded. Wherever possible, farmers should be encouraged to maintain their own records of their use of farm inputs and of their production.

1.14.6 Protecting the Environment

Ecological considerations combined with sound agricultural practices should have an important role in contract farming, although the sustainability of the farming system as it relates to the physical and social environment usually receives little attention from either agribusiness or governments. Environmental issues can very not only from country to country but also from district to district and farm to farm. Deforestation, the depletion of water resources and soil degradation are major concerns that accompany any agricultural development. However, agribusiness is frequently interested only in a single crop whereas farmers usually have permanent multicropping system and must take the sustainability of these into account when assessing the value of contract farming.

Environmental degeneration as a result of any form of farming can become a major problem if it is not controlled. The cultivation of crops on thin soils on very steep terraces encourages high levels of erosion. Twenty-five percent of crops in one contract farming venture in China were grown on land totally unsuitable for intense cultivation. All participants of the contract-sponsors, the local managers and the village committees allowed production on steep slopes without any regulation or apparent concern.

1.15 Contract Terms

Under the different models discussed above contract could be of several types such as product specification, resource providing, price or risk sharing, market access, etc. Product specification contract includes details of the quality characteristic of the product. Resource providing contract mentions the commitment of the firm to supply resources to be used in the production process such as seed, fertilizer, pesticide, etc. Price sharing usually involves a minimum profit margin above the calculated cost of production. It guarantees a margin or specifies a sharing of the margin above the calculated costs. A contract may include one or more of the above features. Contract farming can be structured in a variety of ways depending on the commodity, the objective and resources of the sponsor and the experience of the farmers. Contracting out production is a commercial decision to facilitate an adequate supply within a designated period and at an economic price.[21]

1.16 Features of a Farming Contract

Though contract may vary across commodities and

regions some of the basic elements are common to all contracts. The major features in a farming contract are duration, quantity and quality of output, use of inputs and cultivation practices, inputs and services provided by buyers, delivery arrangements, price, payment schedule etc. Contract for short duration crops such as vegetables are normally on seasonal basis. Long-term agreements may be found in plantation crops such as tea, coffee, rubber, cocoa, oil palm, etc. Since the gestation period between planting and production for these crops is longer and their economic life stretches over decades no contract can foresee all the contingencies. Therefore, contract in these crops may have provision for amendments to meet the unfolding situations as the when they arise.[22]

1.16.1 Quality of Output

Market dictates the quality of the products. The same is translated into commodity traits that could be achieved through use of specific inputs and cultural practices. The sustenance of the buyer firm would depend on its ability to cater to the market expectations. Therefore, the cultural practices the farmers must follow in order to meet the quality requirements may also form part of the contract. The contract also spells out clearly the quality of produce the farmer has to deliver. The firm may supply the necessary inputs and services in order to make sure that the farmer is not at a disadvantage to fulfil the contract obligations due to non-availability of these inputs.

Inspection at different stages ensures that the terms and conditions of the contract are implemented effectively. It helps in identifying and removing potential problems resulting in realization of desired quality of output. Inspection can be viewed as a preventive function. It is an opportunity to determine the need for technical assistance, guidance and training on concurrent basis such that product quality is maintained. Contracts may specifically mention the right of the staff of the company to visit the plots. Farmers are expected to facilitate these visits and agree to follow the advice of the staff regarding practices and operations to be carried out.

1.16.2 Price

Price is an important feature of any contract. Indian agricultural is characterized by large variations in price not only over the years but also within a year/season. Further, distress selling and exploitation of farmers by trade were part of the Indian agricultural scene. This had necessitated government intervention in the form of minimum support price and procurement. However, this was restricted mainly to cereals and some other crops. Several horticulture and plantation crops are subject to market volatility. Most of the farmers enter into contract in order to have assured price and thereby more definite or stable income. The firms also benefit from stable prices as it would help them in managing their resources optimally.

In most cases price is predetermined but it could be flexible. The price may be linked to the market price with incentive component for special efforts made by the farmers to supply the required grade. It may be a fixed price plus bonus for meeting quality and quantity of output. Since the firm may not be able to fully monitor the effort of the farmer the reward is linked to the realized outcome (Tsoulouhas and Vukina 1999). Therefore, contracts by linking the price and outcome are able to supplant the need for complete supervision and control. This results in enormous saving to the firm.

1.16.3 Quantity

Every firm strives to use its processing capacity to the optimal level. Therefore, they try to ensure regular and uninterrupted flow of raw material. The information about the quantity available to the firm confers several advantages to it. It could better plan its activities such as transport, logistics, manpower, finance, etc. for overall efficiency. Therefore, quantity that the farmer has to supply is mentioned in the contract. However, assessing the precise quantity in crops is not possible. Therefore, most of the contract mentions the area under the contract and the farmers are expected to supply the entire quantity of produce to the firm. The contract mentions the penalty to be levied in case the farmer fails to supply full or part of the produce. The firm calculates the acreage to produce the required quantity by taking into account the average yield. In case of bumper crop the firm may not be able to procure all the produce and there are instances where the firms resorted to unhealthy practices to avoid procurement.

1.16.4 Resource Providing Contract

As mentioned earlier if the contract includes supply of inputs then it is called resource-providing contract. A firm may provide inputs for several reasons, namely, i) to ensure use of recommended inputs, ii) market failure for the inputs in their area of operation, and iii) to ease the credit constraints for the farmers. Contract farming is explained as an institutional response to imperfections in the market for credit, insurance, information, factors of production and raw product.

1.16.5 Delivery of Produce

Contract may have details of the delivery arrangement. The produce may be brought to the processing plant by the farmers or may be lifted from the farm gate by the buyer. Not only who makes the transport arrangement but also who bears the cost of transportation is spelt out. The nature of crop largely determines the nature of delivery of the produce. For example, gherkins must be processed within 10 hours of harvesting. It was difficult for the individual farmers to bring the small quantity daily to the processing plant situated beyond a certain distance. Also rejections at the factory would have resulted high cost to growers. Thus the firms arranged to lift the produce daily at specified timings from the collection centres organized near to producer farmers. The collection centres were as far away from the factory as over 200 km.

1.16.6 Payment

The payment arrangement is another important feature of the contract. It could be in cash or by cheque. It may be in lumpsum or in two or three instalments. It could be immediate payment or spread over a month or two. It is important for the firm to ensure that the farmer understood the mode and time of payment otherwise it may lead to unwarranted friction between the two parties. In case of tripartite arrangement where payment may be routed through the financing bank it is important that the farmers are told that the payment is net of the loan outstanding he might have raised from the bank for the purpose. The banks must recover the loan raised for that particular crop and should not link it to any other liability the farmer might have with the bank.

1.16.7 Dealing with Default

In case the farmer is not able to abide by the agreement there should be provision in the contract through which the firm might take action. In most cases it is penalty or recovery of cost. In case the farmers action results in loss to the company it would be recovered from the farmers. Similarly if there is a loss to farmer because of poor quality inputs supplied or lack of technical advice or delay in acceptance of produce etc. the company must compensate. However, there is generally no such provision in the contract.

1.16.8 Contingencies

The major advantage to the firm in contract farming is that the production risk is entirely that of the farmers. However, even in instances beyond the control of the farmer there is no provision in the contract to ease the burden of the farmer. Some contracts have act of God clause in the contract and provide contingency contracts or give priority to those farmers in the subsequent season. Even if crop fails because of the inherent defects in the inputs supplied, such as seed, the company takes no responsibility. In case of broiler chickens the growers were penalized for mortality beyond permissible percentage irrespective of the cause of death.

1.16.9 Large vs Small Farmers

Ideally processing firms may like to deal with small number of large farmers rather than large number of small farmers in order to reduce the transaction cost in monitoring, supplying input, procuring outputs, billing, payment, etc. However, this need not always be the case. It may depend on the nature of the commodity and the quality expectations of the firm. For instance, Pepsi Foods preferred small number of large farmers to achieve its procurement target even if they were spread over a large area. On the other hand, in case of gherkins the primary concern of the firm was quality of the fruits supplied. Gherkins being a labour-intensive crop the company preferred small framers with family labour for their programme to ensure timely performance of crucial tasks and achieve quality.

1.17 Constraints in the Contract

For the neoclassical economists and proponents of agribusiness the contract ensure a sort of mutualism between the parties. Freely entered into the contract allows growers to make better use of their specific endowments in imperfect markets and to arrive at combinations of income, effort and risk reflecting their resources and tastes. Sharing of the transaction cost advantage between the firm and the farmers is the crux of contract farming. The distribution of this advantage depends heavily on factors like bargaining power, availability of alternatives and access to information. The strength of a party in any one of these factors leads to its opportunistic behaviour which is defined as unanticipated non-fulfilment of a contract, thus leading to strains in the contractual relationship and may result in failure of the contract.

Under classical contract law contracting entails comprehensive contracting whereby all relevant future contingencies pertaining to the supply of goods or services are described and discounted. It corresponds to ideal market transactions in economics. The emphasis is on legal rules, formal documents and self-liquidating transactions. However, not every transaction fits into the classical contracting scheme. In long-term contracts expected under conditions of uncertainty are ones for which complete presentation may be prohibitively costly or not possible at all. Not all the future contingencies can be anticipated at the outset and adaptation for such contingencies foreseen. This is called bounded rationality. That is, economic actors though rational are not hyper rational. They experience limits in formulating and solving complex problems and in processing information. The incompleteness of contract may lead to ex post opportunistic behaviour of one party. Williamson called it self-seeking with guile.

Recognition that the world is complex, that agreements are incomplete, and that some contract will never be reached unless both parties have confidence in the settlement machinery characterizes neoclassical contract law.

In agribusiness an ex post advantage for one party can arise in various ways such as change in weather affecting production, price, change in technology, changes in consumer preferences due to emergence of alternatives and built into the contract. When an agribusiness firm is not an exclusive buyer of the commodity (monopsony) farmers behave opportunistically. The situation can arise when there are rivals in the market or the commodity has alternative uses. In seed industry, in India, poaching by rival firms into each others programme offering farmers a higher price was common. Even though the farmer was under contract with the firm he was lured by the higher price. Similarly, tomatoes produced by farmers for a processing firm under contract in the Punjab were diverted to the open market when the prices were high and the farmers supplied the entire quantity to the firm when they were lower. When many farmers indulge in such practices it is not prudent to drag all the farmers to court as it would affect the future goodwill in the area of operation of the firm. Likewise there are several instances in which the firms renege on contract. For example a popular chocolate manufacturer introduced cocoa contract farming in Kerala promising certain price, a match manufacturer entered into contract growing of poplar trees in Haryana, a paper unit entered into contract with farmers in Karnataka for bamboo production. As the farmers were trapped in the contract for huge investments these firms tried to exploit the farmers by reneging on their commitments.[23]

1.18 Advantages and Problems of Contract Farming

Well-managed contract farming is an effective way to coordinate and promote production and marketing in agriculture. Nevertheless, it is essentially an agreement between unequal parties. Companies, government bodies or individual entrepreneurs are on the one hand and economically weaker farmers on the other. It is, however an approach that can contribute to both increased income for farmer and higher profitability for sponsor. When efficiently organized and managed contract farming reduces risk and uncertainty for both parties as compared to buying and selling crops on the open market.

The advantage, disadvantages and problems arising from contract farming will vary according to the physical, social and market environments. More specifically the distribution of risks will depend on such factors as the nature of the markets for both the raw material and the processed product, the availability of alternative earning opportunities for farmer, and the extent to which relevant technical information is provided to the contracted farmers. These factors are likely to change over time, as will be distribution of risks.[24]

1.18.1 Advantages for farmers

The prime advantage of a contractual arrangement for farmers is that the sponsor will normally undertake to purchase all produce grown, within specified quality and quantity parameters. Contracts can also provide farmers with access to a wide range of managerial, technical and extension services that otherwise may be unobtainable. Farmers can use the contract arrangement as collateral to arrange credit with a commercial bank in order to fund inputs. Thus, the main potential advantages for farmer are: [25]

Provision of inputs and production services; Access to credit; Introduction of appropriate technology; Skill transfer; Guaranteed and fixed pricing structures; and Access to reliable markets.

1.18.1.1 Provision of Inputs and Production Services

Many contractual arrangements involve considerable production support in addition to the supply of basic imports such as seed and fertilizer. Sponsors may also provide land preparation, field cultivation and harvesting as well as free training and extinction. This is primarily to ensure that proper crop husbandry practices are followed in order to achieve projected yields and required qualities. There is, however, a danger that such arrangements may lead to the farmer being little more than a labourer on his or her own land. It is often difficult for small-scale farmer outside the contract the context to again access to imports. In many countries a vicious circle has developed whereby the low demand for inputs provides no incentive for the development of commercial distribution networks and this, in turn, further adversely affects inputs availability and use. Contract farming can help to overcome many of these problems through bulk ordering by management.

1.18.1.2 Access to Credit

The majority of smallholder producers experience difficulties in obtaining credit for production inputs. With collapse or restructuring of many agricultural development banks and the closer of many export crop marketing boards, which in the past supplied farmer with inputs on credit, difficulties have increased rather than decreased. Contract farming usually allows farmers to access some form of credit to finance production inputs. In most cases it is the sponsors who advance credit through their managers. However, arrangements can be made with commercial banks or government agencies through crop liens that are guaranteed by the sponsors, i.e. the contract serves as collateral. When substantial investments are required by farmers such as packing or grading sheds, tobacco barns or heavy machinery, banks will not normally advance credit without guarantees from the sponsors. The tendency of certain farmers to abuse credit arrangements by selling crop to buyers other than the sponsor (extra-contractual farming), or by diverting inputs supplied by management to other purposes, has caused some sponsors to reconsider supplying most inputs, opting instead to provide only seeds and essential agrochemicals. The policies and conditions that control advances are normally described in attachments to contract.

1.18.1.3 Introduction of Appropriate Technology

New techniques are often required to upgrade agricultural commodities for markets that demand high quality standards. New production techniques are often necessary to increase productivity as well as to ensure that the commodity meets market demands. However, small-scale farmers are frequently reluctant to adopt new technologies because of the possible risk and cost involved. They are more likely to accept new practice when they can rely on external resources for material and technological inputs. Nevertheless, the introduction of new technology will not be successful unless it is initiated within a well managed and structured farming operation. Private agribusiness will usually offer technology more diligently than government agricultural extension services because it has a direct economic interest in improving farmers' production. Most of the larger sponsors prefer to provide their own extension rather than rely on government services.

1.18.1.4 Skill Transfer

The skill farmers learns through contract farming may include record keeping, the efficient use of farm resources, improved methods of applying chemicals and fertilizers, a knowledge of the importance of quality and the characteristics and demands of export markets. Farmer can gain experience in carrying out field activities following a strict timetable imposed by the extension service. In addition, spoiler effects from contract farming activities could lead to investment in market infrastructure and human capital, thus improving the productivity of other farm activities. Farmers often apply techniques introduced by management (ridging, fertilizing, transporting, pest control, etc.) to other cash and subsistence crops.

1.18.1.5 Guaranteed and Fixed Pricing Structures

The returns farmers receive for their crops on the open depend on the prevailing market prices as well as on their ability to nutritive with buyers. This can create considerable uncertainty which to a certain extent, contract farming can overcome frequently, sponsors indicate in advance the prices to be paid and these are specified in the agreement on the other hand, some contracts are not based on fixed prices but are related to the market prices at the time of delivery.

1.18.1.6 Access to Reliable Markets

Small-scale farmers are often constrained in what they can produce by limited marketing opportunities, which often makes diversification into cultivate unless they know they can sell their crop and traders or processors will not invest in ventures unless they are assure that the required commodities can be consistently produced. Contract farming offers a potential solution to this situation by providing market guarantees to the farmers and assuring supply to the purchasers. Even where there are existing outlets for the same crop, contract farming can offer significant advantages to farmers. They do not have to search for and negotiate with local and international buyers, and project sponsors usually organize transport for their crops, normally from the farm gate.

1.18.2 Problem Faced by Farmers

For farmers the potential problems associated with contract farming include; increased risk; Unsuitable technology and crop incompatibility; Manipulation of quotas and quality specifications; Corruption; Domination by monopolies; and Indebtedness and reliance on advances.[26]

1.18.2.1 Increased Risk

Farmers intering new contract farming ventures should be prepared to balance the prospect of higher returns with the possibility of greater risk. Such risk is more likely when the agribusiness venture is introducing a new crop to the area. There may be production risk particularly where prior field test are inadequate, in lower than expected yields for the farmers. Market risks may occur when the company's forecasts of market size or price levels are not accurate. Considerable problems can result if farmers perceive that the company is unwilling to share any of the risk, even if partly responsible for losses. In Thailand, for example, a company that contracted farmer to rear chickens charged a levy on farmers' incomes in order to offset the possibility of a high chicken mortality rate. This was much resented by the farmers, as they believe that the poor quality of the day-old chicks supplied by the company was one reason for the problem.

1.18.2.2 Unsuitable Technology and Crop Incompatibility

The introduction of a new crop to be grown under conditions rigorously controlled by the sponsor can cause disruption to the existing farming system. For example, the manager may identify land traditionally reserved for food crops as the most suitable for the contracted crop. Some time as the harvesting of food crops, thus causing competition for scarce labour resources. Particular problems may be experienced when contract farming is related to resettlement programmers. Two factors should be considered before innovations are introduced to any agricultural environment. The first is the possible adverse effect on the social life of the community. When tobacco growers in Fiji were encouraged to cure tobacco themselves rather than sell it in the fresh green form, it was found that they were unable to handle the highly technical curing operation with any intermittent social commitment and customary obligations that overrode contractual responsibilities and eventually resulted in cancellation of their contracts. The second factor is the practically of introducing innovations or adaptations. The introduction of sophisticated machines (e.g. for transplanting) may result in a loss of local employment and overcapitalization of the contracted farmer. Furthermore, in field activities such as transplanting and weed control, mechanical methods often produce less effective results than the traditional cultivation methods. Field extension services must always ensure that the contracted crop fits in with farmers' total cropping regime, particularly in the areas of pest control and field rotation practices.

1.18.2.3 Manipulation of Quotas and Quality Specifications

Inefficient management can lead to production exceeding original targets. For example, failures of field staff to measure fields following transplanting can result in gross over planting. Sponsors may have unrealistic expectation of the market for their product or the market may collapse unexpectedly owing to transport problems, civil unrest, change in government policy or the arrival of a competitor. Such occurrences can lead managers to reduce farmers' quotas. Few contracts specify penalties in such circumstances. In some situations management may be tempted to manipulate quality standards in order to reduce purchases while appearing to honour the contract. Such practices will cause sponsor-farmer confrontation, especially if farmers have no method to dispute grading irregularities. All contract farming ventures should pay attention to grievances relating to such issues.

1.18.2.4 Corruption

Problems occur when staff responsible for issuing contracts and buying crops exploits their position. Such practices result in collapse of trust and communication between the contracts. Management needs to ensure that corruption in any form does not occur. On a larger scale, the sponsor can themselves be dishonest or corrupt. Government have sometime fallen victim to dubious or "Fly-by-night" companies persuading the government and other investors to set up a new contract farming company and then sell that company overpriced and poor quality processing equipment. In such cases farmer who make investment in production and primary processing facilities run the risk of losing everything.

1.18.2.5 Domination by Monopolies

The monopoly of a single crop by a sponsor can have a negative effect. Allowing only one purchaser encourages monopolistic tendencies, particularly where farmers are locked into a fairly sizeable investment, such as tree crops, and cannot easily change to other crops. On the other hand, large-scale investment, such as for Nucleus Estate, often require a monopoly in order to be viable. In order to protect farmers when there is only a single buyer for one commodity, the government should have some role in determining the prices paid. Ducker suggests that privately managed monopolies under public regulation are preferable to non-regulated private or public monopolies. The greatest abuses do tend to occur when there are public monopolies, where buying prices are set by the government, or where farmers have made long-term investment in perennial crops. The Kenya Tea

Development Authority (1999) experienced serious unrest amongst its growers, reportedly because of the Authority's inefficient extension services and alleged 'Manipulation' of farmers.

1.18.3 Advantages for Sponsors

Companies and government agencies have a number of options to obtain raw materials for their processing and marketing activities. The benefits of contract farming are best examined in the light of the other alternatives, namely spot market purchases and large-scale estates. The main potential advantages for sponsors can be seen as:

Political acceptability; Overcoming land constraints; Production reliability and shared risk; Quality constancy; and Promotion of farm inputs.

1.18.3.1 Political Acceptability

It can be more politically expedient for sponsors to involve smallholder farmers in production rather than to operate plantations. Many governments are reluctant to have large plantation and some are actively involved in closing down such estates and redistributing their land. Contract farming, particularly when the farmer is not a tenant of the sponsor, is less likely to be subject to political eroticism. As a result of the restructuring of their economics, many Indian state governments have promoted contract farming as an alternative to private, corporate and state owned plantations. In recent years many countries have seen a move away from the plantation system of production to one where small-scale farmer grow crops under contract for processing and or marketing. The decision to choose contract farming does not make a company totally immune from criticism.

For example, the considerable opposition to the role of multinational corporations in India in the late 1990s had a negate effect on investment in contract farming by foreign agribusiness corporations.

1.18.3.2 Overcoming Land Constraints

Most of the world's plantations were established in the colonial era when land was relatively plentiful and the colonial powers had few scruples about either simply annexing it or paying landowners minimal compensation. That is, fortunately, no longer the situation. Most large tracts of suitable land are now either traditionally owned, costly to purchase or unavailable for commercial development. Moreover, even if it were possible for companies to purchase land at an affordable price, it would rarely be possible to purchase large enough parcels of land to offer the necessary economies of scale achieved by estate agriculture. Contract farming, therefore offers access to crop production from land that would not otherwise be available to a company, with the additional advantage it does not have to purchase it.

1.18.3.3 Production Reliability and Shared Risk

The failure to supply agreed contract could seriously jeopardized future sales. Plantation agriculture and contract farming both offer reasonable supply reliability. Sponsor of contract farming, even with the best management, always run the risk that farmers will fail to honour agreement. On the other hand, plantation agriculture always runs the risk of labour disputes. In the case of horticulture production some companies do prefer estate rather than contracted production. Working with contracted farmers enables sponsors to share the risk of production failure due to poor weather, disease, etc. The farmer takes the risk of loss of production while the company absorbs losses associated with reduced or non-existent through-put for the processing facility. Where production problems are widespread and no fault of the farmer sponsor will often defer repayment of production advances to the following season. Both estate and contract farming methods of obtaining raw material are considerably more reliable than making purchases on the open market. The open market is rarely an acceptable option for organizations that have significant assets tied up in processing facilities and need to justify their investment. For example, it is hardly ever an acceptable option for companies who market regular shipments horticulture produce to supermarket and export. Companies must ensure that crops are on consistent basis: a factor that is normally assured under a well-directed contract farming scheme.

1.18.3.4 Quality Consistency

Market for fresh and processed agricultural produce required consistent quality standards. Moreover, these markets are moving increasingly to a situation where the supplier must also conform to regulatory controls regarding production techniques, particularly the use of pesticides. For fresh produce there is a growing requirement for 'Traceability', i.e. suppliers to major markets increasingly need to be confident of identifying the source of production if problems related to food safety arise. Both estate and contracted crop production require close supervision to control of crops within a single project and have to be transplanted, harvested and purchased in a uniform manner so as to achieve product consistency. Agribusinesses producing for market demand high quality standards such as fruit and vegetable for export. It is often find that small-scale farmer and their families are more likely to produce high quality products than farmers who must supervise hired labour. Also contract farming makes quarantine controls over management. It is easier for quarantine authorities to inspect a limited number of exporters of a single commodity, who closely supervise farmers, than to inspect hundreds, or sometimes thousands of individual producers selling through open markets. Much of the production of 'organic' foods is being done on act, as an integrated operation facilitates a clear crop identity from farmer to retailer. In some highly sophisticated operation containers are now being loaded on the farm for direct delivery to the supermarket.

1.18.3.5 *Promotion of Farm Inputs*

An example of an unusual but, nevertheless, interesting benefit for sponsors comes from the Philippines. A feed milling company experienced difficulties in marketing its feed, which was more expansive than that produced by competing companies. To solve this problem it developed rearing schemes for pigs and poultry under contract in order to provide a market outlet for its feeds and to demonstrate their performance to other farmers living near the contracted farmers.

1.18.4 *Problems Faced by Sponsors*

The main disadvantages faced by contract farming developers are :

Land availability constraints; Social and cultural constraints; Farmer discontent; Extra-contractual marketing; and Input diversion.

1.18.4.1 *Land Availability Constrain*

Farmers must have suitable land on which to cultivate their contracted crops. Problems can arise when farmer have minimal or no security of tenure as there is a danger of the sponsor's investment being wasted as a result of farmer-landlord disputes. Difficulties are also common when sponsors lease land to farmers. Such arrangements normally have eviction clauses included as part of the conditions. Some contract farming ventures are dominated by customary land usage arrangements negotiated by landless farmers with traditional landowners. While such a situation allows the poorest cultivator to take part in contract farming ventures, discrete management measures need to be applied to ensure that landless farmers are not exploited by their landlords. Before entering into contracts, the sponsor must ensure that access to land is secured, at least for the term of the agreement.

1.18.4.2 Social and Cultural Constraints

Problems can arise when management chooses farmers who are unable to comply with strict timetables and regulations because of social obligations. Promoting agriculture through contracts is also a cultural issue. In communities where custom and tradition play an important role, difficulties may arise when farming innovations are introduced. Before introducing new cropping schedules, sponsors must consider the social attitudes and the traditional farming practices of the community and access how a new crop could be introduced. Customary beliefs and religious issues are also important factors. For example, Ester for some Christians is an inappropriate time for sowing vegetable crops. Harvesting activities should not be programmed to take place during festivals, and failure to accommodate such traditions will result in negative farmer reaction. It must also be recognized that farmers require time to adjust to new practices.

1.18.4.3 Farmer Discontent

A number of situations can lead to farmer dissatisfaction. Discriminatory buying, late payments, inefficient extension services, poor agronomic advice, unreliable transportation for crops, a mild season change will all normally generate dissent. If not reality addressed such circumstances will cause hostility towards the sponsors that may result in farmers withdrawing from projects.

1.18.4.4 Extra-contractual Marketing

The sale of produce by farmers to a third party, outside the conditions of a contract, can be a major problem. Extra-contractual sales are always possible and are not easily controlled when an alternative market exists. For example, a farmer co-operative in Croatia bought cucumbers, red peppers and aborigines on contract. The co-operative advances to the farmers included all necessary production inputs. Unfortunately to buyers offered cash to farmer as opposed to the prolonged and difficult collection of payments negotiated through the co-operative. Sponsor themselves can sometimes be a cause of extra-contractual practices. There are several companies working with the same crop they could collaborate by establishing a register of contracted farmers. Managers must beaware of produce being sold outside the project and also be ware of produce from outside being channeled into the buying system. This occurs when non-contracted take advantage of higher prices paid by an established sponsor. Non- contracted crops are filtered into the buying system by outside farmers through friends and family who have crops contracts. Such practices make it difficult for the sponsors to regulate production targets, chemical residues and quality aspects.

1.18.4.5 Input Diversion

A frequent problem is that farmers are tempted to use inputs supplied under contract for purpose other than those for which they were intended. They may choose to use the inputs on their other cash and subsistence crops or even to sell them. Clearly this is not acceptable to the sponsor, as the contracted crops yields will be reduced and the quality affected. A step to overcome such problems includes improved monitoring by extension staff, farmer training and the issuing of realistic quantities of inputs. However, the knowledge market usually makes the majority of farmers to the agreement. Unless a project is very poorly managed, input diversion is usually an annoyance rather a serious problem.

1.19 Scope of Contract Farming in India

Indian agriculture is predominantly a small holder's occupation. More than 80 percent of the holdings are of size less than two hectares and these are getting further subdivided and smaller. The income from such small holdings is dominated by small food needs and crops occupy more than 83 percent of the cropped area. The emphasis on self-sufficiency centred production led to low value addition. Even if one assumes that these farmer can cultivate the best possible crops, the return remains meagre.[27] The problem gets further complicated as these farmer choose to remain close to their land and try to supplement their income by working as agricultural labour and rearing one or two milk animals. The share of workers engaged in agriculture fell by 14 percent in four decades, that is from 72 percent (in 1951) to 64 percent (in 2010-11). At the same time, the share of agriculture in National GDP decreased sharply from 55 percent to 18 percent for the same period.[28] This had exacerbated the rural and urban disparity in development and living standards. Several studies that investigated the problem confirm that the small farmer over the decades were more or less unanimous in finding that the major bottlenecks faced by them were lack of access to credit, poor marketing channels for agricultural outputs, weak extension service, etc. The crop insurance schemes in India had not been successful.[29]

The liberalizations of the economy in the 1990 and the WTO agreements have created a new set of challenges to the farming community in general and small farmer in particular. Farmer had been pulled by increasing demands of the markets and the state into a nexus of relationship that extends beyond the farm to national and international level. The interaction between small holders and more powerful economic and political organization is not new. What characterizes the contemporary situation is the variety of forces the small farmers must deal with. The size, complexity and impersonality of these organizations have resulted in a qualitative change in the nature of small holders' relationship to the outside world.[30]

Contract farming is viewed as a way to overcome some of the problems faced by small and marginal farmers. Apart from providing credit, input and extension service contract farming can introduce these farmers to the international market by organizing production of High Value Food (HVF). Contract farming is missing market for credit, insurance, information, factors of production in an environment of pervasive risks.[31]

The growth in agri-processing has great potential to trigger development in other sectors of the economy through though hardly exploited in India because of supply side constraints. It is estimated that only 2 percent of the fruits and vegetables produced in India are processed. It is often stated that 40 percent of fruit and vegetable go waste. At least 20 percent of food in value terms is squandered.[32] Processors of agricultural commodities most often requires a qualitatively homogenous product, but agricultural output is characterized by seasonalty, perish ability and variability. Therefore, it is imperative that the processing firms procure their raw materials in time, in the right quantity and quality.

However, there are several intermediaries between the firm and the farmer. It is estimated that there are at least six to seven intermediaries in fruit and vegetable marketing in India. The presence of a number of intermediaries in the supply chain results in the weak transmission of market signals about the quality and price to the farmer. The middlemen essentially pool the available surplus from the farmers paying little attention to quality. Consequently, the processors often find it difficult to get good quality raw material in sufficient quantity. On the other hand, farmers lack information about the market, that is, consumer preferences such as taste, flavour, price, etc. Further, they are not adequately rewarded for their efforts in producing quality products. Hence, there is little incentive for them to continue to do so if the processors themselves try to procure the quality raw material from the farmers at different locations, the search and information cost would be high. Further, they have to incur bargaining and decision cost on each transaction. However, there is still always the risk of procuring inferior raw material despite best efforts. Therefore ideally standards by acquiring and leasing in sufficient land, however, organizational constraints in many cases would not permit such an arrangement. Further, because of land willing legislation it is not possible to acquire large tracts of land. Hence, instead of vertical integration vertical co-ordination or contract farming is the more ideal solution for firms to get quality raw materials. Contract farming is an intermediate institutional arrangement that allows firms to participate in production and exert control over the production process without owning or operating the farm. Contract farming enables a processor to procure the necessary raw material in the right quantity, quality and in time with least cost.[33]

In India though contract farming is not new can be traced back to the colonial period. Goods were produced by Indian farmers for English factories. Seed production has been carried out through contract farming by seed companies quite successfully for more than four decades in the country. However the concept of contract farming has come a long way from such origins. Since the last couple of decades, contract farming is viewed as a tool to provide technology, extension service, credit, etc. to the farmers. Contract farming is getting prominent policy support to give a fillip to the fledgling agro-processing industry.

There are several agricultural and horticultural crops such as tomatoes, potatoes, chillies; gherkins baby corns, onions, cotton, wheat. Basmati rice, groundnut, flowers, medicinal plants, etc. produced under contractual arrangements with the farmers in India. Big corporate houses and several small players are involved in contract farming. Broiler chicken production in the state of Tamil Nadu is entirely under contract arrangement. Though most of the arrangements are bilateral between the firm and the farmer, there are tripartite and multipartite agreements as well, which include commercial banks and input suppliers. Contract farming in most of the crops mentioned above is mostly on a pilot basis. Recently many states started contract farming in a number of crops in an attempt to diversity the cropping pattern of the states to fulfil the government's objective of moving more hectares away from the crop rotation. Several companies are practising contract farming like Pepsi, Green Agropack, Reliance Agrotech, AV Thomas Group Kochi, HLL Coimbatore Costs and coatings Ltd., Ion Exchange Enviro Farm Ltd. L&M Group etc.

1.20 Need for Contract Farming in India

In our country the farmers face the problems of traditional technology and management practices, little bargaining power with input suppliers and produce markets, inadequate infrastructure and market information, lack of post-harvest management expertise, poor package of produce and inadequate capital to grow quality crop. They are waiting for change for better living standards.[34] The present marketing system has failed to provide a conductive environment to commodities having no government procurement /MSP like vegetable, fruits, medicinal plants, and floriculture, pluses and oilseeds crops. A slight increase in their production leads to price crash the existing agricultural marketing system in forward and backward linkages. The entry of private sector under set market rules and regulations may help overcome these bottlenecks. The public and private sectors can lend a helping hand by promoting contract farming instead of buying land from small and marginal farmers, which renders them landless. Contract farming with small farmers particularly when the farmer is not a tenant of the sponsor, is much more acceptable. The lack of market infrastructure results in about a 30 percent of our fruits and vegetable production go as waste with Rs. 28,810 crore annually, which is more than what the UK consumes in a year.[35] In such a scenario, contract farming is emerging as a variable global model of farming as farmer, price risk and post-harvest losses is significantly reduced with this. The small farmers are normally reluctant to adopt new technologies because of the possible risks and costs involved. They are more likely to accept new practices when they can rely on external sources in this respect.

The farmers get exposure to world-class agro-technology in the form of planting material and technical advance at their doorstep. Thus the farmers acquire new skills, both technical and managerial, through contract farming inculcate the concept of commercial cultivation.[36] Contract farming helps small farmers to participate in the production of high value crops like vegetables, flowers, fruits etc. and benefit from market led growth. Extensive areas are required by the agro-processors for an intensive cultivation to build an uniform method of cultivation that would reduce their production and transaction cost with the growers.[37] Contract farming facilitates more and more private companies to develop backward linkages with the farmers. Access to crop loans at attractive terms through tie-ups with banks is facilitated through contract farming and, there is a possibility and tendency amongst the farmers to go in for alternative cropping system for better monetary returns framers find it easy to get the inputs like credit, technological and extension services, post-harvest processing facilities and more importantly the marketing of their produce with assured cash returns under one roof.[38] With a buyer in Singh, the reliance of farmers on middlemen is almost eliminated. More important, contract farming reduces the transaction cost, especially the search cost and information cost about the availability of raw material. Regular supply of quality produce allows companies to plan their long-term strategies.

Further, development countries are specifying quality for imports of agricultural commodities and processed food from developing countries. We need to incorporate this food quality system in our food processing units. Otherwise, the sanitary and phyto-sanitary (SPS) agreement can act as a non-tariff barrier for our exports. Contract farming will help farmers to reap the benefits of globalization of agricultural trade.[39]

1.21 Role of Government in the Contract Farming

Government have to play an important role if contract farming is to be successful. A relevant legal framework and an efficient legal system are preconditions. Moreover, government can do much to foster success by developing linkages between investors and farmers and can play an important role in protecting farmers by ensuring the financial and managerial reliability of potential sponsors. The role of national government and their local agencies can be divided into regulatory role and development role.

1.21.1 Enabling and Regulatory Role

Contract farming depends on either legal or informal agreements between the contracting parties. In the context of contract farming the enabling aspect of the law is perhaps the most important. Laws of contract in particular, allow the evolution of commercial transactions beyond direct barter exchanges. Legal mechanisms for granting a group of individuals recognition a legal entity have also been central to the development of commerce. A classic example is the limited liability company. However, in the context of contract farming, a sponsor entering into agreement with a cooperative also needs to be assured that the cooperative is on a sound legal footing.[40]

Government need to be aware of the implications of all laws and policy decisions on agribusiness development and how these policies influence contract farming. Approaches to the government by the companies eventually resulted in the ban being lifted and this permitted the establishment of two contracts farming ventures to supply the rapidly growing fast food industry. Thus a simple policy reform ultimately benefited the sponsors and a large number of small-scale farmers.

While it may not be considered a precondition it is desirable that governments play an arbitration or dispute resolution role. Other government enabling activities to sustain contract farming may include:

(a) Provision for training in technological and managerial skills at all levels, if sponsors do not provide those services.

(b) Initiations and facilitation of research studies into the product under contract, in collaboration and consultation with the sponsors state research institutes can particularly benefit smaller ventures, especially those managed by individual developers who cannot sustain their own plant breeding programmes, etc.

(c) Provision of agricultural extension services to ventures that do not employ their own field staff. Small scale developers cannot afford the luxury of their own extension service and thus need to make use of government services.

At the national level, it is a precondition that specialized services are available to provide institutional support to production. Processing and marketing, government services, such as quarantine controls, plant pathology clinics and research stations are important for contract farming. Such services are particularly necessary for companies that invest in high value crops for export or in organic farming. Businessmen, particularly those involved with exports, frequently complain about the red tape and the costs involved with complying with excessive bureaucratic regulations and procedures. A simplification of official documentation, for example, could have a positive impact on the outlook of potential investors.

1.21.2 Development Role

As contract farming grows its importance should perhaps reallocate development resources towards its promotion. For example promotion of contract farming comes from India where the regional office of a government owned bank organized a meeting of bankers, agribusiness executives and the government extension service in order to explore possibilities of creating market linkages for agricultural product. This led to a major poultry producer contracting 2,200 farmers in 164 villages to grow maize and soybeans for feed purposes. Finance is provided by the banks, with a tripartite agreement being signed by farmers, the company and the bank.[41]

Where contracted farmers are organized into cooperatives or groups, governments can play an important role by carrying out activities to string the managerial skills of these organizations. Although the performance of agricultural cooperatives managerial capability should in theory, greatly enhance its business performance, the transfer of technology to farmers and its marketing skills.

The government has a role to play in ensuring that companies proposing to invest in contract farming are bonafide and are planning long-term partnership arrangements with farmers, rather than short-term operations which may leave farmers with considerable debts. Sponsors must have demonstrated financial strength, proven managerial competence and technological experience. Before promoting and launching projects, sponsors should create a suitable management and administrative structure and the purchase or lease of land for offices, processing facilities and transport needs should be organized in advance. Some projects may involve considerable capital investment and elaborate infrastructure such as that required for sugar milling, tobacco processing, vegetable canning and seed production.[42]

The Indian government to create enabling environment for growth especially in agriculture soon after independence, the government established research stations to develop new seeds etc., made provision for cheaper credit, invested in irrigation projects and developed market infrastructures. Over the time the market environment changed significantly after opening up of economy in 1991. The international trade in agricultural commodities increased. Tariffs were lowered under WTO and greater emphasis was on market led growth. This changed environment along with budgetary constraints and reduced inflow of foreign aid compelled the government to reduce its role. Under the circumstances contract farming was taken as means to develop markets, transfer technology, supply inputs and credit. But the strategy will differ from crop to crop and location, commercial decision between the producer and the contractor and its capability in creating enabling environment is limited. Similarly, contract farming as means to generate employment has limited effect and that too when new enterprise is more labour intensive. Nevertheless, government can play the role of a facilitatator where contract farming enhances export earning, reduces imports, helps diversification of cropping pattern, etc. The role of government should be confined to improving infrastructure facilities such as link roads, adequate electricity, water, finance, etc.[43] It may promote development of storage / cold storage, transport, processing at local level, and amend AMC act to permit direct procurement from farmers. The government must provide legal framework for protection of farmers especially marginal and small farmers and dispute setting agency at local level.

1.22 Importance of Contract Farming in Different Stages of Market Development

Based on stylized facts from developing countries, the importance of contract farming as an institution for facilitating market exchange differs at each stage of market development. Contract farming can be subdivided as.

Stage 1: Transformation from substance to commercial agriculture. The main function of contract farming is facilitating transformation from subsistence to commercial farming.

Stage 2: Development of agro-industry and crop diversification. Contract farming is essential in the growth and development of the agro-processing industry.

Stage 3: Mass production and spot market transaction. The market function well and the importance of contract farming is relatively limited.

Stage 4: Production differentiation and globalization. Contract farming functions as an institution to address market failures in the globalized market.[44]

1.23 Significance of the Study

Over the last five decades Indian agriculture has undergone a sea change altering significantly the rural landscape. Transformation is not only due to technological changes such as credit, inputs, extensions as well as development of infrastructure for marketing the output. The changes in the institutional set up were med by deliberate government policies in order to accelerate agriculture development and thereby augment rural income. In our country the farmers face the problems of traditional technology and management practices, little bargaining power with input suppliers and produce markets, inadequate infrastructure and market information, lack of post-harvest management expertise, poor package of produce and inadequate capital to grow a quality crop. Researchers feel that contract farming may help in solving all these problems.

Many project evaluation type studies show that contracting helped farmers to become better farmers, gave more reliable income generated in employment especially for women, provided new skills of farming, this way with patron-client relationship between large and small producers. So the present topic is chosen to study the helpfulness of contract farming in solving the problem of input supplies, marketing of produce income increasing product price etc.

1.24 Objectives of the Study

1. To study the progress of contract farming in India and Maharashtra.
2. To study cropping pattern of selected farmers participated in contract farming.
3. To study the impact of contract farming on economic development of selected farmers.
4. To study the effect of contract farming on agricultural production of selected farmers.
5. To study the changes in processing industries due to contract farming.

1.25 Hypotheses

1. Contract farming is helping the farmers in getting higher income.
2. Farmer gets security of selling production in proper time.
3. Due to contract farming farmers get higher price of goods than market price.

1.26 Research Methodology

The study is based on primary as well as secondary data. The primary data has been collected from field survey of contract and non-contract farmers covering four contracting companies, two processing companies and two seed companies. 25 contract farmers from each company and an equal number of non-contract farmers of the same area have been selected. The selected contracting companies are Bejo-Sheetal Seeds Pvt. Ltd. and Maharashtra Hybrid Seed Company Ltd. (Mahyco) working on onion and cotton seed farming respectively; Jain Irrigation System Limited and Pepsi-Co India Holding Pvt. Ltd. working on white onion and potato for processing contract farming respectively. Respondents are selected by using simple random sampling method and were interviewed personally using questionnaires. Due to the time and financial constraints we randomly select four contracting companies to collect the primary data. A majority of the contract growers have been associated with leading processing and seed companies. The survey data is based on recall memory of the contract growers but it is also supplemented by the data about the growers' inputs, output and prices for the production. The secondary data has also been collected from basic data on performance of contracting companies, books, journals periodicals, government reports and newspapers, etc.

The tools of analysis that are used include simple growth rates, trend analysis, ratio analysis, percentage, average etc., are used. For analysing the performance of contracting crops, simple growth rates of different parameters have been calculated.

1.27 Presentation of the Study

The present study consists of five chapters. The first chapter "Introduction" consists of agriculture economics, role of agriculture in India, meaning of contract farming, advantages and problems of contract farming, scope of contract farming in India, need for contract farming in India, the role of government in contract farming and importance of contract farming in different stages of market development, the objective of the study, research methodology adopted for the study, and significant of the study had been given in the this chapter.

The second chapter presents the review of current and relevant literature on the relevant subject. The national and state level literature on contract farming is reviewed in this chapter.

The third chapter is discusses agriculture in India, trends, market for agriculture products, consumption of food and agricultural achievements after independence.

The fourth chapter is devoted to present the performance of contract farming in India and Maharashtra. History of contract farming in India and Maharashtra is also discussed. This chapter also deals with Maharashtra contract Farming Act 2006 and performance of contract farming in Maharashtra.

The fifth chapter presents a case study of Maharashtra. In this chapter comparison in contract farmers and non-contract farmers and selected contracting companies performance, selected farmers' economic condition and effect on crop pattern and effect of contract farming on selected farmers had been also discussed.

The sixth chapter deals with findings of the present study and the policy measures.

Notes:

1. Sadhu and Singh (2007), *Fundamentals of Agricultural Economics,* Himalaya Pub. House, Mumbai.

2. Ibid.
3. Datt and Mahajan(2012) *Indian Economy*. S. Chand and Company Ltd., New Delhi.
4. op.cit. Sadhu and Singh.
5. Dhaka, J.M. (2009), *Economics of Agricultural Production and Farm Management*, Aavishkar Publishers and Distributors, Jaipur.
6. op.cit. Sadhu and Singh.
7. op.cit. Dhaka, J.M.
8. Eaton and Shepherd (2001) Contract Farming, Partnership for Growth, FAO Agricultural Services, Bulletin 145, Rome.
9. Rajmanohar, T.P. and Kumaravel K.S. (2006), *Contract Farming in India: An Introduction, IcFai* Books, IcFai University Press, Agartala, Tripura.
10. Singh S.(2003), Contract Farming in India, Impact on Women and Child Workers Gatekeeper Series No. 111, London.
11. op.cit. Eaton and Shepherd.
12. Roy and Ewell Poul (1963), *Contract Farming*, The Interstate Printers and Publishers Inc. (Denville, Illinois).
13. Nigel Key and James MacDonald (2006), *Agricultural Contracting. Trading Autonomy for Risk Reduction*, Amber Waves, February.
14. Joy Harwood et al. (1999), Managing Risk in Farming: Concepts, Research and Analysis, Agricultural Economic Report No. 774, USDA.
15. op.cit. Rajmanohar, T.P. and Kumaravel K.S.
16. Singh and Bhagat (2004), "Corporate Initiatives in Indian Agriculture", *Indian Management*, February.
17. Kamal Mathur, and Vinayagam S.S. (2011), Training Programme on Agricultural Marketing Management for Officials of Maharashtra Agriculture Competitiveness Project (MACP), Government of Maharashtra, CCS National Institute of Agricultural Marketing, Bambala, Kota Road, Jaipur.
18. Paty, B.K. (2005), "Contract Farming in India: Progress and Potential", *Agricultural Marketing*, Vol. XLVIII, No.1.

19. Sarkar, A.N.(2003), Techno-Economic Feasibility Study on Contract Farming in Maharashtra, Vaikunth Mehta National Institute of Cooperative Management, Pune.
20. Sharma, Premjit (2007), *Contract Farming*, Gene-Tech Books, New Delhi.
21. Singh Gurdev (2003), *Contract Farming in India: Text and Cases*, Oxford & IBH Publishing Co. Pvt. Ltd., New Delhi.
22. Ibid.
23. Ibid.
24. op.cit. Eaton and Shepherd.
25. Shoja Rani, B.N., *Globalization and Contract Farming in India Advantages and Problems*, www.dspace.iimk.ac.in./bitstream/520/1/6337-647pdf
26. Ibid.
27. Asokan, S.R. and Singh G. (2001), "Small Farmers;An Enlarlaged Species", *Political Economy Journal of India*, 10 (142), 1-6
28. op.cit. Datt and Mahajan.
29. Deshpande, R.S. (2008), *Contract Farming and Tenancy Reforms Entangled without Tether*, Concept Publication Company, New Delhi.
30. Glover, D. and Kusterer K. (1990), *Small Farmer, Big Business; Contract Farming and Rural Development*, London, Macmillan.
31. Key and Runsten (1999), Contract Farming, Smallholders and Rural Development in Latin America: The Organisation of Agro Processing Firms the Scale of Out Grower Production, World Development, 27(2) 381-401.
32. Mahendra, S. et al. (2005), "Food Processing and Contract Farming in Andhra Pradesh: A Small Farmer Perspective", *Economic and Political Weekly*, June, 25.
33. Asokan, S.R. and Singh G. (2004), Scope of Contract Farming in India, paper presented at a seminar on contractual and cooperative farming held at GAU, Anand.
34. Balasubramanian, U.A. (2004), Contract farming, Newsletter, *IMAGE*, Chennai, AISSUE-17.
35. op.cit., Deshpande, R.S.

36. Rangi and Sidhu (2004), "Development of Market Infrastructure for Globalization in India", *Indian Journal of Agriculture Marketing,* Vol. 18(3) pp I-22.
37. op.cit. Balasubramanian, U.A.
38. Channaveere Gowda, B.N. (2011), "Contract Farming and Contractual Arrangement A Descriptive Analysis", *Southern Economist.*
39. op.cit. Deshpande, R.S.
40. FAO (1999), "Law and Markets – Improving the Legal Environment for Agricultural Marketing, *Agricultural Services Bulletin,* No. 139, Rome.
41. National Bank for Agriculture and Rural Development (NABARD), (1999), News Review, Jan-March, Volume 15, No. 1:56.
42. op.cit. Eaton and Shepherd.
43. Singh, G. and Asokan S.R. (2005), "Contract farming" in Ramesh Chand (Ed.) *India's Agricultural Challenges: Reflections on Policy Technology and Other Issues,* Centrad.
44. Sununtar, S. (2008), Global Partnership in Poverty Reduction: Contract farming and Regional Cooperation, ADB Institute Discussion Paper No. 89.

2

REVIEW OF LITERATURE

In this chapter an attempt has been made to review some of the existing literature on contract farming conducted in different states in India and the world as well. Some of them are as follows:

Singh[1] has conducted a study on Contract Farming and Agricultural Diversification in the "Indian Punjab: A Study of Performance and Problems". He made an attempt to find the role of contract farming in agricultural diversification and development in terms of its practices and implications for producers and the Punjab economy. The paper focuses on the nature of contracts, and studies the perceptions of both the farmer and the firm of the working of the contract system and its effect on the local economy. The researcher summarizes that the studies on contract farming helped farmers for the betterment, gave more reliable income, generated employment especially for women, provided new skills in farming, and did away with the patron-client relationship between large and small producers. Contract farming has several disadvantages too: poor extension services, low prices to farmer due to haphazard pricing of the products, inherent higher risk to cultivators, frequent delays in payment, week bargaining power of farmer, sole dependence on companies for inputs as credit, overexploitation of groundwater and the threat of the environmental and finally, the fact that companies often move to new pastures (virgin plots) to exploit land water resources at the least cost, leaving farmer cultivator high and dry. One of the reasons for contract farming coming into existence in India was the Land Ceiling Act which stipulated that "agribusiness firms cannot own and cultivate land for their raw material requirements, to overcome the difficulties encountered in procuring from the open market, especially in perishables". Therefore, the only option for agribusiness firms was to go in for contract farming safeguarding their interests. The study reveals that for the success of contract farming, there is need for institutional and organizational innovations in the rural sector. Contract farming should be under scrutiny from time to time; wide publicity should be given to land available for contract farming competitiveness; legal protection to be provided to growers under contract farming, and the fair trade commission should monitor contract farming practices on continuous basis.

Dilip[2] has conducted a study "Contract Farming in Tomato: An Economic Analysis" and focuses on cost, returns and resource use efficiency, and the effect of contract farming on price, production and income of farmers as also yield variation, marketing costs and the possible losses to farmers. The study was conducted in the block of Sirsa district in Haryana, where the contract system has been in practice since 1989. Two processing firms, vis., HLL and Nijjer Agro Foods Ltd (NAL) were studied. A sample of 50 contract farmers were interviewed out of 125 tomato growers under the contract system , 50 non-contract farmers were also interviewed during 1999-2000. The study reveals that the processing firms preferred large farmers contract farming. The cost incurred, yield and gross return obtained by contract farmers were almost double compared with that of non-contract farmers. The uncertainty over yield and price was much less under contract farming. Surprisingly, the price received for tomato by non-contract farmers was found to be higher than that of contract farmers. Transportation cost was a major component of marketing costs. Farmers demanded that the contract between the farmer and the corporate should be enforceable by law is necessary through fresh legislation by the government. Overusage of inputs like fertilizers and pesticides should be brought down to ensure plant protection and to secure higher yields and farmers need to be educated in this regard. A crop insurance scheme needs to be introduced for tomato farming which induces risk due to higher incidence diseases and pest attack beside possible adverse climatic conditions.

Kiresu et al.[3] has published paper "Contract Farming Opportunity of Small and Marginal Farmers in the Context of Trade Liberalization". This paper brings out the true picture of Indian agriculture in general, and the exact position of small and marginal farmer in particular. They have highlighted several miss-matches in Indian agriculture viz-a-viz the agricultural scenario of developed countries. They recommend contract farming in view of its advantages to both the farming community and contractors as one of the better options for fulfilling the objectives of the liberalized trade regime.

Asokan and Singh[4] have undertaken a study on Role and Constraints of Contract Farming in Agro Processing Industry. They stated that the contract farming is a dynamic partnership between agribusiness firms and farmers, which benefit both and it acts as vehicle for transfer of technology. There were two types of contract existed between the firm and farmer, viz. marketing and production contracts. Marketing contract is the oral or written agreement between contractor and a grower that sets a price and an outlet for the commodity before the harvest or before the commodity is ready to be marketed. In this contract most of the management decisions remain with the growers since they retain ownership till the final disposal of the commodity. The producer bears all the risks of production, shares only the price risk with contractor. The second type of contract is production contract which specifies the quality and quantity of particular commodity to be procured, and the contracting firm has supplied all the inputs to growers. The contracting firm monitors the production practices and quality of the products.

Kumar and Singh[5] observed the Success and Failure of Contract Farming in Himachal Pradesh: A Case Study of Cauliflower Seed Production. They studied success and failure of contract farming in Himachal Pradesh for cauliflower seed production in the agricultural year 2002 -2003. The study was based on the data collected from 45 farmers of Saffron valley of Himachal Pradesh. National seed Corporation (NSC) firstly introduced the contract farming in Saffron valley in 1966 and it remained in operation up to 1977. After withdrawal of NSC from the area the producers are dependent on the private firms for the marketing of seed. In the present system the net returns per hectare were relatively higher in cauliflower seed (Rs.1,11,994 / hectare) followed by tomato (Rs. 68,972 / hectare) peas (Rs.28,068 / hectare) and capsicum (Rs. 21,180 / hectare). The production of cauliflower seed had reduced the seasonality of employment in agriculture lean period and utilizing the ideal family labour. The private firms operative in the area are successfully attracting the firms for the production of cauliflower seeds as they are providing technical know-how, timely supply of mother seed and credit and assured market. The problems faced were absence of written legal agreement, lack of prior price information, near monopoly of big firms, dedications made to account the moisture content and foreign material in the seed.

N. Nagaraj[6] has conducted study "Contract Farming and Related Issues". He focused on economics of contract farming of green chilies, baby corn and poultry in Karnataka and their impact on income, employment and access to technology and credit by contract farmers and non-contract farmers. This study focused on economic analysis of contract farming to compare income, technology and credit access of contract and non-contract farmers and to evaluate advantage of contract farming for small holders and to compare advantages of contract farming under foreign firms and domestic firms.

Multistage sampling method was used to choose sample farmers. In the first stage, based on the concentration of area under baby corn and chili contract farming, one domestic firm and one foreign firm were selected. In the second stage, discussion was arranged with the production manager of the company and a cluster of villages participating in contract farming was chosen. Finally based on the farmers details maintained by the firm, around 180 contact farmers, 45 each growing baby corn and 45 each growing green chilies under foreign contracting firm and domestic contracting firm were selected. A sample of 40 farmers who are not involved in contract farming but cultivating baby corn and green chilies are chosen as control. The socio-economic analysis of sample respondents indicated that they were young to middle aged. More than 90 per cent of sample farmers were educated. There was not a marked difference with respect to age, family, size and education. The size of land holding was higher (7.41 acres) among non contract farmers than contract farmers (4.6 acres in foreign contract and 3.5 in domestic contract). The irrigated area was also higher among non-contract farmers than contract farmers. The contract had higher proportion of area under irrigation.

Domestic contract farming firm had oral contract with farmers while foreign contract farming firm had both written and oral agreements. Both the firms take care to see that the contract area is between 0.5 acre to 2 acre per contract farmer under the contract crop per season. Firms supplied necessary input to contract farmers, thus reducing the working capital to the tune of 30 per cent. Farmers' share of purchased inputs was around 50 per cent.

The imputed cost owned inputs including family labour accounted for around 20 per cent for both contract and non-contract farmers. In the case of baby corn, around 51 per cent of the gross cropped area of farmers was under contract by domestic firm as against 36 per cent by foreign firms, which in chilies was 72 per cent of area by domestic firm as against

35 per cent in the case of foreign firm. In both the crops harvesting consumed major labour where 80 per cent of the labours employed were women. Crop loan borrowed by non-contract farmers was 33 per cent higher than contract farmers, as they had to buy material inputs. The production cost of baby corn per acre was Rs. 8,499 for contract farmers under domestic firms and Rs. 9,653 for non-contract farmers. Similarly, production cost of chilies was Rs. 26,657, Rs. 24,464 and Rs. 23,493 per acre for farmers under foreign, domestic contract firms and non-contract firms, respectively. For baby corn, the farmers under domestic contract firm realized higher productivity of 22.59 quintals per acre compared to 19.54 quintals per acre for farmers under foreign firm followed by 16.19 quintals per acre for non-contract farmers. There exists inequity in income distribution between contract and non contract farmers as there was greater variation in the production of baby corn across contract and non-contract farmers. The inequity in distribution of income was higher for non-contract farmers when compared to contract farmers as validated by gini co-efficient within the contract farmers, the small farmers had lesser instability of income compared to large farmers indicating that small and medium performed better and realized higher production and better incomes.

Some major problems faced by the contract sample farmers in production and marketing of broilers has been indicated. According to the opinion of the sample contract farmers, the major problems experienced were delays in the chick supply, high mortality rate, delay in lifting birds and inadequate batch size. Around 6 per cent of farmers contracting international firm, 25 per cent contracting national firm and 20 per cent of local farmers opined poor quality chicks as the major problem. Around 8 per cent of farmers contracting international firm, 20 per cent contracting national firm and 5 per cent of local farmers opined high cost of inputs as the major problem. On the other hand 32 per cent of farmers contracting international firm, 18 per cent contracting national firm and 15 per cent local farmers expressed that there are no problems in contract farming.

Rajmanohar and Kumaravel[7] published a book *Contract Farming in India: An Introduction*. They introduce the theory of contract farming in general and with reference to India in particular. They also tries to highlight some of the socio-economic studies of farmers related to contract farming in India. Valuable experiences are too dealt within this book. It also describes in detail the general modus operandi, internal functions and monitoring mechanisms of contract farming suitable for both firms and farmers. This book has been divided into two sections titled concepts and Indian experiences. Since contract farming has attained a major role in commercializing Indian agriculture, it is imperative to know the concepts involved in contract farming from the point of view of both the firms and the farmers. Hence, the first section of the book titled 'Concepts' is devoted to an introduction of the general concepts of contract farming which highlight the theoretical application conditions. The second section titled 'Indian Experience' is intended to share some of the contract farming experience in different conditions in different areas of India.

Kumaravel[8] has published paper "Contract Farming Concepts and Issues". In this article he has covered various definitions, models, types, advantages and disadvantages of contract farming. He also specially deals with the issues emerging out of contract farming, the successful implementation and practice of contract farming in India. He concluded that the corporate intervention in agriculture through contract farming arrangements is taking a vital/lead role in linking the corporate firms and the farmer. India has potential benefits in contract farming due to its diversified nature and comparative advantage in agricultural. The options available for India to explore in contract farming are many. Successful contracts not only lie with the integration of the socio-economic environment in which the firms operate but also with proper selection of crops. Not all the crops are suited for contract farming. Crops which are well-suited in Indian conditions for contract farming are horticultural crops including export oriented fruits and flowers, medicinal crops, cotton and oilseed corps.

MacDonald's[9] in "Why Deals Use Contract? The Economics of Contract" deals with the drawbacks of spot markets and reasons for farmers opting for contracts. The economics of contracting is well dealt within this article. It enlists and explains the positive points of contracting vis-a-vis reducing risk and providing incentives, reducing transaction costs in some spot markets, clarity in asset specification, reduced costs of search, measurement and monitoring and economy involved in cost due to contracts. It mainly focuses on two sources of income risk – yield (or production) risk and price risk and the need for minimizing such risks by contractual arrangements. He observes that spot markets will fail to respond to changes in consumer demand, if prices do not reflect the attributes of products that consumers prefer. Parties will rely on contracts, when the transaction costs of using contract fall below the cost of using spot markets.

Sukhpal Singh[10] undertaken the article integrates Contract Farming with Respect to Agricultural Development Focusing on India. It is a working paper of CENTA entitled "Contract Farming for Agricultural Development – Review of Theory and Practice with Special Reference to India". In this article, the author throws light on some of the finer points of contract farming with reference to the agricultural development of India. According to the author, a farmer may prefer a contract due to the easy access to additional sources of capital or the fixed price or the free access to new technology and inputs. The article points out some of the drawbacks of contract farming such as firms favouring large farmers and better endowed regions, little bargaining power of farmer, encouraging 'Reverse tenancy', interlocking of markets, equity and efficiency implications leading to food insecurity and ecological degradation. It also pinpoints some of the problems faced by contract growers like undue quality cut on produce by firms, delayed deliveries at the factory, delayed payments, low price and pest attack on the crop with no compensation. Various model involved in contract farming with respect to India are also discussed in this article. He concluded that given the nature of modern farming involving tremendous amount of technological input and market orientation which require capital resources, it is but inevitable to involve private corporate business interests in agricultural development through contract farming system. Contracts require frequent and independent scrutiny so that they remain competitive both with similar contract and with open market transactions. Wide publicity of contract terms will help to stimulate competition. From the producers point of view, specific points to be considered in negotiating the contract terms include the method of determining the producers price, adjustments for quality differentials, allowance for climatic variations, farm practices, credit terms, provisions for renewal and termination of contract and for arbitration. The other tools of mitigating loss of control used by farmers in the first world have been the petitioning of the state of intervention to regulate the contract, the formation of producer bargaining units, and the formation of farmers markets. There have also been experience of complete failure when co-operative or state agencies were contractors. Working with farmer co-operative for better and more sustainable contract procurement by private agribusiness firms seems to work for both the parties. This is an experiment being tried out by Marico Industries in Maharashtra state of India in safflower oilseeds. The company provided working capital, infrastructural facilities, managerial inputs, and contract job crushing which helped the crushing unit co-operative to become viable.

Gurdev and Asokan[11] in their study "Contract Farming in India", focuses on the nature of contract farming and the practical problems in its application with respect to Indian conditions and also suggests some valuable solutions. The authors opine that contract farming in India is undergoing a lot of teething problems mainly due to poor design, unsuitability of crop and a lot of apprehension on the farmers' side. The article reveals that gherkin production in Karnataka and broiler chicken production in Tamil Nadu under the contract arrangement have been successful for more than a decade without much problem as farm size did not prove to be a limiting factor in both the cases. The article also suggests a few solutions for free and fair contract. The study concluded contract farming arrangements seem to be successful in crops where the firm and the farmers are locked in asset-specific investment with little room for opportunistic behaviour of either party, Innovative pricing mechanism, that is, rewarding the farmer according to his efforts, assessing the quality of the product as far as possible, objectively contributes to the success of a scheme, transparency by the firm in dealing with the farmers with regard to price, weight measurement, grading and payment builds trust and contributes to the longevity of the arrangements.

Sunil Khairnar and V. Yeleti[12] the published paper, "Contract Farming in India: Impact and Implications" describes some of the theoretical aspects of contract farming with reference to India. It also deals with existing forms of contract farming and their problems, the role of government parameters for optimal contractor ship etc. The article also points out the peculiar approach to its program including banks such as ICICI and SBI for providing agricultural credit and Hindustan Lever as buyers and Cargil to lift the product. The authors list some of the prominent examples of contract farming in India. They concluded that the advantage of contract farming is biased towards the agribusiness firms involved in the contract and the case for contract farming in India as an option for small and marginal farmers does not quite exist. However, this should not rule out the beneficial effects of contract farming schemes, especially in efficient market outcomes, and indirect positive economic welfare such as rural employment generation both on the farms and in the processing plants. It can be said, though not conclusively, that landless, small and marginal farmers do benefit through the evolution of off-contract practices like 'reverse tenancy' and 'sub-contracting', and ready market for surplus tradable labour. The entry of an agribusiness firm and the evolution of contract farming arrangements in an area can bring to the farmers' access, hitherto hard-to-avail credit, farm inputs, and more necessarily new technology, new crops, and better farm practices.

Pratap and Joshi[13] paper "Vertical Co-ordination in High Value Food Commodities: Implications for Smallholders" trie to evaluate the significance of high value crop under contract and non-contract farming, by selecting three firms viz., Nestle India Limited – a multinational firm for milk and milk products. Venkateshwara Hatcheries Limited (VHL) – a private sector domestic firm engaged in contract broiler farming and Mother Dairy Fruits and Vegetables Ltd. (MDFVL) a wholly owned subsidiary of public sector entity (namely, National Dairy Development Board), which sources fruits and vegetables through producers' associations. Prominent findings of this study are the considerable reduction of transaction costs due to organized institutional arrangements under contract farming and improved market efficient with regard to smallholders. A common feature that the three models have shown is that they offer technical support for production and guarantee an assured market to the producers. In broiler farming, the firm adds in terms of major inputs and exercises substantial control over the production process, but on producers decision. Transaction cost as a result of contract farming has been reduced by over 90 percent in the case of milk and vegetables, and 58 percent in the case of broilers. The net revenue realization by contract producers has been 2 to 4 times higher in milk and vegetables and 1.1 times in broilers.

Prasad B.V.S.[14] in this paper "Contract Farming in India: Option and Implications for Small and Large Farmers", discusses contract farming experiences of Punjab in particular and India in general. The author suggests that small farmers can lease out their land in fevour of medium and large farmers and the large farmers can take some land on lease in order to make contract farming more effective. The article evaluates contract farming from a small versus large farm perspectives, measures the level of crop diversification in the farming, the role of corporate-led contract farming in raising productivity–profitability and in boosting growth in the agricultural sector. The article concludes with the observation that contract farming has been able to diversify the cropping pattern as well as increase the productivity of farms in Punjab. He concluded that contracting are very promising in the early years. Farmers benefit from improved technology and higher productivity, quality and production. However, once farmers deploy themselves into the new technology, problems start cropping up. If the market price is more advantageous than the contract price, farmers renege on the contract. Generally the contracts are not written and the legal enforcement system is too tedious for both growers and firms.

www.manage.gov.in[15] published an article by unknown author in SPICE magazine of MANAGE entitled, "Contract Farming Ventures in India: A Few Successful Cases". The major success stories of contract farming in India are dealt within this article. They are the Pepsi Foods Ltd. of Punjab in packaged food products; the Appachis of Tamil Nadu involved in integrated cotton cultivation and Ugar Sugar Works Ltd. of Karnataka in sugar production. The article discusses some of the bottlenecks and drawbacks of contract farming in India with respect to both farms and firms. The criticisms leveled against farms / farmers are, a limited number of farmer participation in the field, seeds production inputs purchase, choice of technology packages and availing of appropriate technical guidance etc. On the firms' part, the drawbacks pointed out are low employment generation, introduction of lesser labour saving farm practices, low level of commitment in rural development, lack of transparency and communication in price fixation and payment schedule, etc.

Arbind Gupta[16] has published paper "Re-spinning Strategies". He tries to resolve the problems occurred in the cotton supply chain. The article highlights the contract farming projects in cotton which has witnessed a growth in the yield of cotton cultivation by 20-40 % and an average increase of 18-45 % in net income in the states of Haryana, Maharashtra and Andhra Pradesh. Some of the constraints faced in contract farming of cotton are briefed in this article, like lack of awareness by farmers, small size of land holdings, meagre participation by mills and ginners and lack of credit and crop insurance. He concluded that domestic textile mills are too busy with upgrading their production base to meet the challenges of changed market scenario, and once they are through with this process in coming few months, they will shift their focus to the raw material sourcing in a major way.

Mahendra Dev's[17] article deals with the food processing sector of Andhra Pradesh. It is entitled, "Food Processing and Contract Farming in Andhra Pradesh: A Small Farmer Perspective". In this article conducted a study on Oil Plam and Gherkin cultivation in West Godavari and Chitoor districts respectively. He states that contract farming operations have by and large solved the problems of quality raw materials supply. Oil palm growers were keen on an assured minimum price whereas the gherkin growers were totally dependent on export demand. A few solutions are put forth by the authors to streaming the contract farming system of Indian agroprocessing industries. They concluded that the participation of small farmers in oil palm cultivation is almost negligible. However, it is surprising to note that the crop was introduced in the state with an intention to help the small farmers get additional income. That was the reason for the higher average age of plantations of marginal farmers and

SCs. But later, sensing good profits, large farmers entered the cultivation. On the other hand, the long gestation period (four years), high investment needed for the crop despite subsidies, or special package for cultivation of intercrops as in coconut and the lack of separate line of credit seem to have alienated the small farmers from oil palm cultivation. In gherkin, participation of small farmers was considerable. This may be because of labour-intensive nature of the crop and drip irrigation facility created. Other countries where the processors favoured small farmers for contract farming because of low cost production in some crops and areas, directions of the government and availability of family labour.

Prabhakaran's[18] study "Private Sector Partnerships in Poultry Production and Marketing in India: A Case Study of Tamil Nadu" is based on their earlier FAO project. The major players involved in contract poultry farming in Tamil Nadu are Suguna, Pioneer, Shanti and Selvam Hatcheries. The major private sector partnership witnessed in broiler production was the one between the integrator / firm and the contracted broiler production. The type of contract in terms of farmers obligation and the contractors obligations and criteria for calculation the incentives accrued by the contract farmers, like productivity score feed conversion ration are highlighted in the article. Similarly, regarding integrators, the advantages such as lesser cost of production and better profit margin are also discussed.

Ramesh T. and Cracy C.P. in their[19] article "Contract Farming: Experiences of Ghekin Cultivation in Tamil Nadu" define the scope of contract farming arrangements in gherkin cultivation in the study area of Triunelveli, Dharmapuri and Dindigul districts of Tamil Nadu. Various metrics on contract farming arrangement are also discussed extensively. The major reasons for success of contract farming in gherkin and the defects in gherkin cultivation with respect to contract farming are well presented in this article. Some of the benefits of contract farming to the processor / firm and farmer are also discussed in this article in detail. They concluded that oral contractual arrangements prevailed in gherkin cultivation and mutual trust on other party is the key for successful contracts. The terms and conditions of the contract are determined by the processor and growers have little say in deciding the contractual obligations. The value of physical inputs supplied by the processor on credit ranged between 17 to 26.5 percent of the cost of cultivation while farmers's own assets and contribution ranged between 25 to 40 percent of cost of cultivation. The farmers are satisfied with the technical guidance and supervision provided by the field supervisors employed by the processor. These field officers ensured that the contractual relationship is smooth and progressing.

Singh[20] had published a book *"Political Economy of Contract Farming in India"*. He focuses at the logic, process and implications of contract farming arrangement from the producers and local economy's point of view with help of a field study in the Indian Punjab. The study defines the concept of contract farming and traces its logic as a system. The implication of contract farming arrangement for the primary producers as reported in various standard of literature from theory and practices angles, are discussed for contract growers, food production, availability and security effect an environment, social and economic differentiation and on gender. The objectives of this study were, to explore the nature of contract, a cross classes of farmers and companies; to study the farmers and the firms perception of the working of the contract system and problem, if any, and to examine the effect of contract system on the local economy and the community; and the sustainability of the contract system. The methodology used for the understanding the contract system looks at the performance and problems of the contract farming system in the given context based on case studies of firms and on interview, survey of contract growers of different crops. The primary survey of contract growers was conducted in district of Amritsar, Jalandhar, Patiala and Bhatinda in Punjab and the Sirsa district in Haryana and four crops such as tomato, potato, chilies and green mustard and four contracting companies H.L.L., Nijjer, Pepsi, and markfed. This provides a breeder contextual analysis of the contract farming arrangement in terms of its political economic aspects. Finally, major conclusions from the study and policy suggestions for better design and management to contract farming system are discussed. The analysis of case studies in Punjab reveals that though contracting has led to better income for the farmers and more employment for labour to begin with, it is not a smooth sailing for firms and unlikely to be sustained due to lack of trust between firms and farmers and tendencies towards agribusiness normalization and monopolization by firms. A comparison of contract systems of local and multinational firms shows that the local firm is better able to relate to the growers due to its local language contracts and local origins which is evident in larger proportion of its growers willing to continue with it compared to the growers of the multinational. One of the major issues in the farming sector of Punjab has been that of farmer participation in agro-industrial development as it is belived that the capital farmers have accumulated under the Green Revolution regime, significant investible surpluses which need to be given an outlet for investment. That purpose is certainly not being served by the contract farming model of agricultural change, as these firms are the only beneficiaries of value addition surplus and do not share the extra profits with farmers in any way. An analysis of the labour conditions under contract farming system shows that the labour issues in contract farming are still not addressed in research on contract farming. Since contract production is primarily carried out with female labour about and increasingly child—there is a need to address the whole question of changing agrarian production structure under contract farming from a gender perspective with focus on issues of transfer of skills, choice of technology, organization of labour, working conditions and terms of work.

Shoja Rani[21] has published a paper "Globalization and Contract Farming in India: Advantages and Problems". She focuses on contract farming history and advantages, disadvantages for farmers and sponsors and lastly conclusions. She conclude that there are some problems in contract farming to both. For successful implementation of contract farming having co-ordination consciousness and acting in an organized manner are advisable for both sides. Government attitudes and incentives are also important aspects in contract farming.

Gahukar[22] has published a study "Contract Farming for Organic Crop Production in India" and focuses on organic crop production through contract farming. In the world there has been increasing demand for organic food and fiber. In India efforts are being made for organic crop production through contract farming. Experiences showed that farmers are benefited from teaching guidance, supply of quality farm inputs and assured purchasing at remunerative price. This venture if executed by a tripartite agreement would bring about favourable changes in the present conventional agriculture to make it sustainable and commercial like-wise consumers would get certified organic product at reasonable price. Author explains some perspectives that the Indian food market is valued at Rs. 6,50,000 crore but only 106 of farm products are exported in comparison to USA (12 percent), the Netherland, Canada (6 percent) U.K., Brazil, Italy (3 percent). In organic farming some challenges have given convincing farmers about the economic benefits of contract farming through field demonstrations should be taken up urgently. Organic farming on contract basis requires a long term approach as it is based on the trust of farmers, for which grass roots intervention is critical for its success. Certification cost for organic product is comparatively high and need to be reduced drastically, facilities for storing and verification of quality of agriculture commodities at village level are lacking. Banks are ready to finance contract farming in organic agriculture to only those farmers who are not defaulters.

Tripathi et al.[23] have "Contract Farming in Potato Production: An Alternative for Managing Risk and Uncertainty". This study was based on the primary data collected from 54 respondents of Haryana and the study area is district of Karnal, Kuruksheta and Ambala, and the contracting company is DCM Shriram Consolidated Ltd. (DSCL). They focus on cost of potato cultivation and comparative study of yield and price. The cost of cultivation (17 to 24 percent high), crop yield, gross income and net income over various costs have been found higher under contract farming as compared to the non-contract system of potato production. The benefit cost ratio is almost double under contract farmering as compared to that in non-contract farms. The profitability could be increased by the rational use of irrigation under contract farms and manure and fertilizers non-contract farms to manure a non-contract farms. The yield and price uncertainty has been found higher for non-contract than contract farms. In the contract farm crop yield has been found 8.84 percent higher than non-contract farming and the average price received by the potato growers is much high (390/9) in the contract than non-contract farms (179/9). No price uncertainty has been observed in case of contract farming system of Potato production. It is revealed that resource use efficiency can be reduced and price uncertainty minimized through adoption of contract farming in potato production.

Singh[24] has published a paper "Multi-national Corporation and Agricultural Development: A Study of Contract Farming in the Indian Punjab". He examines the role of the MNCs in agricultural development in institutional economics perspective by analysing the performance of the contract system; exploring the nature of contracts; studying the farmer and the firm perceptions of the functioning of the contract system; and looking into the effect of contract system on the local economy in Punjab. The case studies are based on primary survey of contract farmers in the state of Punjab with the help of an interview schedule prepared for the purpose and discussions with official of the MNC subsidiaries involved in processing and marketing of three crops (potato, tomato and chilies) being procured under contract. The primary survey of contract growers was conducted in Amritsar, Jalandhar, Patiala and Bhathinda districts in Punjab.

Setboonsarng's[25] paper "Global Partnership in Poverty Reduction: Contract Farming and Regional Cooperative" focuses on the evaluation contract farming, its define, advantages and disadvantages the importance examines strategies for mitigating contract farming challenges and looks of the different types of Asian contract farming schemes, discusses how contract farming can be a viable and finally recommendation for the successful promotion of contract farming. He stated major concerns: monophony control, the burden of labour management, contract enforcement, bias towards large farmers, requirement for increased management skills, increased risk and health and environment implication.

Ashaltha and Devraja[26] have conducted a study on Opportunity for Contract Farming in Banana: A Case Study at Tamil Nadu State. In Tamil Nadu banana production is cultivated in many districts from contract farming. Authors focus on India as the largest producer of banana in the world with an annual production of 16.8 million tonnes. Most of it is consumed internally and hardly 0.1 per cent of the produce is exported. Tamil Nadu has the largest area and production under banana cultivation and stands second in productivity next to Maharashtra. Around 60 to 65 per cent of the banana product in Tamil Nadu is consumed within the state and remaining 35-40 per cent of the produce is marketed to different country markets, mostly Trivandrum from where it is exported. The farmers in Tirunelveli district and other parts of Tamil Nadu are aware of the likely benefits of contract farming and are enthusiastic about the implementation of the concept. There are few corporate really interested in venturing in to contract farming in this area. A consortium of exporters if farmed can give a big boost to banana contract forming in southern district to Tirunelveli and Tuticorin. Author has done the case study in four districts in Tamil Nadu. These are Trichy, Coimboture, Tirunelveli and Tuticorin, and participate in contract farming with some corporate firms in collaboration. There are firms like Southern Petrochemical Industries Corporation for supply of tissue culture seed material, Mahindra Shubhlabh Services Ltd. for inputs and Bhuvi Care for technical services.

Rangi and Sidhu[27] had published a paper "Contract Farming in Punjab". They examines some of the policy issues related to contract farming in the Punjab state scheme. The data was culled out of the report of Punjab Agro Food-Grain Corporation Ltd., Chandigarh, and covers many advertisements in the newspaper on contract farming as also responses of the few contract farmers who were interviewed. Again after a gap of 16 years, the S.S. Joshi committee has been reconstituted. The committee recommended that in 10 lakh hectares now under paddy and wheat crops, rotation should be introduced to replace paddy / wheat by crop that consumes less water to check the adverse effects on the ecology and also to meet the demand for such products in the country. "Vegetable Crops are more labour intensive and can provide 4-5 times more employment opportunities in rural areas, as compared with wheat and paddy crops" says the report.

Sharma[28] has published a paper "India's Agrarian Crisis and Smallholder Producers' Participation in New Farm Supply Chain Initiative: A Case Study of Contract Farming". He tries to understand socio-economic implications of corporate led initiatives in agriculture (mainly contract farming) in the state of Punjab, which has more experience in contract farming compared to the other states. The results indicate that contract farming is a good initiative for medium and large scale farmers producing for the market but the long-term success of such initiatives will depend on how a large number of small and marginal farmers can be linked to restructured markets under changing market and policy environment. The study points out that it is important to provide an integrated set of services including credit and not just seed and limited extension services partnership between public and private sector companies / organizations is needed in order to provide these integrated services. More important is to improve bargaining power of smallholder producers while also reducing transaction costs for companies through promotion of producers groups / association / co-operatives. Small farmers will be able to effectively participate in the changing markets and establish links with new market chains (super markets agribusiness companies, processors, exporters etc.) only if they have access to basic infrastructure, quality inputs and services and are organized. The focus of study has to examine impact of corporate-led agricultural growth through a case study of recent experiments with contract farming in food grains in Punjab. The study has production Basmati rice and confined two districts namely Ludhiana and Jalandhar, covering about 50-60 farmers. However, finally a small sample of about 40 farmers growing Basmati rice is used for the present case study. The study is based on a small sample size.

Sharma[29] in his paper "India's Agrarian Crisis and Corporate-led Contract Farming: Socio-Economic Implications for Smallholder Producers" discusses India's agrarian crisis and the role of corporate led contract farming in addressing that crisis. A two stage 'Heckman Model' is used to explain determinants of participation in contract farming, and whether participation in contract farming affects farm income. The results indicate that contract farming has a positive impact on crop productivity and farm income. The socio-economic factors that influenced participation in contract farming has education, age, farm size, access to institutional credit, source of off-farm income and membership to an organization. Factors related to the likelihood of participation in contract farming are slightly different from the factors affecting farm income. The study has been conducted in three districts of Punjab namely, Amristar, Jalandhar and Ludhiana. Initially 150 farmers were selected through stratified random sampling. He concluded that there is a need to assist farmers to have better education, access to timely and quality inputs such as extension services, institutional credit, and better opportunities of off-farm income to improve financial status, to provide these inputs and services, partnership between public and private sector companies is needed. Collaboration between public and private sector for providing extension services can take place easily. Small farmers will be able to participate in the changing market effectively and establish links with new market chains (Supermarkets, Agribusiness Companies, Processors, Exporters, etc.).

Sachiko and Dinghuan[30] have examined the impact of contract farming on income. They found that the contract farming is seen by proponents as a way to raise small farm income by delivering technology and market information to small farmers, incorporating them into remunerative new markets. Researchers have been a critic on contract firm, however, sees it as a strategy for agribusiness firms to pass production risk to farmers, taking advantage of an unequal bargaining relationship. There is also concern that contract farming will worsen rural income inequality by favouring larger farmers. This study examines these issues in Shandong province, China, using survey data collected from 162 apple and green onion households, including both contract farmers and non-contract farmers and interviews with four contracting firms in 2005. Using a 'Probit Model' to estimate participation in a contract farming scheme, they observed little evidence that contracting firms prefer to work with larger farmers, though all farms in the area are quite small. Furthermore, using a Heckman selection-correction model to control for possible bias, researcher finds that contract farming earn significantly more than independent farmers after controlling for household labour availability, education, farm size and other characteristics. Finally, they concluded that the way contracting companies contribute in farm income varies between commodities; contract apple growers receive higher price yields (presumably due to better quality). These results suggest that contract farming can help small farmers raise their incomes and gain access to the growing urban and export markets.

Singh[31] has published a study "Contract Farming in India: Impact on Women and Child Workers". This paper draws on case studies of hybrid cottonseed production in Andhra Pradesh and vegetable farming in Punjab to examine the labour conditions in contract farming in India. He argues that agriculture is becoming increasingly 'feminized' as men move out of the sector more quickly than women, and as women become the preferred labour type for many employers. While these new labour arrangements have led to marginal increases in real income for some women workers, they have also changed relationship between workers and employers, workers and work and led to differentiation within labour. Women's wages are generally lower than men, working condition poorer and their bargaining power more limited. Of greater concern is the issue of child labour; one of the major problems in contract farming throughout the developing world. India is one of the main users of child labour in the Asian region with almost 80 percent of working children employed in the agricultural sector. The majorities of that child worker are girls. They are preferred by employers for their docility, obedience and nimble fingers. The cotton seed case study reveals that children, mainly girls, who might be as young as six, and work from 8.30 am to 6 - 7 pm. These children might be continuously employed for six to nine months a year. Yet their employers or contractor have no requirement to take care of them; if any health problems arise, the children are simply replaced with a new group. With no social security obligations, there is hardly any cost involved for the employers. Children miss out on their schooling to work in the fields, yet child labour under contracting is not subject to any legal or public disapproval. The author argues for the need to take a gender perspective to address the whole question of a changing agrarian production structure under contract farming especially, the issues associated with transfer of skills, choice of technology, organization of labour, working conditions and terms of work. Author suggests that banning child labour is not the answer. Instead conditions for these children need to be made more tolerable, and their education and skills need to be built so as to release them and their families from the vicious cycle of poverty and exploitation. He also calls for industry regulated codes of contract along with legal provisions, to increase the voice and influence of contract labourers.

Singh and Joshi[32] have written a paper "Grower Heterogen City and the Gains from Contract Farming: The Case of Indian Poultry". They focuses on contract farming in poultry in the southern state of Andhra Pradesh in India. In particular, it estimates and evaluates the gains from the contract relationship to both parties. Previous literature has paid greater attention to grower benefits from contracting but even here quantitative estimates are scarce. In poultry integrators' gain is lower production cost and interest in arbitrage. But grower margins are not significantly different between contract and non-contract production. Despite this contract growers gain appreciably from contracting in terms of lower risk and higher expected returns. In terms of observed and unobserved characteristics contract growers have relatively poor prospects as independent growers. With contract production, these growers achieve incomes comparable to that of independent growers. Efficiency wage type arguments might be responsible for this outcome. They concluded from the gains to both integrators and growers from contracting in poultry production as poultry is produced by contract and independent growers. The latter becomes the benchmark to assess the gains for both parties. For integrators contract production is more efficient. While they possibly also gain farm interest arbitrage, the surprising finding is that grower margins do not very much between contract and non-contract growers. Therefore, a lower grower margin is not the strategy by which integrators sustain contract production. The poultry case study suggests that contract farming is a useful institutional arrangement for the supply of credit, insurance and technology to growers all of which are otherwise very demanding problems. For many commodities however contract farming in India is not legal because of the agricultural production marketing acts that make it mandatory for commodities under the act to be wholesaled in regulated markets. Removing the prohibition would be important to widen the scope of contract farming. Some believe that contract farming should be regulated to ensure that processors live up to the promises made in the contract regarding the quality of inputs and provision of credit and the buy-back arrangements. Note, however, that this is not an issue in the poultry example where the processor supplies 97 percent of the value of inputs. As a result the interests of the processor and the grower are closely aligned.

Phil[33] has published a paper "Smallholder Contract Farming in Developing Countries". He focuses on smallholders' contract farming. Smallholders may enter contract to reduce transaction costs of accessing new markets, borrowing, managing risk, acquiring information or increasing employment opportunities. The success of contracts reflects both the contracting environment and management practices. The contracting environment includes the strength of markets for contracted output, government macro policies, technical sophistication in production and attenuation of land ownership while important management elements are farm groups, selection of participants for contract, managing contract default and conflict resolution. Direct benefits from contracting accrue to smallholders from improved access to markets improved technology, better management of risk and opportunities for employment of family members. Indirect benefits occurs farm empowerment of women and increased commercial acumen on the part of smallholder contract farming is the focus of this paper. Potential to improve the welfare of small holders, however, is not a sufficient condition for such improvement. Small farmers can be excluded from contract because of awarding contracts to larger farms be adversely affected by the second round effected of contract on income and prices and suffer surrounding of markets that lie outside of contracts. Institutional developments that might ameliorate these types of exclusion are anti-trust legislation, policies to directly improve the contracting environment, policies to address specific problems smallholders face in entering contracts and participation by NGOs in contact facilitation.

Kumar[34] has published a paper "Resources Provision Productivity and Contract Farming: A Case Study of Punjab". He makes an attempt to evaluate the models of contract framing system in Punjab (PAFC and the direct Contracts Models) with the given objective of resource provision to the farmers especially that of the small growers. The objectives of the paper are: to evaluate contract farming from a small versus large farmers perspective; to measure the level of resource provision by contract farming in the case of Punjab; to see the role of contract farming in raising productivity / profitability and in boosting growth in the agriculture of the state.

He concluded that the companies preferred large growers for contract to avoid problems of dealing with too many small growers. Contract farmers of all the categories tired to maintain immunity against risk by lying at least two-third of their operated area under non-contract crops. The productivity data clearly showed a visible superiority of contract farmers over their counterparts non-contract farmers in all size classes.

The superiority of contract holders over others was more dominant in the case of crop productivity. From the above findings, one reaches to the conclusion that the experiment of contract farming in Punjab has certainly benefited the farming community in general, although the system is biased towards medium and large farmers. About the performance of companies under direct contract were operating in a more judicious way and disseminating the scientific farming through their research and extension staff.

Singh[35] has published a "Understanding Practice of Contract Farming in India: A Small Producer Perspective". He examines the nature, problems and potential of contract farming in India from the perspective of small and marginal producers, under commercialized and globalized agriculture as small farmers withholdings of less than 2 ha accounted for 82 per cent of all operational holdings in 2000-01, and 39 per cent of the total area. Large holdings of more than 4 ha declined to only 6.4 per cent by 2000-01 and accounted for 37 per cent of the area. The average holding size come down to 1.32 ha in 2000-01, with the average size of marginal holdings being only 0.4 ha and that of small holdings 1.41 ha. Of the total, 64 per cent are marginal (i.e. between 1-2 hectares each). In this situation, if any mechanism has to help agricultural development, it has to involve and work with this overwhelming majority of farmers. The paper defines the concept of contract farming and its rationale and profiles of various models of contract farming practised in India and examine their performance and focuses on important policy, legal and institutional mechanisms for promotion of contract farming and for facilitating small farmers' participation in contract farming in India. The paper concludes that by emphasizing that contract farming is context specific and only a means of agricultural development, not an end in itself.

Birtnal[36] has published a paper "Making Contract Farming Work in Smallholder Agriculture". He concluded that Indian agriculture is dominated by smallholders and 86 per cent have land holdings less than or 2 ha, and their average size of land holding is 0.53 ha. In the developing countries like India diversification towards high-value agriculture appears to be a possible option, at least in the short to medium run. The food basket of Indian consumer is changing fast. Sustained economic and income growth, and a fast growing urban population are fuelling rapid growth in demand for high value food product like fruits, vegetables, milk, meat, egg, fish and beverages. He has tried to identify and collected some facts underlying the success of contract farming and to brief overview of the potential advantages and disadvantages associated with contract farming and had identified factors that were critical to the success of some contract farming schemes in India. He also concluded that the agribusiness firms while improving their own profits should ensure that contract crop/commodity is more remunerative for farmers than without it; and the marketing and transaction costs associated with farmers' disposal of produce and acquisition of inputs, technology and services are lower with contract farming. Second, for high-risk commodities firms must share production and marketing risks to the extent possible, and also assist farmers managing production risk. Third firms should abstain from a tendency of extracting monopsony and monopoly rents. Fourth, firms should base their pricing strategy on the market trends and create incentives for farmer for better efficiency and product quality as to manage problem of extract contractual sales or any problem of moral hazards.

Dodamani and Kunnal[37] have conducted a study "Value Addition to Organically Produced Naturally Coloured Cotton under Contract Farming". They have analysed the value addition to naturally-coloured cotton at different stages of processing. They have found that during ginning one quintal of colour cotton yielded 35 kg lint, 64 kg seed and 1 kg of waste. This lint underwent spinning process and yielded 29.69

kg yarn and 5.31 kg waste. The yarn underwent the weaving process and yielded 28.96 kg cloth and 0.98 kg waste. The 29.96 kg cloth has been found equivalent to 106.28 metres of cloth. While preparing (cuttings) shirts, 1.28 metres of waste material was obtained. Finally, 42 shirts were made form 105 m of cloth. They found that an additional value of Rs. 5,875 had generated through processing Kapas into cotton garments (shirts). Its break-up at different levels of processing has been recorded as follows: ginning, Rs.3,27 (5.57 percent); Spinning Rs. 7,81 (13.30 percent); Weaving Rs. 1,626 (27.68 percent); and garments manufacturing, Rs. 3,140 (53.45 percent).

NABARD Project[38] has conducted a project on Contract Farming as Means of Value-Added Agriculture. Contract farming is seen as an effective means of generating supplies for processing industries and exporters, with a substantial potential and its widespread practice abroad. Maharashtra Economic Development Council decided to examine in-depth issues connected with contract farming to facilitate contract farming arrangements to help achieve objectives of agriculture and horticulture development. This study was undertaken by National Bank of Agriculture and Rural Development and assigned to Management Analytics, an independent research and consulting organization. The study has defined the applicability, equitability and enforceability of contract farming. It would attempt to identify crops and regions suited for contract farming, components of contracts, credit requirements and suitable institutional arrangements for disbursal and recovery, safeguards to ensure contract performance, measures against performance and arbitration procedures to resolve experiences and remedies. It involved four in-depth case studies of commodities grown under contracts (poplars under the Wimco programme in the North, mainly Punjab / Haryana), tomatoes and chillies under Pepscio / HLL Nijjer programmes in Punjab and sun-sip / seafoods (Ex-Wimco) in Andhra Pradesh and Karnataka; seed multiplication under JK Agri-genetics, Proagro and Nath seeds in Andhra Pradesh, Maharashtra, Gujarat, Sugarcane cultivation and processing under Prawarangar and Warnanagar co-operatives in Maharashtra, Modi Sugar in Uttar Pradesh and Sakthi Sugars in Tamil Nadu. Sample surveys of about 50 contract and other growers for each commodity systems in the study area were also conducted as a part of the study.

Braja Bandhu Swain[39] has a conducted study "An Evaluation of Constraints or Contract Framing System: A Case Study of Orissa". He has analysed to study how the contract farming system explores the agricultural development in Indian agricultural and why we need this type of system. This study is based on the following objectives the nature of contractual between industry and farmers, what are the constraints for contract system to increase the area under the crop cultivation. This study used the Logit model by taking the farmers cultivating and not cultivating sugarcane in a village of Orissa where the village economy is closely associated with a sugar industry. The farmers of this village are cultivating sugarcane and supplying to industries under forward agreement to provide the key inputs needed in the process of cultivation of sugarcane and often with cost recovery upon farm product delivery. He also concluded that the company should handled the uncertainty existed in market in respect to sugarcane that the company should procure all amount of sugarcane produced by farmer in right time. Company should give assured price and all input needed in the process of sugarcane cultivation to farmers. In return farmers should handled the output uncertainty in sugarcane cultivation and farmers should supply the sugarcane to company. In other words for success of the agreement, the company should run for long period of time by which farmers can change the cropping pattern from the paddy to sugarcane. The model shows that if the company will take some initiative in the areas like credit, irrigation facilities, the farmer, who does not cultivate sugarcane, may shift to sugarcane cultivation and area under cultivation of sugarcane will increase. From this process there can be change in the cropping pattern of agricultural and farmer can earn more income, which leads to develop the economy.

Shiv Kumar and Puran Chand(2004)[40] studied on prevailing practices and dimensions of contract wheat seed farming in Haryana state. Assured incentive price for wheat seed motivates a farmer to enter into contract production with a company. This study is based on the primary as well as secondary data. Appropriate proportionate sample farmers (160) were drawn from the public and private seed agencies. Simple tabular and factor analysis techniques have been used. The Pepsi and the Tamil Nadu price fixation models have employed for the study. In this paper, a study has been done of prevailing approaches of contract seed production under deferent sectors, distribution of different categories of contract farmers and their comparative net returns under different production environments, and discerning and quantifying the dimensions of contract seed production. Public agency contracted medium and large farmers whereas private agency contracted all farm sizes. Nearly 30 percent of small farmers were covered by the private agency under the Pepsi model. The wheat seed farmers of private agency received all inputs, production technology and extension services whereas the farmers of public agency were provided only the seeds. The net gains of medium and large wheat seed farmers of public agency were respectively more by Rs. 47.76 and Rs. 48.21 per quintal over the corresponding grain farmers. The net gains of small, medium and large wheat seed farmers of the private agency were higher by Rs. 54.10, Rs. 27.99 and Rs. 37.76 per quintal over the corresponding categories of grain farmers, respectively. The net gain of small wheat seed farmers of the private agency has been reported as Rs. 235.28 per quintal, which is the highest across different categories of farmers. The overall net gains of farmers of public agency under the Tamil Nadu model and of private agency under the Pepsi model are of Rs. 185.44 and Rs. 170.88 per quintal, respectively. The assured price has explained 37.68 percent and 23.60 percent of the variance in public and private seed agencies, respectively. The contract production procedural support provided to farmers of private and public agencies could explain 28.64 percent and 6 percent of the variance, respectively. Management of risks (10.15 percent) and physical infrastructure (8.27 percent) at farmers fields of public agency ranked almost equal in importance but trailed far behind in order of importance by farmers of private agency in making the choice.

Shiv Kumal et al.[41] studied on mode of operation and performance of contact farming of cottonseed in Haryana. The quality of cottonseed matters most for the successful product development. The quality cottonseed production is monitored by the Haryana State Seed Certification Agency in the state. The study has reviewed the prevailing contract cotton farming models; has studied mode of operation of cotton contractual arrangements; has analysed the production matrix, growth and contributions, and has discerned and quantified variations in intensive structure of public and private seed firms. It has used both primary and secondary data. Appropriate statistical tools, viz. exponential growth model, index, etc., have been used to study the data. All categories of farmers have been brought together under the management of private seed agency for production of cottonseed of a single variety on a large homogeneous block. Contract cotton farming has fully vetted the legal agreement with their growers. The public and private agencies pay incentive price to farmers which is higher than the prevailing market price. Farmers of private agency are free from intricacies of input and output markets, receive all technology and technical know-how and have facilities for production and consumption loans, whereas farmers of public agency are trailed far behind in terms of these benefits. Private agency has flourished at the expanse of public agency since contract cotton is incentivized by private contractors under flexible and farmer-friendly production regime. The study has concluded that the private agency has sharpened its competitive edge while the public agency has lagged behind in competitive race perhaps due to obsolescence of technology, weak management, capital constraints, etc. Moreover, the favourable changes in socio-economic and legal framework of government policies have encouraged active participation of the private sector in cottonseed business. The commitment driven contract farming has emerged as a viable alternative farming model, in the post-WTO regime, which provides assured and reliable input service to farmers and desired farm produce to the contracting firms.

Singh S. (2000 b)[42] has conducted a study "Theory and Practice of Contract Farming". A review in the paper focuses the role of contract farming in agricultural diversification and development in terms of its practice and implications for the producers and the local economy, in Punjab, India. The study highlights role of contract farmers and the contracting companies (HLL, Pepsi and Nijjer) in three different crops (tomatoes, potatoes and chilies). The main benefits of contract farming as perceived by the contract farmers were better and reliable income, new and better farming skills, better soil managements and outlet for bulk sales. The study also identified the faults of the contracting system both at company and farmer level. About two-thirds of the HLL growers and more than 50 per cent of the Nijjer growers did not face any major problem in contracting. The others reported problems were poor co-ordination of activities, poor technical assistance, delayed payments, outright cheatings in dealings and manipulation of norms by the firm. Some of the Pepsi potato farmers had a few problems with the company system. But the large, numbers of them (60%) were happy. The study also highlighted the implication of contract farming on cropping pattern, land lease market sustainability, farm income and employment despite, various problems and conflicts between company and growers, 62 per cent of HLL, 80 per cent of Nijjer and 68 and 73 per cent of Pepsi (potato and chili respectively) farmers wanted to continue contract respectively.

Conclusion

Most of the studies reviewed above have indicated that the results of contracting are very promising in the early years. Farmers benefits from improved technology and higher productivity, quality and production. Some study indicated that contract farming helped farmers for the better, gave more reliable income, generated employment especially for women, provided new skills. In the review also they indicated that contract farming has several disadvantages too: poor extension services, low prices to farmer due to haphazard pricing of the produce, inherent higher risk to cultivators, frequent delays in payment, weak bargaining power of farmer, sole dependency on companies for inputs as credit, over-exploitation of ground water and the threat of the environment. Some studies indicate generally the contracts are not written and the legal enforcement system is too tedious for both growers and firms. Today in India new national agriculture policy (NAP) favours such types of private sector participation through contract farming and land leasing to accelerate technology transfer, accumulate capital flow and organize assured market for crop production, especially of cotton oil seeds, horticultural crops, food grain crops and fruits. Agribusiness companies need an assured and regular inflow of supplies to operate their processing facilities efficiently and often, they require the commodities to be processed to satisfy certain quality standards. The conditions that favour contracting are an opportunity for reducing price and sales volume uncertainties, the need for the standardized farm market to provide such produce, etc. The review of study indicate that the way contract contributes to farm income varies between commodities, contract growers receive higher prices yields presumably due to better quality. The reviewed studies also revealed that contract farming has a positive impact on crop production and farm income. The socio-economic factors that influenced participation in contract farming has education, age-farm size, access to institutional credit, source of off-farm income and membership to an organization.

Most of the studies reviewed above have indicated that changing agrarian production structure under contract farming, especially issues associated with transfer of skills, choice of technology, organization of labour, working conditions and terms of work. Some studies stated that several state governments, including Andra Pradesh, Gujarat, Karnataka, Punjab and Tamil Nadu have already started promoting contract farming with desired changes in the policy and the market front. They have started changing laws to enable and support such contractual relationship and providing companies interested in it with a variety of incentives, subsidies and tax rebates including lifting of land ceiling. There is a need for developed agriculture sector and increasing production and income by using optimum utilization of resources for the development of agriculture sector in the various state. Since study has so for been conducted for studying contract farming in Maharashtra therefore, the present study is a sincere effort to study contract farming in India, specially in Maharashtra.

Notes:

1. Sukhpal Singh (2000), "Contract Farming for Agricultural Diversification in the Indian Punjab: A Study of Performance and Problems, *Indian Journal of Agricultural Economics*, 56 (3), July-Sept.

2 Dilip, B.K., R.K. Grover and K.N. Rai (2002), "Contract Farming in Tomato : An Economic Analysis", *Indian Journal of Agricultural Economics,* April-June, Vol. 57, No.2.

3. Kiresur, V.R., S.A. Patil and H.S. Vijayakumar (2002), Contract Farming: An Opportunity for Small and Marginal Farmers in the Context of Trade Liberalization, PII, *Agricultural Economics Research Review.*

4. Asokan, S.R. and Singh, Gurdev (2003), "Role and Constraints of Contract Farming in Agro-Processing Industry, *Indian Journal of Agricultural Economics,* 58 (3).

5. Hemant Kumar and Ranveer Singh (2005), "Success and Failure of Contract Farming in Himachal Pradesh: A Case Study of Cauliflower Seed Production". *Indian Journal of Agricultural Marketing,* (19 (2).

6. N. Nagaraj, M.G. Chandrakanth and C.P. Gracy (2008), Contract Farming and Related Issues Department of Agricultural Economics, University of Agricultural Sciences, Bangalore.

7. Rajmanohar, T.P., Kumaravel, K.S. (2006), *Contract Farming in India. An Introduction.* ICFAI. Books. The ICFAI University Press, Agartala.

8. Kumaravel K.S. (2006), "Contract Farming: Concept and Issue", in Rajmanohar T.P., Kumaravel K.S. (eds) *Contract Farming in India an Introduction,* ICFAI, Books. The ICFAI University Press, Agartala.

9. James MacDonald et al. (2006), "Why Use Contract ? The Economics of Contracts", in Rajmanohar T.P., Kumaravel K.S. (eds) *Contract Farming in India an introduction,* ICFAI, Books. The ICFAI University Press, Agartala.

10. Sukhpal Singh (2006), "Contract Farming for Agricultural Development-Review of Theory and Practice with Special Reference to India", in Rajmanohar T.P., Kumaravel K.S. (ed.) *Contract Farming in India an introduction,* ICFAI, Books. The ICFAI University Press, Agartala.

11. Singh and Asokan S.R. (2006), "Contract Farming in

India", in Rajmanohar T.P., Kumaravel K.S. (ed.) *Contract Farming in India an Introduction,* ICFAI, Books. The icfai University Press, Agartala.

12. Khairnar S. and Yeleti V. (2006), "Contract Farming in India: Impact and Implications", in Rajmanohar T.P., Kumaravel K.S. (ed.) *Contract Farming in India an Introduction,* ICFAI, Books. The ICFAI University Press, Agartala.
13. Pratap and Joshi (2006), "Vertical Coordination in High-Value Food Commodities: Implications for Smallholders", in Rajmanohar T.P., Kumaravel K.S. (eds) *Contract Farming in India an Introduction,* ICFAI, Books. The ICFAI University Press, Agartala.
14. Prasad B.V.S. (2006), "Contract Farming in India: Options and Implications for Small and Large Farmers", in Rajmanohar T.P., Kumaravel K.S. (eds) *Contract Farming in India an Introduction,* ICFAI, Books. The ICFAI University Press, Agartala.
15. Spice MANAGE (2006), "Contract Farming Ventures in India: A Few Successful Cases, in Rajmanohar T.P., Kumaravel K.S. (eds) *Contract Farming in India an Introduction,* ICFAI Books. The ICFAI University Press, Agartala.
16. Arbind Gupta (2006), "Respinning Strategies", in Rajmanohar T.P., Kumaravel K.S. (eds) *Contract Farming in India an Introduction,* ICFAI, Books. The ICFAI University Press, Agartala.
17. Mahendra Dev and Chandrasekhara Rao (2006), "Food Processing and Contract Farming in Andhra Pradesh: A Small Farmer Perspective", in Rajmanohar T.P., Kumaravel K.S. (eds) *Contract Farming in India an Introduction,* ICFAI, Books. The ICFAI University Press, Agartala.
18. Prabakaran R. and Serma Saravana Pandian (2006), "Private Sector Partnerships in Poultry Production and Marketing in India: Case Tamil Nadu", in Rajmanohar T.P., Kumaravel K.S. (eds) *Contract Farming in India an Introduction,* ICFAI, Books. The ICFAI University Press, Agartala.

19. Ramesh T. and Gracy C.P. (2006), "Contract Farming Experience of Gherkin Cultivators in Tamil Nadu", in Rajmanohar T.P., Kumaravel K.S. (eds) *Contract Farming in India an Introduction,* ICFAI, Books. The ICFAI University Press, Agartala.
20. Sukhpal Singh (2005), *Political Economy of Contract Farming in India,* Allied Publishers Pvt. Ltd., Mumbai.
21. Shoja Rani, B.N. (undated), Globalization and contract farming in India-Advantages and problems, www.despace.iimk.ac.in/bitstrem/2259/520/1/6337-647+pdf
22. Gahukar R.T. (2007), Contract Farming for Organic Crop Production in India, *Current Science,* Nagpur, Vol.93, No.12.
23. Tripathi R.S., Ram Singh and Sube Singh (2005), "Contract Farming in Potato Production : An Alternative for Managing Risk and Uncertainty", *Agricultural Economics Research Review,* Vol. 18.
24. Sukhpal Singh (2002), "Malti-National corporations and Agricultural Development: A Study of Contract Farming in the India Punjab", *Journal of International Development,* 14.
25. Sunantar Setboonsarng (Feb. 2008), "Global Partnership in Poverty Reduction: Contract Farming and Reduction-contract Farming", Contract Farming and Regional Development. A study of contract farming and regional cooperation ADB institute. ADB Institute Discussion paper No. 89.
26. Ashalata and M. Devaraj (June-2006), "Opportunity for Contract Farming in Banana: A Case Study at Tamil Nadu State", *Agricultural Situation in India.*
27. Rangi, P.S. and Sidhu, M.S. (2003), "Contract Farming System, Punjab State Policy Issues", *Productivity,* October-December, Vol. 44, No. 3.
28. Vijay Paul Sharma (Aug. 2007), India's Agrarian Crisis and Small Holders Producers Participation in New form Supply Chain Initiatives: A Case Study of Contract Farming, Indian Institute of Management, Ahmadabad.

29. Vijay Paul Sharma (2008), "India's Agrarian Crisis and Corporate-led Contract Farming: Socio-economic Implications for Small Holder Producers", *International Food and Agribusiness Management Review,* Volume 11, Issue 4.
30. Sachiko Miyata Dinghun Hu (2007), Impact of Contract Farming on Income International Food Policy Research Institute, Discussion paper 00742.
31. Sukhpal Singh (2003), *Contract Farming in India: Impact on Women and Child Workers.* Gatekeepat Series No. 111 IIED3 London.
32. Bharat R., Pratap S.B., Joshi P.K. (June-2007), Grower Heterogeneity and the Gains from Contract Farming: The Case of Indian Poultry. Indian Statistical Institute, New Delhi.
33.. Phil Simmons, Overview of Small Holder Contract Farming in Developing Countries. www.google.com
34. Parmod Kumar, Resources Provision, Productivity and Contract Farming : A Case Study of Punjab. www.google.com
35. Sukhpal Singh, Understanding Practice Contract Farming in India: A Small Producer Perspective. www.google.com
36. Pratap B., Birtnal, Marketing Contract Farming Work in Small Holder Agricultural. www.ncap.res.in/contract-%20 farming/.... /5.1% 20 pratap %205%20 Brithal, pdf.
37. Dodamani M.T. and Kunnal L.B. (2007), "Value Addition to Organically Produced Naturally Coloured Cotton Under Contract Farming, *Agricultural Economics Research Review,* Vol.20, pp.521-528.
38. NABARD Research Project, Contract Farming as means of value added Agricultural. www.google.com
39. Braja Bandhu Swain, An Evaluation of Constraints of Contract Farming System: A Case Study of Orissa, www.google.com.
40. Shiv Kumar and Puran Chand (2004), "Prevailing Practices and Dimensions of Contract Wheat Seed Farming in Haryana State", *Agricultural Economics Research Review,* Vol. 17 July–Dec.

41. Shiv Kamal et.al. (2007), "Mode of Operation and Performance of Contract Farming of Cotton Seed in Haryana", *Agricultural Economics Research Review,* Vol. 20 Jan.-Jun.
42. Sukhpal Singh (2000), "Theory and Practice of Contract Farming A Review". *Journal of Social and Economic Development,* 2(1), pp.228-246.

3

PERFORMANCE OF CONTRACT FARMING IN INDIA

3.1 Introduction

In India, it has long been realized that the economic condition of a vast majority of the farming community cannot be changed unless Indian farmers, especially the small and marginal ones, diversify their pattern of cropping according to the fast changing tastes of the global community. Diversification and technology upgradation is needed more importantly and urgently in growing fruits, vegetables, and other high cash crops to stabilize income and employment in the farming sector. Dynamism in the agricultural sector can be brought by way of its reduction in cost of cultivation through productivity gains, i.e., cutting cost directly or by raising returns to the producers by value addition. For increased value addition in the agricultural sector it is essential to create more scope for processing and marketing activities[1].

The experience of agricultural development in India has shown that the existing systems of delivering of agricultural inputs and purchase and use of agricultural output have not been efficient in reaching the benefits of better linkages between agriculture and agro-processing industry to the farmers or the agro-industry. The timely, quality and cost effective delivery of adequate inputs still remains a dream despite the marketing attempts of the corporate sector and the developmental programmes of the state. The farmers are unable to sell their produce remuneratively. There is plenty of distress among farmers both in agriculturally grown as well as backward regions manifested in farmer suicides. Agriculture markets in India which are found to be both inefficient and imperfect, may not be able to ensure fair and reasonable returns to all the players. There are temporal and spatial variations in the markets and the producers share in the consumer rupee has been quite low in general, except a few commodities[2]. In the era of liberalization and globalization policies, the role of the state in agricultural marketing and input supply is being reduced and an increasing space is being provided to the private sector to bring about better marketing efficiency in input and output markets. On the other hand, processor, and/or marketers face problems in obtaining timely, cost effective, and adequate supply of quality raw materials. Contract farming is a step towards achieving both these objectives of cost reduction and value addition by providing the farmers with better seeds and other inputs improved marketing channels and technical know-how.

In India though contract farming is not new it has come to limelight in the late 1980s with the entry of Pepsi in the processing of tomato in Punjab. Currently there are nearly 50 processor / exporters practicing contract farming for different commodities. There are very successful cases like gherkin in Karnataka, peppermint and roses in Punjab, broilers and coleus in Tamil Nadu, organic cotton in Gujarat and some less satisfactory ones like safflower in Maharashtra, Basmati paddy in Punjab and wheat in Uttar Pradesh.

Gherkin was introduced in Karnataka by Global Greens as new crop for which there was no domestic market. Though over time competitor emerged but all of them adopted contract farming. Though mint was not new in Punjab, A.M. Todd introduced peppermint on contract arrangements as sole producer of pepper mint oil. Similarly, rose cultivation was introduced in Punjab by R.T. Aromatic oils for rose oil and other derivatives for niche market in Canada. Similarly semi Labs was the sole commercial users of coleus roots for medicinal purpose. Broiler production was a case of more comprehensive forward co-ordination by hatcheries. Though the activity itself was not very stable it helped the hatcheries to survive. Organic farming was introduced under broader objective of fair trade. Thus, for the six success stories market imperfections clearly existed or were created for sustainability[3].

3.2 Contract Farming: Past and Present in India

Contract farming system in ancient Greece was the widespread practice with specified percentage of particular crops. During the first century, China also recorded various farms of share cropping. In the United State of America (USA) as recently as the end of the nineteenth century, i.e. in the first decade of the twentieth century, formal farmer corporate agreement were established in colonies controlled by European power. For example, Gezira in central Sudan, farmer were contracted to grow cotton as part of a larger land tenancy agreement[4]. In India it was also practised in colonial period when commodities like Colin indigo were produced by Indian farmer for English factories. The colonial period saw the introduction of cash crops such as tea, coffee and rubber, poppy and indigo in various parts of the country. Cotton exports during the US Civil War, British settlers and East India Company compradors wanted to develop India as an exporter of other commercial crops as well. The settlers took to plantation crops - tea, coffee, rubber - in the more salubrious climate of hills in the South and the North-east, while poppy (for opium exports to China) and indigo found favour with compradors in the Gangetic and Central plains. Tenants and yeomen peasants alike were attracted by ready purchasers who offered what was deemed to be an attractive price for these new crops since no markets existed for them. This was the beginning of contract farming in India in the second half of the nineteenth century[5]. Given the prevailing land-tenure systems, these arrangements soon degenerated into near-indenture systems for the cultivators. Farmers were bound to grow the crops, and accept whatever price was offered, after paying for the inputs provided by the buyer, again at a price of his choice. In a sense, these arrangements were variants of longstanding moneylender landlord and renters dominated cultivation of most crops in India. The facts that the crops grown were of no consumption value to the farmers and that they had no access to any other buyer made them even more exploitative. Mahatma Gandhi's championship of the cause of the indentured indigo growers of Champran in Bihar immediately following his return to India in 1916 is a major milepost in the history of contract farming.

Other crops and regions did not suffer from such extreme privation, but contract growing had earned a poor reputation. The Assamese population still feels that through contract growing of tea, it first lost its land ownership and eventually, it had to compete against "outside" (read Bihar and UP) migrants for unskilled labourers' jobs on these very lands. The Southern plantations, however, did not cause such traumas. Thus, when the erstwhile Imperial Tobacco Company (present-day ITC) wanted to introduce the cultivation of Virginia tobacco in coastal Andhra Pradesh through contract farming in the 1920s, it received a warm welcome. It had, of course, taken great care to structure what seemed to be a fair contract system, through well-defined roles for the company and the participating farmers. It recruited trained persons to propagate the idea of tobacco cultivation first through mass contact and demonstrations. It targeted the relatively better-off and educated farmers. When farmers began to sign up, these staff became the nucleus of extension and procurement personnel. It had a large corporate presence in the midst of the growing area, through its warehouses and factories were in Guntur. For several decades it was the largest employer in the area and its presence was considered benevolent. Nevertheless, some 50 years later, farmers began to feel that the balance of power was hopelessly tilted in favour of what was among the largest private companies in the country.[6] The contract system was finally abolished by an Act of Parliament in 1984, and replaced by open auctions. Organized seed trade emerged in the 1950s. Those in the business had no choice but to multiply seeds on growers' lands, since their business could not own land and large enough parcels were hard to come by in the areas best suited for this purpose, anyway. Initial informal arrangements developed into proper contracts, which stipulated various obligations of both sides including supply of basic materials, adherence to prescribed practices, supervision and quality-checking and exclusivity of selling at prescribed prices. The seed business could not possibly have developed at all without contract farming. At the same time as the leading cigarette company had to give up contracts for tobacco (1984), the leading match company, Wimco, facing an acute shortage of matchwood, introduced poplar in North India as a farm-forestry crop through an elaborately-designed contract farming system. It had roped in major public banks for providing term-finance to participating farmers and insurance companies to cover plant mortality. Its deployment of a large, well-qualified extension staff and novel measures to provide finance and cover risks led to a quick acceptance of the exotic trees in Punjab, Haryana and Uttar Pradesh. A competitive market emerged within a decade and the corporate arm responsible for this function became a profitable provider of planting material. As a pioneering processed food exporter, Wimco also experimented with contract cultivation of tomatoes to supply its paste factories in Karnataka and Andhra Pradesh, with far more United and temporary success. Its competitor, Kissan Foods, later acquired by Hindustan Lever, also had the same experience. Later entrants, such as the Bhilai Engineering

Corporation in Madhya Pradesh and Nijjer Agro Foods in Punjab have had somewhat better experiences and even today continue with contract farming in limited fashion. The soft drinks giant PepsiCo had to commit to exports of processed foods as a pre-condition for its entry into India in the 1990s. It chose to set up a tomato processing facility in Punjab to meet this obligation and launched a major contract farming programme to introduce the crop on a large scale in the state, which was not a tomato-growing area. PepsiCo's foray attracted much attention; nevertheless, it sold the facility to Hindustan Lever in 2000, along with the contract farming programme.[7] While tomato (and eventually chili) farming caught on in Punjab, the commercial interest of these large companies waned, since PepsiCo no longer had to export only tomato paste following economic reforms, and Hindustan Lever found recently that it could not compete with cheap Chinese imports. The great interest generated in food processing in the 1990s also translated into an equally strong interest in contract farming as possible means of raw material supply. Most of the projects were based on fruits and vegetables, all but a handful of which never got off the drawing boards. Most of these projects were, however, very poorly designed, without proper analysis of markets and economic viability, as were their contract schemes. Nevertheless, small pockets of successes do exist: gherkins and flower processor/exporters in Karnataka, oleo-resin and spice extract plants in Kerala, medicinal and herbal supplement processors in the foothills of the North. The current period has witnessed another flurry of interest in contract farming, this time into subsistence and food crops as well. Hindustan Lever's foray into the wheat flour market was large enough to encourage it to promote contract farming through other agencies. Rallis undertook to provide planting material and other inputs and State Bank of India and ICICI Bank financed wheat farmers in Madhya Pradesh, which Hindustan Lever agreed to buy through its own agents. Exporters of Basmati rice found lucrative and booming export markets and structured their own similar contract schemes. The present Punjab government pushed agriculture diversification from the traditional paddy-wheat combination in a big way. It invited processors and contract agencies to participate in the programme in the state in a big way. These projects differ from the earlier ones substantially. Ultimate buyers now employ contract farming agencies (which are divisions or subsidiaries of major agribusiness firms such as Rallis, Mahindra and Mahindra, Escorts or DCM) to interface with the farmers. These agencies work on a fee from farmers and buyers alike to supply inputs and extension. The state government acts as an honest broker between the buyers and agencies, and allocates areas of exclusive operation to them. These activities got off to major start in kharif 2003 in Punjab, with a coverage of over 1,000,00 ha land under reintroduced maize and basmati paddy. The Punjab initiative is closely watched by various other states, notably Haryana, Madhya Pradesh and Gujarat, which would want to replicate it should the results from Punjab appear satisfactory (table 3.1).

Throughout this period, several other arrangements incorporating many features of contract farming were also tried. The two most important such enterprises both originated out of a concern for obtaining a better deal for farmers at the mercy of monopolistic buyers. Both these started in 1948-50, espoused a co-operative form of organization, were built on a fruitful partnership of enlightened farm leaders and urban educated elite, and are shining examples of synergy between small-scale conventional production units and large-scale modem processing plants. Sugar co-operatives in Maharashtra and milk co-operatives in Gujarat both catered to their members' production needs initially and offered them better prices through the processing plants they owned. Over the next five decades, these projects were replicated many times. The oldest ones are the most successful ones today, with vastly expanded scope of activities and services for the membership.

Table 3.1
Mileposts in Chronology of Contract Farming in India

Period	Events
1850s - 1860s	Cotton exported to Britain after disruption of US supplies.
1860s	Plantations for tea and coffee in the hills of the North-east and the South, indigo and poppy cultivation in plains.
1910s	Distress and unrest among indentured contract farmers.
1930s 1948-50	Virginia tobacco contract farming in Andhra Pradesh Sugar co-operatives emerge in Maharashtra and milk co-operatives in Gujarat incorporating many elements of contract farming.
1950s	Emergence of seed business based on contract farming.
1980s	Poplar introduction through contract farming; also tomato contract farming.
1990s	Tomato introduced in Punjab through contract farming.
1990s	Numerous, mostly abortive, efforts at introducing contract farming in Horticulture.
2000s	Variants of contract farming introduced for wheat in MP and crop diversification in Punjab; emergence of specialist contract farming firms.
2003-04	Contract farming accepted in new policy framework for agriculture reforms.

Source : Deshpande C.S. (2005), Contracting Farming As Means of Value-added Agriculture, Department of Economic Analysis and Research, National Bank for Agriculture and Rural Development, Mumbai.

Not surprisingly, they enjoy unwavering member support. Equally importantly, a number of other private, successful processors of sugarcane and milk in other states (UP and Punjab) have incorporated most of the co-operative measures benefitting the farmers in their approach and have earned farmer loyalty as well. Contracts have been extended to non-crop activities as well. Smaller poultry farmers for both eggs and broilers function as contracted franchisees of the larger operators in many parts of the country, most notably in the Namakkal area of Tamil Nadu. Major shrimp farming firms in Kerala and Andhra Pradesh and mushroom growers of Tamil Nadu have also availed of production contracts with smaller individual units, much the same way as large industrial producers of consumer goods or pharmaceuticals routinely use smaller firms under contract to them to manufacture products to be sold by them under their own brand name.

The earlier, colonial-period negative image not with standing, contract farming is thus seen to be serving some useful purpose in India in its own limited sphere. Ironically, even though it was earlier held to be an instrument of exploitation of the smaller producer by the infinitely larger and more powerful buyer (as it is even now perceived in some instances), it is considered to be a major corrective to market imperfections. Contracts and similar arrangements evoke very positive responses wherever they have succeeded, even as failures outnumber successes. The fact that contract farming finds an important place in the reforms to agriculture policies presently under discussion is an eloquent testimony to its currency and appeal right now.[8]

3.3 Practice of Contract Farming in India

Contract Farming is fast evolving as a mechanism of alternative marketing in the country. Punjab, Karnataka, Maharashtra, Madhya Pradesh, and Tamil Nadu have been the front runners in this regard. The experience of contract farming in India shows that there is considerable saving in consumption of inputs due to the introduction of improved technology and better extension services. Contract farming has usually allowed the farmers some form of credit to finance use of production inputs. In some cases, viz. Apache Model of contract farming for cotton in Tamil Nadu, there are arrangements for loans from commercial banks.

Contract farming has been successful in effecting crop diversification in many states. Studies of tomato contract production in Punjab and Haryana, Cucumber in Andhra Pradesh and cotton in Tamil Nadu found that the net returns from those crops under contract being much higher than those under non-contract situations though production cost in tomato was much higher than the contract system. It will be observed that different commodities covered under contract farming in different states are both traditional ones like basmati rice, wheat, maize, red gram, bengal gram, groundnut, sesame, cashew nut, coconut, onions etc. and non-traditional ones like medicinal plants (Ashwagandha, Dhavana, Coleus, Safed Musli) and Gherkins. An illustrative list of states/corporate involved in different crops in contract farming in India is given Table No. 3.2 Contract farming is spread across crops, regions and agencies (public, private and multinational) in India. There are different models being practised by different players in the sector which range from bi-partite to multi-partite and intermediary based. The table shows that most of the crops covered under contract farming are those with some market failure either in terms of farmer involvement or the market signals. Most of these are high value crops which require new and higher investments for producing for the market. Therefore, they need risk coverage – both production risk and market risk and, more of the latter.[9]

The role of the seed sector has been substantial in the advances that India made in agriculture in the last four decades. The expansion of seed industry has occurred in parallel with growth in agricultural productivity. Given the fact that sustained growth to cope with increasing demand would depend on the pace of development and adoption of innovative technologies, the seed would continue to be a vital component for decades to come. The organized seed industry of the country is just forty years old. Yet, its growth has been phenomenal. India is one of the few countries where the seed sector is already reasonably advanced. The private seed industry is no more confined to just production and marketing of seed. It has as well acquired technological strength to cater

Table 3.2
Company and Cropwise Spread of Contract Farming in India

S. N.	Company	Type of Linkage	Crop / Product	Farmers (N) acreage (acre)	Ave-rage area under come
			Maharashtra		
1	Field fresh foods	Direct contract farming and thru franchisee	Baby Corn and sweet corn	1000, 4000 acres	4
2	DFV (P & PAG)	Contract farming	Banana	2150, 8600 acres	4
3	Sanghar exports	Contract farming (for Bharani group N & E)	Banana	100, 400 acres	4
4	Jain Irrigation	Contract Farming	White Onion	2385, 2887 acres	2.3
5	Pepsi	Contract farming direct / indirect	Potato		1.33
6	Siddhi Vinayak agri	Contract farming thru	Potato	1000 1500	1.5
7	MSSL	Contract Farming	Grapes	400 2000	5
8	Trikaya foods	Pacholi / lettuce			
9	Deepak fertilizers	Contract Farming	Grapes / prom-enade onion / banana	2000 farm	
10	Tina oils & Chemicals	Contract Farming	Soybean / sunflower	60,000 236000	4
11	Biotor (formerly Jayant)	Contract Farming	Castor	25000 1,00,000 acre (6500 in mah)	4
12	C & M Group, Nashik	Contract farming	Soyabean and Maize	2200 Farmers	

			Karnataka		
1	Global Green	C.F.	Gherkin	1000 640	0.64
2	Intergarden	C.F.	Gherkin	4460 Farmers (2001)	-
3	Vishal	C.F.	Vegetables	1200 4800 acres	4
4	Namdhari Fresh	C.F.	Guar (cluster bean)	80 acres	
5	AVT mecormick	C.F.	Chilly 2125 acres	430 2125 acres	5
6	Pepsi	C.F. Direct / indirect	Potato	1500 1995 acre	1.33
7	Sami Labs	C.F.	Med, Plants	-	-
8	Himalaya Heal care	C.F.	Ashwa-gandha	1750	-
9	Mysore S.N. C. Oil Company	C.F.	Dhavana	-	-
10	Atural Remedies Pvt. Ltd.	C.F.	Coleus	-	-
11	M/s Bharti Associate	C.F.	Gherkins Processing	750 680 acre	0.80
			Tamil Nadu		
1	Global Green	C.F.	Gherkin	11000 7040 acre	0.64
2	T.N. Project	C.F.	Guar (Cluster been)	80 acres	-
3	Shakti Soya	C.F. indira	Soybean	-	-
4	Super Spinning	C.F.	Cotton	-	-
5	Apachi Cotton	C.F.	Cotton	-	-
6	Cauvery Oil palm	C.F. Direct	Palm	209 4375 acre	21
7	Suguna Poultry and Hatcheries	C.F.	Chicken	15000 across 8000 villages and 11 states	-
8	Venketeshwara Hatcheries	C.F.	Chicken	15000 across 8000 villages and 11 states	-
9	Swati Hatcheries	C.F.	Chicken	Of the total broiler production 37 % in under contract farming and 78 % of it is from South India	-

Andhra Pradesh					
1	Global Green	C.F.	Gherkin	6300 4000 acre	0.64
2	AVT McCormick	C.F.	Chilly	430 2125 acres	5
3	Sresta natural products (24 letter mantra)	C.F. direct and thru N.G.O.	Organic Produce	1800 3600 acre	2
4	Dabur India	C.F.	Amla (India gooseberry)	1042 acre	-
5	Palm Oil (Godrej Palm Tech SICAL, Radhika)	C.F. Direct	Palm	95000 acres	-
6	Venkateshwara hatcheries	C.F.	Chicken	-	-
7	Nandan Farms (P) Ltd Hyderabad Joint venture spearhead National Products	C.F.	White Viagra	-	-
Punjab					
1	U.B. Group	Thru Pepsi	Barley	400 3200	8
2	Field Fresh foods	Direct C.F. and thru franchise	Baby corn and sweet corn	600 2400 acres	4
3	Pepsi	C.F. direct/ indirect	Potato	2000 2660 acres	1.33
4	Biotor	C.F.	Castor	4000 16000 acres	4
5	A.M. Todd	C.F.	Mint	500 2500 acres	5
6	Satham Overseas	C.F.	Basmati	-	-
7	Markfed	C.F.	Basmati	-	-
8	LT overseas	C.F thru Pepsi	Basmati	2500 6250	-
9	Pepsi	C.F.	Basmati	300 2000 acres	6.67
10	Sattuj Agri	C.F.	Organic Basmati	30 1320	44
11	Nijjer Agro Foods Ltd.	C.F.	Tomato and Chilly	1000 tomato farm 700 chilly farm 3000 acre 1400 acre	3 2

12	Vardhaman led consortium of spinning mills of North India & State Bank of Patiala	C.F.	Cotton	-	-
13	Nestle India Ltd.	C.F.	Milk	-	-
14	Punjab Agro Food Park Ltd. A joint venture of Punjab Agro Export Cooperation and JDMA, a corporate body	C.F.	Green vegetable and exotic vegetable	-	-
Gujarat					
1	DFV P & PAG	C.F.	Banana	1000 4000 acres	4
2	Me Cains Foods India	C.F.	Potato	750 F	-
3	Pepsi	C.F. Dim indirect	Potato	1500 F 1995	1.33
4	Biotor Formerly Jayant	C.F.	Castor	5000 f 20,000 acre	4
5	HUL	C.F. Direct	Chicory	1700 4500 acres	2.5
6	Agrocel	C.F.	Organic Basmati / Cotton Seasame	1300 2080 farmer	1.6
7	Amit Green acre's	C.F.	Organic Cotton and Seasame	500 3200	6.4
8	Patel Farms	C.F.	EMU	35 farmers	-
9	Champion Agro	C.F.	Baby Com	2500 acres	-
10	Reliance Group	C.F.	Processing of Medicial Plants and Alovera.	-	-
Madhya Pradesh					
1	Garlico Industries	C.F.	Garlic and White onion	-	-
2	Maikal Biore	C.F.	Organic Produce	1700 12885 acres	7.6

3	Mahima	C.F.	Organic Produce	600 10,000	16.7
4	Pratibha Syntax	C.F.	Organic Cotton	2700 22000	8.1
5	Cargil India Ltd.	C.F.	Wheat maize and Soybean	700 2800	4
6	Ion Exchange Enviro Farms Ltd (IEEFL)	C.F.	Fruit, Vegetable Cereals spices and pulses	-	-
7	ITC IBD	C.F.	Soyabean	500 5000 acre	10
8	HLL	C.F.	Wheat	400 4800 acres	12
9	Rallies India Pvt. Ltd.	C.F.	Wheat	-	-
10	Reliance Bio Science Ltd.	C.F.	Aromatic Oils (Lemon grass, palmarosa citronella, tulsi	-	-
Rajasthan					
1	U.B. Group	Thru Pepsi	Barley	900 7200	8
2	SAB miller	C.F.	Barley	8150	-
Uttar Pradesh					
1	Safal (NDDB)	C. F thru associations	Vegetables	150 associatio ns 18000 farmers	-
2	A M Todd	C.F.	Mint	500 2000	5
3	Rallis	C.F.	Wheat	19000 acres (2003)	

West Bengal					
1	Pepsi	C.F. direct / indirect	Potato	6500 2600 acres	1.33
2	Arambagh Hatcheries	C.F.	Chicken	-	-
3	M/s. Dabar India Ltd.	C.F.	Pineapple	-	-
Haryana					
1	Pepsi	C.F.	Potato	1500 1995	1.33
2	Satluj Agri	C.F.	Organic Basamati	10 440 acre	44
3	Agrocel	C.F.	Organic Basamati Cotton	900 1440 acre	1.6
4	A.M. Todd	C.F.	Mint	400 2000 acre	5
5	HAFED	C.F.	Basmati	-	-
6	L.T. Oversease	C.F. thra Pepsi	Basmati	1500 3750 acre	2.5
7	Satnam Overseas	C.F. thra Pepsi	Basmati	-	-
Uttarakhand					
1	Dhawan Intl	Direct	Med plants	-	-
2	Voc B	C.F.	Organic Basmati	440 500 acre	1.1
Kerala					
1	Herb India	C.F.	Safed Musli Steevia	-	-
2	Nadukuda Pvt. Ltd.	C.F.	Pineapple	-	-
3	M/s. Agreen Co, palikunnu kanur	C.F.	Pineapple	-	-

Source: Working Group Report of the Sub-Committee of National Development Council (NDC) on Agriculture and Related Issues. Nov. 2006, Planning Commission, New Delhi.

to the varietal needs of tomorrow. The Indian seed industry is currently valued around Rs 2,500 crore ($ 500 million) and is expected to be around Rs 3,750 crore ($ 750 million) by 2006. There are about 150 organized seed companies in India today. Several companies have Government of India (DSIR) recognized research and development departments and have produced and released a large number of varieties and hybrids in several crops. The contribution of private research in terms of value is steadily increasing. The share of research hybrids in total turnover of crops like pearl millet, sorghum-sudan grass, sunflower, maize, sorghum and cotton was about 70 per cent in 1997-98 compared to 46 in 1990-91. Private R&D's real investment in research has quadrupled between 1986 and 1998. Subsidiaries and joint ventures with multinational companies account for 30 per cent of all private seed industry research.[10]

3.4 Seed Industries and Contract Farming in India

The National Seeds Corporation was established in 1963. The Government of India enacted the Seeds Act in 1966 to regulate the growing seed industry. It stipulated that seeds should conform to minimum levels of physical and genetic purity and assured percentage germination either by compulsory labeling or voluntary certification. It also provided a system for seed quality control through independent state seed certification agencies placed under the control of the respective state departments of agriculture. This was a most eventful time for Indian agriculture, not only because of introduction of high-yielding cereals, particularly wheat and rice, but also for many other positive developments related to seed such as, constitution of seed review team, enactment of Seeds Act, 1966 and the formation of National Commission on Agriculture. The private sector also made significant entries into seed business in this period. The eighties witnessed two more important policy developments for the seed industry, namely, allowing MRTP/FERA companies to invest in the seed sector (1987) and the introduction of a new policy on seed development in 1988. The 1991 Industrial Policy made a radical departure from the earlier one on foreign investment. It identified seed production as a high priority industry. The New Policy on Seed Development greatly liberalized import of vegetable and flower seeds in general and seeds of other commodities in a restricted manner and also encouraged multinational seed companies to enter the seed business. Over two dozen companies initiated research and development activities and have made substantial commitments for investment on research and development in response to this policy initiative. The investments are expected to increase with increasing volumes of seeds of proprietary hybrids and preparedness of farmers to pay higher price for quality seed. The Seeds Act 2001 was finalized on the basis of the recommendations of Seed Policy Review Group. It replaced the previous Act of 1966 and Seed (Control) Order of 1983.

3.5 Current Status of the Seed Industry in Contract Farming

India's seed industry has grown in size and level of performance over the past four decades. Both private and public sector companies/ corporations are involved in seed production. Two central corporations, the National Seeds Corporation (NSC) and the State Farm Corporation of India (SFCI) and 13 state seed corporations comprise the public sector. There are around 150 national and multi-national private seed producing and selling companies. The industry has grown impressively from a modest beginning in seed production in 1962-63 to over 5 lakh ha by 1995-96. The quantum of seed produced and sold went up five times from 14 lakh quintals to 70 lakh quintals in this period. The area planted with bought seed was about 10 per cent in 1990-91, with a volume of around 6 lakh tonne valued at Rs 680 crore. These seeds comprised of proprietary hybrids, public-bred hybrids and open-pollinated varieties (OPV). In terms of quantity and value, OPV seeds were the largest, followed in order by public hybrids and proprietary hybrids. Although proprietary hybrids had only a 32 per cent share of the market, their share in the value was 76 per cent. The 1998-99 estimates present a different picture, with proprietary hybrids growing at the expense of public hybrids. The area planted under bought seed increased only by 3 per cent over that of 1990-91; the market size, however, expanded significantly in terms of both quantity and value. The total market for purchased seed was 8.64 lakh tonne, valued at Rs. 2,250 crore. The volume of proprietary hybrid seed was estimated to be around 51,000 tune, valued at Rs 600 crore ,in 1998-99 as against 19,300 tonne and Rs 95 crore respectively in 1990-91. The volume of public hybrids fell to 39,000 tonne in 1998-99 as against 60,000 tonne in 1990-91. The OPV volume increased by 51 per cent. The present contribution of OPV in the total bought seed market has grown, indicating greater use of bought seed by farmers. The price paid by farmers for all hybrid seeds is higher than that in 1990-91. This trend suggests that farmers do not consider the seed price to be a constraint to its use, so long as it ensures higher return through higher productivity and other value-added traits.

3.6 Growth of Contract Farming of Seed Industry in India

Public seed companies (NSC, SFCI) had large captive farms on which they could multiply seed, but private seed companies could not own land to multiply their own seed. Their search for a suitable solution led to contract farming in select parts of the country. This solution was adopted by both Indian and multinational companies. The first large-scale activity started under the aegis of Mahyco in the early 1970s, mainly in the Marathwada region of Maharashtra. It spread to neighbouring areas of Andhra Pradesh, Vidarbha and Karnataka. These states/areas dominate the seed business even today, save for the hybrids of cold-weather crops. The original selection may have been based on the promoters' familiarity, but it has been proven sound by the agro-climatic factors and relative isolation which make controlling conditions easier, as well as hardworking and loyal peasantry.[11]

The original contracts were mostly with individuals. At present, almost all companies follow a group approach. The main features of the contract system are:

1. On-farm multiplication of seeds requires observance of both a specified package of practices and adequate isolation and other quarantine procedures to maintain

the genetic identity of planting material. Hence, multiplication is taken up on contiguous blocks which could be effectively isolated from the remainder of agricultural activity in the vicinity;
2. Seed producers find it useful to contract all farmers of the area that they want to operate in;
3. Companies have identified their respective zones of operation and groups of farmers for reproduction;
4. Companies specify areas, supply parent seeds, provide advance at times, supervise production, and estimate likely crop size;
5. Company staff ensures that standard contracted practices are followed on farm through well-scheduled supervision visits and tests;
6. The initial direct contact with farmers is now replaced by organizers, who become effective interfaces between companies and contract farmers. They are responsible for a group of farmers, and meeting the group target. They could be local financiers or suppliers of other inputs. Any revisions are invariably implemented through organizers.

In the 1980s, changes in the national agricultural policy allowed private companies to operate in the seeds production sector. They were also allowed to import commercial seed and germplasm for vegetables. A considerable number of domestic firms and MNCs entered into seed production ventures in the country. Mahyco (the largest Indian company in seed production) Cargil (an MNC), Indo-American Hybrid Seed, Namdhari Seeds, National Seeds Corporation (a sector company), Karnataka seeds corporation (state owned corporation) Rallis and some smaller private firms have been successfully using contract farming for seed production. Public sector companies are engaged in production and sale of seeds of cereals, pulses and oil seeds. Privet sector firms are in the business of hybrid seeds of cotton, vegetables, maize, sunflower and flowers which covers about two-thirds of nearly one billion dollar annual business in seeds in India. These companies follow either direct contract farming with farmers or subcontracted procurement through smaller firms, which in turn resort to directly contracting seed growing farmers. Since seed production is undertaken by a few farmers over smaller areas out of their holding the risk are fewer. Every season the seed are required and supplies are, therefore, stable and this agribusiness is relatively more successful. Due to contract systems adopted by different seed companies differ in their provisions as far as relationship with farmer is concerned.[12]

3.7 Some Studies of Contract Forming in India

Recently, there have been some quick case studies of contract farming system in India. Most of them look at the economics of the contract farming systems in specific crops, compared with that of the non-contract situation and/or competing traditional crops of a given region e.g. in gherkins (hybrid cucumber) in Tamilnadu[13] and Andhra Pradesh[14], Karnataka[15] and tomato in Punjab[16] and Haryana[17], white onion in Maharashtra[18] potato in Maharashtra[19] etc.

The Pepsi in Punjab, for instance, managed to improve tomato yield per hectare by 35-50 percent in 1,600 hectares of cultivated land by working with contract farmers, besides promoting the cultivation of varieties fit for processing. Also for the first time, a winter crop of tomatoes was made possible by Pepsi in Punjab. However, Pepsi soon ran into difficulties due to farmer default. It had contracted with small farmers for the procurement of tomatoes. When the price of tomatoes in the open market went up due to hot weather and consequent wilting of the tomato crop, these farmers sold their produce. Similarly, Wimcos contracts in long gestation crops of mango and poplar have run in to rough weather due to the absence of any tangible benefits to contracting farmers over the long period of 5-7 years. Wimco provides technical assistance, good quality planting material developed at its nurseries, and tie up for institutional finance from 'NABARD' and gives a guarantee to purchase proceeds after harvest, at a remunerative price.[20]

The Green Agro Park (GAP) Ltd. is working with 3,500 small farmers for gherkin production, under contracts in Karnataka state, with 1400 acres under cultivation. The company provides all the inputs and technical advice along with facilities of 100 percent buy back, local pickup and grading and weighment of produce. Most of the farmers cultivate half to one acre of land for gherkins under contract. This gives the company a year round supply of produce to the processed and subsequently exported with the help of and Overseas Spanish Company. The company prefers to work with small farmers as they rely on family lalour which is good for crop care and lowers cost (Sukhpal Singh, 2005.) Reliance Agrotech is into contract farming of cashew, mango, bamboo and teak in Madhya Pradesh. Technology is provided to the local farmers to grow crop which match the Reliance standards and then it is brought by the company for processing and marketing.[21]

HLL is doing chicory contract farming in Gujarat in districts of Anand, Kheda, Mehsana and Jamnagar. Seeds are given free of cost to the farmers. Per acre 40 bags are to be supplied by the farmers to the company and each bag has to contain 50kgs of chicory. Payments will be made within 15 days of delivery of chicory. Two inspections of the crop before harvest are carried out. The crop has to be harvested and cut into different size and dried for 15 days after harvest by the farmer. A price of Rs. 100 for 20kgs of chicory is paid by the company. It is also doing contract farming in dairy in Etah in Uttar Pradesh where the Krishi Pashu Vigyan Kendra set by the company has trained farmers in better animal management, bank loan procedures, the management of reclaimed land and community development programme. Growth centres provide services like villages based payments, dispending hybrid seeds, vaccinations and artificial insemination.[22] Ion Exchange Enviro Farmers Ltd. Pune is engaged in contract farming of organic mango, banana, pineapple, pulses and vegetables around Pune and supplies vegetables. Food World Mittal Farmers, Ahmedabad is into contract farming of safed musli—a medicinal herb.[23] The C&M Group of Nashik is meeting poultry feed plant needs. A total of 14 villages in Dindori taluka, 39 villages in Baglan taluka and 23 villages in Kalwan taluka have been covered during the kharif season.

Shri Bhumi Farmers Pvt. Ltd. is into contract farming and marketing of branded red bananas. It has red bananas on 25 acres of land near Bangalore, of which 10 acres is its own crop on leased land and the other 15 acres under contract farming with farmers. It supplies all the inputs including tissue culture banana plants which are produced from a bio-tech company and supplied to farmers at the rate of Rs. 16 per plant. It provides technical assistance and even support for tube well construction. The best quality graded bananas are brought back at Rs. 7 per Kg.[24]

The model was developed and is being implemented by the Nestle India Limited – a multinational firm – to source milk from small-scale producers. It is well-known that dairying in India is an integral part of rural economy, yet its scale of production is too small for a majority of the households to generate cash benefits. Contracting with such a large number of small-scale producers raises transaction costs to any firm. To reduce the cost of contracting Nestle follows an intermediate model of contract farming where the agreement is done with a local villager, called as an 'agent'. The agent collects milk from small-scale producers, and also facilitates distribution of inputs and delivery of services. Nonetheless, over time there has been some scaling-up of dairying in Nestle's milk shed area perhaps due to availability of an assured market in the form of contract farming. As a result, the firm has also started direct contracting with large producers. The intermediary contracting however remains the dominant form. In fact, majority of dairy processors in India use intermediary contracts to procure milk supplies. The contract farming scheme of the Nestle now covers about one million dairy farmers in over 1500 villages in several districts of Punjab. In 2005, Nestle collected 438 million kg of milk from farmers. Most of the milk collected by Nestle firm is processed into value- added products like baby food, butter, ghee, curd, etc. The firm observes strict food safety and quality standards right from the milk production stage. It has a well-developed traceability and milk chilling systems, and for quality milk supplies it encourages farmers to use milking machines and quality inputs.

The case of contract farming in vegetables relates to the Mother Dairy Fruits and Vegetables Limited (MDFVL) - a wholly owned subsidiary of the public sector parastatal, National Dairy Development Board (NDDB). Horticultural production in India is geographically dispersed; only about 15 percent farm households grow vegetables and 5 percent grow fruits.[25] This means high transaction costs to the firm in securing supplies from scattered producers. To reduce these costs, the MDFVL secures supplies of fruits and vegetables from growers' associations promoted by it. The firm provides technical guidance, services and inputs to association members to ensure that farmers follow best production and marketing practices. MDFVL (earlier called SAFAL) is an organized retail chain and was started in 1988 in Delhi. As of now, the MDFVL secures its supplies from around 300 growers' associations spread throughout the country, and has almost an equal number of retail outlets in Delhi. SAFAL is the brand name for MDFVL products. Recently, the MDFVL has established a 100 percent export-oriented HACCP certified processing plant in Mumbai. The model of contract farming in broilers in India is a replica of what prevails in most other countries. Firms provide day-old chicks, feed, vaccines and services to farmers at no cost to them, and lift entire output by paying fixed growing charges (per kilogram of body weight of bird) in lieu of their contribution to cost (labour, water and electricity charges, litter and rent for poultry shed and equipment). Farmers are thus insured against market risks.

The case of contract farming in broilers relates to the Venkateshwara Hatcheries Limited (VHL) - one of the leading firms in poultry business in India since early 1970s. The firm is engaged not only in contract farming of poultry, but also in manufacturing of poultry feed, medicines, vaccines and value-added poultry products. Recently, the firm has started a retail chain in poultry products with brand name 'BROMARK'.[26]

3.8 Role of Government of India in Contract Farming

There is yet no national policy on contract farming in India, but there are plans to formalize the arrangements in respect of pricing, legalities, pledge financing, warehousing, and the forward and futures markets. The planned steps include:[27]

1. Recording all contractual activities, ideally at the panchayat level.
2. Putting in place an arbitration mechanism.
3. Setting up farmer associations to improve the farmer's bargaining power with the agribusiness firms.
4. Amending the restrictive State Agricultural Produce Marketing Regulations Act (APMC) and the Essential Commodities Act.
5. Tax breaks on procurement.
6. Planning new insurance schemes like the income protection insurance prevalent in the US.

The APMC Act restricts farmers from entering into a direct marketing contract with bulk purchasers as all the produce is to be canalized for sale through the regulated markets only. The government has circulated a Model Act to replace the APMC and several states are in the process of enacting suitable legislation as convenient. This Model Act includes suggested provisions for a contract farming agreement, as follows:

All contract farming agreements should be registered with the market committee or a prescribed officer. Disputes are to be referred to a prescribed Authority and are to be resolved within 30 days; an appellate authority will entertain appeals and will decide such cases within 30 days. The decision of the prescribed/appellate authority shall have the force of a decree of the civil court; All disputes will be resolved only in the above manner and not by any other court of law; No market fee will be levied on direct procurement; Quality of the supply has to be clearly stipulated plus its sampling procedure; and contract farming agreements must give a description of the farm land covered, crop delivery arrangement; optional features include cultivation/ input specifications to be followed, insurance, nature of support services to be provided, farmer management forum and monitoring of quality and yields.

The Tamil Nadu state has drafted a legislation governing contract farming. The legislation includes clauses on the relationship between the contract farmer, the contractor and the processor of food products. The law drafted specifies that any dispute, in the first instance, will not be taken to courts, and be settled by an independent arbitrator appointed by the state government for resolution. The notification in this respect is, however, yet to be issued. The guidelines are expected to be of use to various states in which agri-export zones have been identified. The centre has, so far, sanctioned 48 agri-export zones in various states, to develop as premier centres for agricultural exports. In this context, the policies adopted by the Government of Tamil Nadu and Punjab after having discussions with corporate groups, could also be made useful for the Government of Maharashtra by way of drafting similar policies for promotion of contract farming in the state. The salient features of policies evolved and adopted by the Government of Tamil Nadu and Punjab with regard to contract farming are summarized below; bearing in mind its relevance to Maharashtra in the present context.

3.9 Tamil Nadu Government Policies:

3.9.1 Land Development:

(a) The existing Sec.37-A of the Tamil Nadu Land Reform (Fixation of Ceiling on Land) Act 1961 provides for the state government to exempt any industrial or commercial undertaking to hold or acquire any land in excess of the ceiling area. A decision has been taken to exempt agro-based industry with a view to promote and develop them who are engaged in the cultivation of fruits and vegetables and also the industries which are engaged in the business of value addition viz. grading, packing, distribution, storage processing etc.

(b) Similar exemption will also be made in case of sericulture industry, mainly for the purpose of Mulberry cultivation and also for medicinal plants.

(c) In line with the guidelines issued by the Government of India, participation of private sector through involvement of NGOs and Forest Department for carrying out agri-business (viz. cultivation of fruits and vegetables, medicinal plants) similar arrangement shall be encouraged in order to develop the agro-based industry in the state of Tamil Nadu. The industries proposed to carry-out agro-business in degraded forest lands shall also be considered for exemption under Sec.37-A of Land Ceiling Act. All such cases, proposing to be engaged in any of such agro-based industries, will be considered on a case-to case basis for the purpose of availing exemption under Sec.37-A of Land Ceiling Act.

(d) Any land hold on lease by any person, so proposed to avail the exemption under Sec. 37-A, for the purpose of developing into agro-based industry, will also be considered for exemption.

(e) The cultivable waste land or poramboke land, which are owned by the government will also be made available for the purpose of developing agro-based industry, subject to other conditions being satisfied.

(f) The state government agencies (viz. Agricultural Engineering Division etc.) shall provide machinery and other facilities for the land development required by the above industries, at a concessional rate, on a priority basis. The financial assistance shall also be extended for the land development for the above activities.

3.9.2 Power Tariff

The industries involved in the production of fruits and vegetables shall be leived LT Tariff. III-A under the Tamil Nadu Revision of Tariff Rates on supply of Electrical Energy Act, 1978. The concession shall, however, be restricted to 10 HP. The requests for power connection from entrepreneurs of new floriculture units, will be considered immediately subject to the rules of Tamil Nadu Electricity Board.

3.9.3 Capital Subsidy

Capital subsidy shall be granted to fruits and vegetables industries upto 20 percent of the fixed assets subject to a ceiling of Rs. 20 lakh. The following items shall also be included in the fixed assets in addition to the fixed assets already defined:

- Green-house structure.
- Irrigation and Fertigation equipment.
- Cold room, grading room and mobile refrigerated truck/ van equipment.

3.9.4 Sales Tax

The Sales Tax of marketing of fruits and vegetables shall be exempted.

3.9.5 Pollution Clearance Charges

Exemption will be granted from payment of the charges of Rs. 10,000/- (Rupees ten thousand only) per annum, levied by the Tamil Nadu Pollution Control Board (TNPCB) for clearance required for setting-up of the unit.

3.9.6 Industry Status

The industries involved in processing, cold-chain, storage, tissue-culture units, hybrid-seeds production of fruits and vegetables, sericulture, medicinal plants etc. shall be given industrial status for the purpose of availing of concessions/ incentives / subsidies at par with the other industrial units in the state.

3.9.7 Training Support

In line with industrial training institutes run by the state and private, the government shall establish similar training centres for the artisans, involved in agricultural activities, including cultivation, processing etc.

3.9.8 Technology Development Centre

Government shall encourage private sector to establish technology development centres in order to disseminate modern technology / processing methods etc. to the field level, for which financial assistance/ incentives shall be provided.

3.9.9 State Government Supports

(a) Institutional financial assistance for purchase of refrigerated truck for carrying the fruits and vegetables from the farm / production unit to the marketing centres /sea ports for export etc. This assistance may be made available from TIIC/ state and central sponsored schemes.

(b) Financial assistance shall be made available for establishing value-added centres for fruits and vegetables viz. grading, packing, distribution, storage etc.

(c) The tissue culture units involved in the propagation of mother planting materials for the production of fruits and vegetables shall also be eligible for getting concessions/ subsidies at par with the above industries and also the assets of the mother planting material shall be treated as 'fixed assets.'

(d) The lease period for the degraded forest and cultivable waste lands/poramboke lands etc. shall be provided for the above mentioned activities for a minimum period of 20 years on a case-to-case basis. However, the annual rental value may be reviewed after every 3 years.

(e) Good quality water is most essential to carry-out large scale cultivation of fruits and vegetables, especially in cultivable waste lands and degraded forest lands etc. The state government shall facilitate individual units to meet the water requirement from the available water resources, depending on the availability etc.

3.9.10 Other Supports

Central government agencies will take care of import of certain critical inputs like soluble fertilizers, plant protection chemicals, plant growth-regulators, certain rare species of planning materials, which are specifically required for the export-oriented floriculture production units. However, if the state level canalizing agency is required for such innovation ventures the same will be organized by the state government with a view to save time and money for the individual growers. This will also solve the problem of non-availability of such critical inputs, which will sustain the quality of the product.

3.9.11 Legislation Support

Government has come forward with a legislation with a view to promote production of fruits and vegetables aromatic, herbal, medicinal plants and sericulture through contract or corporate farming which will provide for early settlement of disputes between farmers and promoters by providing for an arbitration machinery and other relevant matters, connected with contract farming.

3.10 Punjab Government Policies

The Punjab government has embarked on an ambitious crop-diversification programme. Alarmed at declining water table and worsening of soil texture due to targeting cultivation of 'other' crops using the concept of contract farming. The Punjab government have managed to cover 31.15 lakh hectars of land under the "Diversification and Contract Farming Scheme" during the Rabi season, 2003-04. The shifting area from wheat crop would cover barely, pulses and oilseeds. Having pioneered in conducting successful demonstration (PepsiCo-tomato) of contract farming in a true professional manner, the Punjab government is now looking forward to "Second Green Revolution" through the instrument of contract farming. The "New Industrial Policy-1996," notified by the Punjab government recognizes agro-based industry as a thrust area and provides a special package of incentives to back it up. Punjab Agro-Industries Corporation (PAIC) has been declared as the Nodal Agency of the state government for promotion of agro-based industries in Punjab. PAIC actively assists the private Indian/ foreign investors in obtaining all kinds of official sanctions, licenses, permits and in arranging for other infrastructural facilities for proper, efficient and economic working of new project, including contract farming project. Special package of incentives provided for promoting agro-based industry, according to the Punjab government's "New Industrial Policy-1996," is as given below:

A-Category Incentives:

1. Investment incentive @ 30 percent of fixed capital investment, subject to a maximum of Rs. 5 million.
2. Sales-tax exemption/ deferment for 10 years subject to a maximum of 300 percent of fixed capital investment.
3. Generator set subsidy @ 50 percent of the cost of captive generator set, subject to a maximum of Rs. 1.5 million.

The above 'A' category incentives are available to the following categories of agro based industries:

1. Freeze-drying and dehydration of fresh fruits and vegetables.
2. Potable/Industrial alcohol from raw materials, other than molasses.

3. Bio-conversion of maize/com into organic chemicals/ compounds, other than starch.
4. Products manufactured from agricultural residues, excluding pulp and paper.
5. Processing of aromatic and medicinal plants for extraction of their oils/ extracts.
6. Tissue culture.
7. Integrated poultry, project involving pure line breeding, grand-parent franchiser breeding and modern hatcheries.
8. Processing of eggs for the manufacture of pastes and powders.
9. Mechanized processing, preservation and packaging of fish and other fishery products.
10. Refrigeration equipment for cold storages and for refrigerated vans, including units developing alternate technology for refrigeration like solar energy etc.
11. Other hi-tech industries in the agro-industrial sector, involving processing agricultural produce / residue available in the state.
12. 'A' category incentives to all agro-industrial units, set-up in SSI sector or in large and medium sector, irrespective of locations, except industries figuring in the negative list.
13. Exemption from payment of electricity duty for a period of 5 years to all new agro-industrial units set-up in the state. Selective 11 agro-based industries to be exempted from payment of electricity duty for 7 years.
14. Generator set subsidy @ 30 percent of the cost of captive generator set, subject to maximum of Rs. 1 million to all new agro-industrial units set up in the state. However, generator set subsidy @ 50 percent of the cost of captive generator set subject to maximum of Rs. 1.5 million shall be allowed to the 11 selective agro-based industries.

15. Subsidy @20 percent of the purchase value of equipment / laboratories for obtaining hazard analysis and critical control (HACCP) and ISO:9000, subject to maximum of Rs. 0.5 million.
16. Expenditure incurred on refrigerated trucks/ vehicles to be considered as eligible for fixed capital investment for computation of subsidy.
17. Exemption from excise duty for wines / liquors / brandy etc. made from 100 percent fruit / potatoes / grains produced in the state.

3.11 Role of Financial Institutions in Contract Farming in India

The Government of India's National Agricultural Policy envisages that private participation will be promoted through contract farming and land leasing arrangements to allow accelerated technology transfer, capital inflow and assured market for crop production, especially of oil seeds, cotton and horticultural crops. National Agricultural Policy of Government of India has also recognized contract farming as an important aspect of agri-business and its significance for small farmers. The Inter-Ministerial Task Force on Agricultural reforms observed that contract farming was becoming increasingly important.

3.11.1 Financial Institutions' Initiative

If farming has to run like a business, a farmer requires input, credit and market. The advance of credit is a vital part of contract farming. Access to credit is not only a big incentive for small-holders in joining contract farming schemes but it also helps them to enter the market. A number of policy initiatives has been taken by the Government of India, Government of Maharashtra, RBI and NABARD in the recent past for the development of agriculture, allied to agriculture and rural sectors in the country as well as in the State of Maharashtra. The initiatives taken up by NABRD/ RBI, with regard to rural credit, are summarized below. :

3.11.2 Policy initiatives by NABARD for contract farming

The recent policy initiative by the NABARD, inter alia, focuses on augmenting and smoothening the flow of ground–level credit for rural development. The NABARD introduced refinements in its policies for extension of short-term refinance, besides fine-tuning the refinance policy for investment credit to meet the emerging needs of important sub-sectors of agriculture. Recognizing the potential and benefits of contract farming arrangements in the agricultural sector, NABARD took the important initiative of supporting such arrangements by the banking sector and developed a special refinance package for contract farming arrangements (within and outside AEZs) aimed at promoting increased production of commercial crops and creation of marketing avenues for the farmers. In order to augment the reach of bank credit and increased the production of commercial crops as also for creation of marketing avenues for the farmers, all contract farming arrangements (within and outside AEZs) are made eligible for availing special refinance package from NABARD. Following are a few amongst such important policy initiatives:

1. Important policy changes in financing Seasonal Agricultural Operations (SAO), included certain relaxations in sanction of credit limits to DCCBs, not complying with Section 11 (1) of Banking Regulations Act, 1949 (AACS), enhancement of quantum of credit limits to DCCBs with reference to multiples of their own funds, certain relaxations with reference to stipulation of minimum involvement (MI) norms etc.
2. In tune with the National Agricultural Policy (NAP), the National Bank liberalized the existing scheme of financing the marketing of agricultural produce, covering even the non-borrowing members of PACS.
3. The existing guidelines for provision of relief by the short-term cooperative credit structure and the RRBs to farmers, affected by natural calamities, have been

revised in tune with the guidelines issued by RBI to the scheduled commercial banks.

4. The other policy initiatives included rationalization of clean cash credit limits by SCBs/DCCBs to cooperative sugar factories for payment of bonus to workers, permitting SCBs/DCCBs to finance activities in service sector etc.
5. The refinance policy for farm mechanization was further liberalized and special impetus was given for financing power tillers. The interest rate on refinance for investment credit has been rationalized and made effective from 1st May, 2000.
6. 100 percent refinance to disbursements made by CBs, SCBs, RRBs and select SCARDBs (having net NPA less than 5 percent).
7. The policy changes in Non-Farm Sector (NFS) refinance included expansion of service sector, regrouping and rationalization of schemes, enhancing limit of composite loan, liberalizing Small Road and Water Transport Finance Scheme, introduction incentives under REDPs, etc.
8. The National Bank has brought the Scheduled Primary (Urban) Cooperative Banks within the ambit of refinance facilities under Section 25 of the NABARD Act.
9. Scheme for setting-up of agri-clinics and agri-business centres by agricultural graduates with support of NABARD refinance has been recently introduced. Banks will provide loans on attractive terms for setting-up of these proposed centeres with refinances facilities from NABARD.
10. Private sector investment in agriculture will also be encouraged, more particularly in areas like agricultural research, human resource development, post-harvest management and marketing.
11. Rural electrification will be given a high priority as a

prime mover for agricultural development. The use of new and renewable sources of energy for irrigation and other agricultural purpose will also be encouraged and promoted.

12. Term facility for repayments (3 years), fixation of higher scale of finance for crops under contract farming, extension of refinance scheme for financing farmers for contract farming in AEZs to contract farming outside AEZs besides coverage of medicinal and aromatic plants.
13. Extension of Refinance scheme for contract farming under Automatic Refinance Facility. Preparation of banking plan for financing diesel gensets to gherkin farmers in Karnataka with TFO-1.71 crore. Area developing project for grapes in Nashik district, Maharashtra with TFO-402 crore. Refinance support extended for contract farming within AEZs and outside to various financing agencies during 2004-05 and 2005-06 was to the tune of Rs. 774 crore and Rs. 268 crore respectively.

3.11.3 NABARD'S Development Initiatives

1. Conducting workshops and exposure visits for better interface among farmers and entrepreneurs and popularization of contract farming concept.
2. Conducting crop specific studies in (Ex. gherkins in Karnataka, grapes in Maharashtra and mango in AP) to understand the gamut of contractual arrangements.
3. Sensitization of stakeholders through state and district level meets and consultations.
4. Sensitization of bankers through tailor-made training programme at Bankers Institute for Rural Development (BIRD) Lucknow.
5. Follow-up with National Agricultural Insurance Corporation for insurance of crops grown under contractual arrangements in AEZs.

6. Initiatives for expansion of scope of contract farming for medicinal plants through corporate initiatives.

3.11.4 Commercial Banks' Participation for Providing Credit Facility

With the present trends of declining interest rates in the deregulated environment and huge amount of deposits build-up on one hand and various incentives being provided by the government to invest in agriculture and allied activities, with mandatory norm of minimum 40 percent lending to agriculture sector, on other hand, commercial bank have equally good prospects to enter the scene. The given scenario is much more opportune for commercial banks, considering that the corporate's entering into the agriculture sector, through contract farming route, is much reserved / cautious in terms of cash lending to the member farmers on a contractual basis. As corporate lending is not picking up, commercial banks are looking for greener pastures. They have hit upon a unique strategy to rise credit off-take and at the same time fulfil their agriculture sector lending targets. Interest rates in contract farming have been going down rapidly, from 12 percent last few year to around 9 percent now. Banks are entering into tie-ups with companies manufacturing farm inputs in order to offer crop finance schemes to farmers who undertake contract farming for the latter.

In the public sector, Union Bank of India and the State Bank of India are aggressively pushing farm credit. HDFC Bank has a contract farming portfolio of around Rs. 50 crore. While UTI Bank is also looking at getting into contract farming in a big way to increase its direct agricultural lending portfolio, ICICI Bank is focusing on contract farming and is tying-up with several companies. Last year, ICICI Bank financed 55,000 farmers to take-up contract farming. The target for this year has been enhanced to one lakh. Hitherto, this shortfall was made good by parking funds in the National Bank of Agriculture and Rural Development's Rural

Infrastructure Development Fund (RIDF). As a matter of change of strategy, banks are now aggressively lending to the agriculture sector, with focus on agro-processing and agri-business.

Union Bank of India has tied-up with Jain Irrigation Systems Ltd.(JISL) to offer crop finance schemes to farmers who undertake contract farming for Jain Irrigation Systems Ltd. This offer at present is open to farmers in the Jalgaon, Dhule and Nandurbar districts of Maharashtra. UTI Bank is looking at contract farming in a big way to double its portfolio of direct agriculture lending- from Rs. 300 crore to Rs. 600 crore.

The State Bank of India (SBI) has tied-up with Rallis India Ltd., in an effort to boost its agriculture sector lending. This alliance with Rallis is the first of such tie-up of State Bank of India with a corporate sector for contract farming. The bank is also currently scouting for tie-ups with other corporate for the stated purpose.

Indian Bank had financed two contract farming projects in Tamil Nadu, aggregating to Rs. 10 lakh and is now planning to tie-up with global processed-food majors and lead domestic companies to improve its lending for selected and commercially viable contract farming activities.[28]

3.12 Role of Policies in Promoting Contract Farming

Contract farming in India is in the infant stage, and the evidence indicates it can be developed as a pro-poor market institution through appropriate policies and strategies. Also there are opportunities for farmers in contract farming. Sustained income growth, a fast-growing urban population and increasing westernization of diets are fuelling rapid growth in demand for high-value horticultural and animal food products, which have a greater scope for production under contracts. Between 2005 and 2025 the demand for different animal food products is projected to increase by 75-110 percent and for fruits and vegetable by 85-90 percent, as compared to a 20 percent increase in the demand for food grains[29]. The demand for processed food products and beverages is expected to grow even faster; the share of processed foods and beverages in the total food expenditure is projected to rise to 15 percent in 2020 from 9 percent in 1999.[30] Besides, export opportunities are also emerging with unfolding of globalization. The share of high-value food products (dairy, poultry, fruits and vegetables) in the total agricultural exports has steadily increased; from 13.5 percent in 2001-02 to 15.9 percent in 2005-06.[31]

Contract farming schemes are organized by large agribusiness firms including processors, exporters and supermarket chains. Developing contract farming thus requires appropriate policies, infrastructure and regulations that facilitate private investment in agribusiness. During the last 15 years the Government of India has taken a number of initiatives, such as de-regulation of food industry, pruning of the list of agricultural items reserved for small-scale industries, 100 percent foreign direct investment (FDI) in food processing, reduction in corporate taxes and excise duties on processed foods, establishment of agri-export zones, priority sector lending to food processing industry, enactment of an integrated food law, de-regulation of agricultural markets, etc. to boost food processing and promote agribusiness and contract farming. The following issues however merit further attention.

3.12.1 Investment in Public infrastructure

A firm's decision to invest in agribusiness, to a great extent, is influenced by the availability of good public infrastructure (roads, electricity, communication network, electricity, etc.). Public infrastructure is essential to reduce marketing and transaction costs and post-harvest losses, and for quick access and dissemination of information. Unfortunately, the public infrastructure in India has remained underdeveloped, leading to a slow growth in private investment in refrigerated transport, cold storages and food processing. This is reflected in the low level of value-addition to agricultural produce; only 2.2 percent of the production of fruits and vegetables, 6 percent of the poultry meat, 21 percent of the buffalo meat and 15 percent of the milk produced in the country are processed into value-added products by the organized sector. The evidence also shows a greater concentration of production of high-value agricultural commodities (in which contract farming is more pronounced) in the areas well-connected with roads and urban centers.[32] Investment in public infrastructure is thus essential to trigger private investment all along the supply/value chain.

3.12.2 FDI in Food Processing

The Government of India allows 100% FDI in food processing but restricts FDI in retailing in general, because of opposition from traders' lobby and some political parties that argue that FDI in retailing would adversely affect livelihood of millions of workers in the unorganized retailing. Restricting FDI in food retailing however may act as barrier to FDI in food processing and thereby to the growth of food processing industry, which is crucial to establish strong backward linkages with agriculture. For example, despite a provision of 100% FDI in food processing the growth in output of food processing sector has remained almost the same as in the pre-FDI period. The government, however, has permitted FDI in single brand retailing in 2006. Evidence from elsewhere shows that FDI in food retailing is beneficial to both consumers and producers.[33] FDI in retailing means rise of supermarkets offering benefits of convenience shopping, and access to a variety of products at lower prices to consumers. Supermarkets procure food commodities from independent procurement companies (dedicated suppliers) who often work with farmers or through contract farming. Such market linkages create opportunities for farmers to have a better access to markets for produce, inputs, services and technology.

3.12.3 Model Act 2003

By enacting the Model Act (The State Agricultural Produce Marketing Development & Regulation Act) in 2003 the Government of India has taken a noteworthy step towards creating a level playing field for the private investment in agricultural markets, agribusiness and contract farming. Its implementation by the state governments has remained half-hearted. Only a few states have amended their existing Agricultural Produce Market Committee Acts on the lines of Model Act, others have done some partial amendments or are yet to decide on the modifications. The implementation of the Model Act, 2003 in its true spirit is likely to promote competition and strengthen industry's linkages with agriculture. It is, however, cautioned that the governments should take appropriate measures to curb any tendency of regional monopsony and collusive oligopsony.

3.12.4 Mechanisms for Dispute Solution

The Model Act, 2003 outlines provisions for regulation of contract farming to protect interests of both agribusiness firms and farmers. However, one of the provisions that merit attention concerns mechanism for dispute resolution. Considering the lengthy legal procedures, the Act provides that disputes between firms and farmers, if any should be mutually resolved or settled by the Marketing Committee with which the contract farming scheme is registered. However, at present a considerable number of contract farming schemes are informal and remain unregistered with the Marketing Committee. Non-registration of contract farming schemes creates a scope for opportunism, breach of contracts and rise in disputes. These problems would appear in a severe form with spread of contract farming, which is likely. Thus, there is a need to (i) enforce registration of contract farming schemes, and (ii) establish a judicial or quasi-judicial body for speedy resolution of disputes.

3.12.5 Grades and Standards

Price and quality of products are two major factors that can render a contract farming scheme a success or failure. Agribusiness firms may reject farm produce or pay a lower price on the ground of its poor quality. This happens because of a lack of well-defined grades and standards for farm produce. Organized retailers, exporters and processors are imposing their own grades and standards on producers. The requirement for developing effective grades and standards and their compliance by both sellers and buyers cannot be ignored with rising demand for safe and quality foods in both the domestic and the international markets.

3.12.6 Promote Farmers

Often, agribusiness firms tend to ignore small farmers in contract farming schemes because of higher transaction costs of dealing with a large number of them. An effective way of involving smallholders in contract farming is to encourage them to organize themselves into cooperatives, self-help groups and growers associations. Such organizational structures help them improve their bargaining power vis-à-vis agribusiness firms, and also generate scale economies in acquisition of inputs, technology, services and information. Non-governmental organizations (NGOs) can also play an important role by acting as intermediaries between firms and farmers.

3.12.7 In Agricultural Research and Extension

Contract farming is more prevalent in high-value agricultural commodities that have a considerable market demand. This implies a greater diversification of agricultural production portfolio, and sets a demand-driven agenda for agricultural research and extension. Agricultural research and extension in India have remained largely in the public-domain. However, increasing participation of the private sector in agribusiness offers considerable scope for public-private partnership in agricultural research and extension to effectively address rising (i) consumers' concerns for food variety, safety and quality, and (ii) farmers' requirement of information, technology and services.

3.12.8 *Investment Capacity and Cope Up with Risks*

Two important factors in scaling-out/up of the contract farming relate to credit and insurance. An overwhelming majority of farmers in India are smallholders. They lack capacity to invest in high-value agriculture and are risk averse. Some activities like poultry and fruit plantation are capital-intensive and riskier, and need institutional support in terms of finance and insurance. Although formal rural credit system in the country is fairly well-developed, institutions to protect farmers against risks have remained under-developed. Hardly around 4 percent farm households in the country insure their farming activities.[34]

3.13 Registration of Contract Farming in India

In the absence of the system of registration of contracts with any authorized agency of the state for the verification of the credentials/track record of the sponsoring companies, there are reported cases of farmers becoming victims of the fly-by-night operators. There is a very low level of awareness about contract farming amongst the different stakeholders. It is probably for this reason that vast areas of the country covering states such as Bihar, Jharkhand, Chhattisgarh, Orissa, West Bengal and the North-East and areas of Himachal Pradesh and Jammu & Kashmir have remained untouched by the major contract farming sponsoring companies. The Model APMR Act, 2003 of the Government of India has recommended the compulsory registration of contract farming with Market Committee. Sponsor is commended to register himself with the Sub Divisional Officer or with an officer prescribed by law. The National Commission on Farmers, however, has given its recommendations not to involve the

Market Committee as a party to contract farming. Accordingly, Market Committee would not be registration authority for contract farming and the contract farming sponsor shall get the contract farming agreement recorded with the Sub-Divisional Magistrate, who, in turn shall ask for such documents as required to verify the credentials of the sponsoring company. Absence of a proper legal framework is a major impediment in popularizing contract farming system in the country. Under the present system, the Contract Act is the only law for contract farming, but the provisions of the Contract Act do not cater to the specific requirements of contract farming in a suitable manner. Besides the costs, procedure and the delay the distance from the courts works as a disincentive to the farmer to invoke the Civil Courts jurisdiction when the need arises. The different types of possible disputes arising out of contract farming can be attributed to refusal to receive delivery of the commissioned goods, delay in payment beyond agreed period, discounting of payment, returning the commissioned goods without any good reason, forced price reduction, compulsory purchase by subcontractors of parent firm's products, and forcing subcontractors to pay in advance for materials supplied by the parent firm etc.

3.14 Contract Farming Model Act 2003 in India

The Government of India has taken a noteworthy step towards creating a level playing field for the private investment in agricultural markets, agribusiness and contract farming. By enacting the Model Act (The State Agricultural Produce Marketing Development & Regulation Act) in 2003 Its implementation by the state governments has remained half-hearted. Only a few states have amended their existing Agricultural Produce Market Committee Acts on the lines of Model Act, others have done some partial amendments or are yet to decide on the modifications. The implementation of the Model Act, 2003 in its true spirit is likely to promote competition and strengthen industry's linkages with agriculture. It is, however, cautioned that the governments should take appropriate measures to curb any tendency of regional monopsony and collusive oligopsony.

In India, the legal reform process is already under way with the Union Government enacting the Model Act for the state Agricultural Produce Marketing (Development and Regulation) Act, 2003 and many states (8 as suggested, and 10 partially like Gujarat, Haryana, Karnataka, Maharashtra, U.P, Delhi and Chandigarh permitting only direct marketing/ contract farming or private/co-operative markets (only Karnataka)) carrying out the amendment in their Acts. This amended act deals with setting up of private markets, selling of produce by growers outside the APMCs (regulated markets), setting up of direct markets, specialized commodity specific markets, regulation and promotion of contract farming, provision for agencies and measures to promote quality, standards, and alternative markets, and public-private partnerships to facilitate more and better linkage between firms and farmers. The amended APMC Act has certain mandatory and optional provisions regarding contract farming. The mandatory ones include aspects like who can undertake contract farming (type of sponsor and of contract grower), details about the land under contract, duration of contract, description of farm produce, and other contract specifications like quantity i.e. acreage, entire crop, or fixed quantity. It also has provisions on produce quality specifications and penalties for lower quality like rejection, or lower price, crop delivery arrangements i.e. at farm/factory gate/collection centre and transport arrangements, pricing and credit mechanisms, and farmer asset/land indemnity. Besides, it makes it compulsory to register contracts with the local authority and specifies a procedure for dispute resolution. On the other hand, the optional features include those relating to farm practices, joint crop insurance, support services to be provided, farmer-management forum for monitoring of contract system performance, and monitoring of quality and yields.

The model contract agreement is quite fair in terms of sharing of costs and risks between the sponsor and the grower.[35] But, it leaves out many aspects of farmer interest protection like delayed payments and deliveries, contract cancellation damages if producer made firm specific heavy investments, inducement/force/intimidation to enter a contract, disclosure of material risks, competitive performance based payments, and sharing of production risks. Also, there are state level variations in the amended Acts as agriculture is a state subject in India. For example, in Gujarat, the amended Act makes the APMC as a party in the tripartite contract (earlier mandatory, but now optional) stating the logic that APMCs have a useful role as facilitator as they have longstanding relationship with farmers and can disseminate the contract farming concept and practice besides monitoring its practice. Though the union model Act exempts contract procurement from market fee, the Gujarat Act makes it mandatory to pay the prescribed cess to the concerned APMC or in case of multi-location operations, to the GSAMB which will apportion it to the concerned APMCs. On the other hand, Bihar has abolished the APMC Act instead of amending it and that makes the agricultural market in the state totally unregulated. Further, it is not known how far the model contract agreement will be adopted by the agencies unless it is conditionality to avail certain other incentives or policies.[36]

3.15 Contract Farming under the Model Act in India

Under the Model Act, the agriculture produce covered under the contract farming agreement may be sold to the contract farming sponsor outside the market yard and in such a case, no market fees should be livable. Disputes arising out of contract farming agreement may be referred to an authority prescribed in this behalf for settlement. The prescribed authority shall resolve the dispute in a summary manner within thirty days after giving the parties a reasonable opportunity of being heard, in the manner prescribed. The dispute redressal authority should be a body at the sub-divisional level comprising a representative of the sponsoring company, a farmers' representative and the Sub Divisional Magistrate of the area under whose jurisdiction the contract farming land falls. It has also been provided that the party aggrieved by the decision of the prescribed authority as above may prefer an appeal to an Appellant Authority within thirty days from the date of decision. The Appellate Authority should be the concerned District Collector and Magistrate. The Appellant Authority shall dispose of the appeal within thirty days after giving the parties a reasonable opportunity of being heard and the decision of the Appellant Authority shall be final. The decision by the authority and decision in appeal as above should have force of the decree of the civil court and shall be enforceable as such and decretal amount shall be recovered as arrears of land revenue. Disputes relating to and arising out of contract farming agreement shall not be called in question in any court of law as recognized by the Model Act. Contents of a contract farming agreement depends on a number of factors such as the nature of the product, the primary processing required, if any, and the demands of the market in terms of supply reliability. Quality incentives, payment arrangements, the extent to which the parties have capital tied up in the contract and the level of control the sponsor wants to have over the production process also influence the nature of the agreement. A contract covering, for example, oil palm, tea or sugar, where significant long-term investment is required from all parties, will be different from a contract covering annual crops such as fruit and vegetables for local supermarket. This may also be the same as one not covering such produce destined for overseas markets, which may have more rigid controls on pesticide use and product quality as well as higher presentation and packaging standards. Although corporate bodies, government agencies and individual developers are, out of necessity, the catalysts of the contract, farmers and their representatives must be given the opportunity to contribute to the drafting of the agreement and assist in the wording of specification in terms farmers can understand. Management must ensure that agreements are fully understood by all farmers. The terms and conditions entered into must be written down for independent examination and copies given to the farmers' representatives. The legal framework of the agreement should comply with the minimum legal requirements of the Indian Contract Act, local practice must be taken into account and arrangements for arbitration must be addressed. Agreements, in the form of a written contract, usually cover the responsibilities and obligations of each party, the manner in which the agreement can be enforced and the remedies to be taken if the contract breaks down. In most cases, agreements are made between the sponsor and the farmer, although in the case of multipartite arrangements, the contracts can be between the sponsor and farmer associations or cooperatives. In the majority of cases, it is highly unlikely that a sponsor will take legal action against a small holder for a breach of contract. The costs involved are inclined to be far in excess of the amount claimed, and legal action threatens the relationship between the sponsor and all farmers, not just those against whom action is being taken. Action by a farmer against a sponsor is similarly improbable. As neither side is likely to seek a legal remedy through the courts, it is important that quick and easy ways of resolving disputes are identified in the agreement. For the purpose, appropriate legal provision will have to be made in the law governing the marketing of agricultural produce (APMC Act) and to inter-alia provide for compulsory registration of all contract farming agreements and the procedure for settlement of disputes arising there from.[37]

3.16 Concepts of Good Farming Contract

In the contract farming to have a written contract preferably in local language using simple and non-ambiguous vocabulary for clarity of terms and conditions and to eliminate changes of misunderstanding because of multiple meanings.

The contract document must be signed by all the parties in the contract and a copy given to each of them for record and use.

A farming contract should preferably be on stamp paper, consistent with existing legal framework for the purpose and registered with local authority. There should be no scope for unfair practices against any party in implementation of the contract. Risk faced by the producer in signing the contract must be made known to him. Dispute if arises must be settled locally by the designated authority.

The committed plot must be properly identified. As quality of produce to be procured is crucial to the processor, this quality must be clearly defined or described. The quality parameters as far as possible must be objectively measurable and quality assessment procedure must be transparent and acceptable to producers. The quality assessment to the extent possible should be made at the farm gate, e.g. grading, weighing etc. in the presence of the producers.[38]

In case the contractor takes part in managing production activity in terms of field inspection of standing crops it must be mentioned in the contract. Farmers should agree to comply with recommendations and action to be taken to realize the potential yield of quality produce. Where inputs are supplied by the contractor who also provides technical information and extension service to growers and in some case carries out inspection of growing crop entire, production should be purchased by the contractor at the agreed price. In a long term contract for plantation crops, price may be linked to future price with a minimum guaranteed price. In case byproducts or residue is delivered to the contractor a reasonable compensation for the same plus his cost of harvesting and delivery must be paid. Timing and place of delivery of produce are important from buyer's point of view and have cost implications for the producers. Hence these must be specified, payment schedule and mode of payment should be part of the contract.

In case of non-compliance of contract by either party,

there should be some penal clause for compensation of losts to the other party, penalty for different types of violations should be provided provision for arbitration by some local authority operating at village level should be made.

3.17 Maharashtra Contract Farming Act, 2006

Contract farming in Maharashtra will get the much needed impetus, following the passage of the bill to amend the Maharashtra Agricultural Produce Marketing (Development and Regulation) Act which has been passed in the State Assembly on Thursday 20 April 2006. The government claimed that contract farming would boost food processing and export of agricultural produce. The contract farming act is designed to encourage the investment in the food processing industry of Maharashtra, which would ensure farmers get the best prices for their produce. The government further said, "food processing industry and exporters of farm produce have always wanted assured supply of quality farm produce. The act will not only assure this would happen, but also iron out vagaries in prices that plague farmers every year." As the new law allows buyers of farm produce to enter into direct agreement with the farmers, the farmers will also be saved from paying commission and other charges to agriculture market produce committees. Food processing units are typically located in areas that are far remote from the place of production and the act will go a long way in creating new employment opportunities in rural areas.

The bill has aimed at providing a viable means of marketing agroproduce to farmers. ITC, Cargil Foods, Metro Cash & Carry, Hypercity and ShopRite have already expressed desire to link contract farming act with the state government. State Minister for Marketing said contract farming would integrate and strengthen the agricultural produce marketing system. The bill provides for compulsory registration of all contract farming sponsors, recording of contract farming agreements under certain conditions, and indemnity to producers title and possession over his land from any claim arising out of the agreement. The minister said contract farming sponsors would be able to provide inputs, credit and technology to the contract farming producer, thereby resulting in improving productivity and quality of the produce. The produce would also be assured of the price, as it would be a part of the agreement.

However under the provisions of new law it has been specifically mentioned that a contractor will have no right over the land of the farmers. The state government clarified under the Act the contractor will have to register has agreement with farmer which will include details like, how much land of farmer would be under contract, for how long and for which crop production. The state will also appoint an authority to arbitrate disputes that would arise between farmers and contractors. The decision of this body can be challenged before the appellate authority. The state government said that under the contract farming the agreement would be of agricultural produce and not for agricultural land. Farmers saatbara utara, on land possession would not change hands under the system and added there was no question of any company which has entered into a contract seizing the land.

This provision has been incorporated in the Maharashtra Agricultural Produce Marketing (Regulation and Development) Act, 1963 vide G.R. dated-16th July 2006. The various Rules regarding this provision are as follows:

Contract farming sponsor shall apply for registration in FORM G to District Deputy Registrar (DDR), C.S. with registration fee Rs. 500. Agreement shall be exclusively for the purchase of agricultural produce only. Sponsor to submit the original copy of agreement to DDR. Prohibition for creation of right, title, interest or ownership in the land and sale under contract farming agreement. Minimum period of agreement shall be for one crop season and maximum period shall not be more than 3 years. Liberty to mutually decide other terms and conditions of the agreement as in FORM I. Dispute arising out of agreement to be referred to DDR. DDR to give decision within 30 days. Appeal to Divisional Joint Registrar within 30 days. Agreement shall not be entitled to be called in question in any court of law.

3.18 Performance of Contract Farming in Maharashtra

In Maharashtra contract farming has been playing a pivotal role and mostly it is taking place in sugarcane / cotton by ginning / factories, seeds companies, while some companies are doing contract farming under the contract act in potato. It has also cultivated cotton and banana. The table 3.3 shows the details of different contract companies working through in the Maharashtra state in 2008-09. PepsiCo India Holding Pvt. Ltd. has been working in Taluka Shirur of Pune District in cultivate potato. It has covered area of more than 1200 hectares nearabout 500 farmers are benefited from it. Marketing facilities are provided and different processing business are established. They produce potato chips etc. The company has also established many branches in different district. These are working in Sangli and Satara district. More than 160 farmers are benefited in Sangli district and more than 750 farmers are benefited in Satara district. The same processing business have been run by the company in both the districts.

NCC Narsinh Cotton Pvt. Ltd. is established in Parbhani district. It cultivates cotton. It has covered more than 6000 hectare of land and more than 285 farmers are benefited. It is running business like ginning / pressing and marketing. NCC Shri Cotton Pvt. Ltd. is established in Hivarkhed Taluka Telhar, dist. Akola. It cultivates cotton. It has covered near about 6300 hectare of land. More than 2300 farmers are benefited from it. It has been working on raw cotton processing. Raw cotton processing is also run by Arvind Limited Akola. It cultivates cotton and it has covered more than 9000 hectare of land, more than 4700 farmers are benefited from it.

NCC Shri Ganpati Cotton Pvt. Ltd. Malkapur dist.

Table 3.3
List of Contract Farming Companies in Maharashtra Year 2008-2009

District	Name and Address of Company / Firms etc.	Name of crops covered with area in hectare	No. of Farmers benefited	Nature of processing and marketing facilities offered, if any
Pune	PepsiCo India Holding Pvt. Ltd. Tal- Shirur Dist. Pune	Potato -1200	499	Potato Processing For Potato Chips-LAYS
Sangli	PepsiCo India Holding Pvt. Ltd. Tal- Shirur Dist. Pune	Potato -1	163	Potato Processing For Potato Chips-LAYS
Satara	PepsiCo India Holding Pvt. Ltd. Tal- Shirur Dist. Pune	Potato -1	759	Potato Processing For Potato Chips-LAYS
Parbhani	NCC Narsinh Cotton Pvt. Ltd. Sur. No. 34 Bhandarwade Pathri	Cotton 6050	285	Ginning /Pressing and Marketing
Akola	1. NCC Shri Cotton Pvt. Ltd. Hivarkhed Tq. Telhar 2. Arvind Ltd, Akola	Cotton – 6299 Cotton 9020	2352 4716	Raw cotton Processing Raw cotton Processing
Buldhana	1.NCC Shri Ganpati Cotton Pvt. Ltd. Malkapur 2. NCC Shri Matosri Cotton Pvt. Ltd. Malkapur	Cotton 48 29.93 Cotton 104 6.6	2065 408	Company himself Company himself purchased from farmers
Dhule	NCC Jaylaxmi Fibers Pvt. Ltd. At.Post. Dhamane, Tq. & Dist. Dhule	Cotton 5452	2488	Purchase of raw cotton from contractor grower at ginning unit
Beed	NCC Abhinandan Cotton Pvt. Ltd. Majalgaon	Cotton 772	231	Purchase of raw cotton from contractor grower at ginning unit
Jalna	NCC Santosh Fibers Pvt. Ltd. Jalna	Cotton 172	33	Purchase of raw cotton from contractor grower at ginning unit
Solapur	Desai Fruits & Vegetable Pvt. Ltd. Kandhar	Banana 39	5	Export

Source : Director of Agriculture Marketing Board Pune.

Buldhana purchases the product of farmers itself. It produces cotton. It has covered 4829.93 hectare of land from it. In Buldhana district another company called NCC Shri Motoshri Cotton Pvt. Ltd. Malkapur has been working on the same project. It cultivates cotton. It has covered 1046.6 hectare of land and more than 400 farmers are benefited from it.

NCC Jai Laxmi Fibers Pvt. Ltd. Dhamane, Tq. District Dhule produces cotton. It has covered near about 5500 hectare of land and nearabout 2500 farmers are benefited from it. It purchases row cotton and makes the process of it. The same business it also run by NCC Abhinand Cotton Pvt. Ltd. Majalgaon district Beed. It cultivates cotton. It has covered nearabout 800 hectare of area and near about 250 farmer are benefited from it. NCC Santosh Fiber Pvt. Ltd. Jalna also runs the same business. It cultivates cotton in 172 hectare of the land and 73 farmer are benifited farmers from it. Desai Fruits and Vegetable Pvt. Ltd. Kundhar district Solapur cultivates Banana. It has covered near about 40 hectare of land but only five farmer are benefited from it. It exports the products in foreign countries.

The Table 3.4 shows the list of difference contract companies working in Maharashtra state. In the 2010-11 Desai Fruits and Vegetable Pvt. Ltd. Kandhar cultivates banana and 172 farmers are working in contract farming Banana and A.S. farms Prop. Amersing Appasaheb Patil A/p. Aerag, Tq. Miraj, District Sangli. The company purchase the crop and supply it to hotels. It produce babycorn, zukeni, sweet corn. More than 50 farmers are benefited from it.

NCC Narsay Cotton Pvt. Ltd. Pathari, district Parbhani produce cotton. It has covered 1854 hectare of land and near about 545 farmers are benefited from it. It purchases row cotton and process it. The same business it also run by NCC Shri Cotton Pvt. Ltd. Hivarkhed district Akola it cultivates cotton. It has covered 14754 hectare of area and nearabout 4155 farmers are involved in cotton contract farming. Arvind Ltd. Akola also run the same business. It has covered 16975 hectare of

Table No. 3.4
List of Contract Farming Companies in Maharashtra Year 2010-2011

District	Name and Address of Company / Firms etc.	Name of crops covered with area in hectare	No. of Farmers benefited	Nature of processing and marketing facilities offered, if any
Solapur	Desai Fruts and Vegetable Ltd. Kandar, Tq. Karmala	Banana	172	Export
Sangli	A.S. Farms Prop. Amersing Appasaheb Patil A/p. Aerag, Tq. Miraj, Dist. Sangli.	1. Babycorn 2. Zukeni 3. Sweet corn	50	Supply of agri. product to hotels
Parbhani	NCC Narsay Cotton Pvt. Ltd. Pathari Dist. Parbhani	Cotton 1854 hectare	545	Ginning / Pressing and Marketing
Akola	1. NCC Shri Cotton Pvt. Ltd. Hivarkhed dist. Akola	Cotton 14754	4155	Raw Cotton Processing
	2. Arvind Ltd. Akola	Cotton 16975	6094	Raw Cotton Processing
Buldhana	1.Shri Ganpati Cotton Pvt. Ltd. Malkapur.	Cotton 16023.6	4320	Company himself purchased from farmers
	2.Shri Matosri cotton Pvt. Ltd. Malkapur.	Cotton 10601.20	3819	Company himself purchased from farmers
Total - 5	**7**	**60207.8**	**19154**	

Source : Director of Agriculture Marketing Board, Pune.

land and 6094 farmers are involved in cotton contract farming. It process the raw cotton.

In the Buldhana district working in contract farming is Shri Ganpati Cotton Pvt. Ltd. Malkapur. It has covered 16023.6 hectare of area and 4320 farmers are involved in the cotton contract farming. The same business is also run by Shri Matosri cotton Pvt. Ltd. Malkapur. It has covered 10601 hectare of land and nearabout 3819 farmers are involved in the contract farming. Company itself purchases cotton from farmers. In the year 2010-11 in Maharashtra the crop cultivated under the contract farming of Banana, cotton in the total area of land 60,207.8 hectare and nearabout 19,154 farmers were involved in contract farming.

The Table No. 3.5 shows the details of contract farming in Maharashtra in the year 2011-12. The PepsiCo India Holdings Pvt. Ltd. is working in various district like Pune, Sangli and Satara. It cultivate the potato crop for processing potato chips- Lays etc. It has covered 1200 hectares land and 499 from in Pune district, 163 farmers in Sangli and 759 farmers in Satara district and produces patato under contract farming.

Conclusion

It is observed that the process of contract farming in India involves, engaging rural Indian farmers for the cultivation of

Table No. 3.5
List of Contract Farming Companies in Maharashtra
Year 2011-2012

District	Name and Address of Company / Firms etc.	Name of crops covered with area in hector	No. of Farmers benefited	Nature of processing and marketing facilities offered, if any
Pune	PepsiCo India Holding Pvt. Ltd. Tal. Shirur	Potato-1200	499	Potato Processing for Potato Chips-LAYS
Sangli	PepsiCo India Holding Pvt. Ltd.Pune	Potato	163	Potato Processing for Potato Chips-LAYS
Satara	PepsiCo India Holding Pvt. Ltd.Pune	Potato	759	Potato Processing for Potato Chips-LAYS

Source : Source : Director of Agriculture Marketing Board Pune.

agricultural produce under strict government policies. The role of contract farming in Indian rural economy involves government and private participation along with the rural workers. Further, it engages a good number of farmers and other rural workers to discharge other agriculture related activities. Contract farming is providing technology, extension services, credit, etc. to the farmers. A number of agribusiness firms have entered into contract farming agreements for a number of agricultural and horticultural crops, such as tomatoes, potatoes, chili, gherkin, baby corn, rose, onions, wheat, basmati, cotton, groundnuts flowers, medical plants, etc. produced in some from of contractual arrangements with the farmers in India. The states like Maharashtra, Andhra, Pradesh, Karnataka, Punjab, Haryana, Madhya Pradesh, Chattisgarh, Rajasthan, Tamil Nadu, Uttarkhand and Uttar Pradesh provide favourable conditions for contract farming and success of contract farming in these states owes to lower total land under marginal fields, better irrigation facilities, soil productivity and yield per hectare.

Contract farming in Maharashtra will get the much needed impetus, following the passage of the bill to amend the Maharashtra agricultural produce marketing (development and regulation). The government claimed that contract farming would boost food processing and export of agricultural produce. The Contract Farming Act is designed to encourage the investment in the food processing industry of Maharashtra, which would ensure farmers get the best prices for their produce. The government further said, "food processing industry and exporters of farm produce have always wanted assured supply of quality farm produce. The act will not only assure this would happen, but also iron out vagaries in prices that plague farmers every year." As the new law allows buyers of farm produce to enter into direct agreement with the farmers, the farmers will also be saved from paying commission and other charges to agriculture market produce committees. Food processing units are typically located in areas that are far remote from the place of production and the act will go a long way in creating new employment opportunities in rural areas.

Contract farming sponsor shall apply for registration in FORM G to District Deputy Registrar (DDR), C.S. with Registration fee Rs. 500. Agreement shall be exclusively for the purchase of agricultural produce only. Sponsor to submit the original copy of agreement to DDR. Prohibition for creation of right, title, interest or ownership in the land and sale under Contract Farming Agreement. Minimum period of agreement shall be for one crop season and max period shall not be more than 3 years. Liberty to mutually decide other terms and conditions of the agreement as in FORM I. Dispute arising out of agreement to be referred to DDR. DDR to give decision within 30 days. Appeal to Divisional Joint Registrar within 30 days. Agreement shall not be entitled to be called in question in any court of law.

The Government of Maharashtra had decided in June 2005 to modify the 1963 APMC act (Distribution) in which contract farming has been included and rename it as Model Act 7. Early implementation of this act would encourage farmers, because despite the present constraint, success with strong linkages between farmers and processors marketing agencies has been achieved. Such partnership is essential so that the objective is fulfilled for a sustainable business relationship and marketing performance.

In Maharashtra, 12 companies were working in 10 district in 2008-09 and area under contract farming was 34880.53 hectare and 14004 farmers were involved. In 2011-12 only one company was working in three district. It has covered 1200 hectare are land and nearabout 499 farmers are culticating potato.

Notes:

1. Rajmanohar T.P., Kumaravel K.S. (2006), *Contract Farming in India: A Introduction*. The ICFAI University Press Agartala.

2. Sukhpal Singh (2005), *Contract Farming for Agricultural Development*. Review of Theory and Practice with Special Reference to India,New concept Information Systems Pvt. Ltd., New Delhi.
3. Deshpande, R.S. (2008), *Contract farming and Tenancy Reforms Entangled Without Tether*. Concept Publishing Company, New Delhi.
4. Eaton, Charles and Andrew W. Shepherd (2001), Contract Farming, Partnerships for Growth, FAO Agricultural Services, Bulletin 145, Rome.
5. Rani, B.N., Globalization and Contract Farming in India Advantages and Problems. www.despace.llmk.ac.in/bitstream/2259/520/1/6337-647+pdf.
6. Deshpande, C.S. (2005), Contracting Farming As Means of Value-added Agriculture, Department of Economic Analysis and Research, National Bank for Agriculture and Rural Development, Mumbai.
7. Jain, R. C.A., Regulation and dispute settlement in contract farming in India, www.ncap.res.in
8. Deshpande R.S. (2008), *Contract Farming and Tenancy Reforms Entangled Without Tether*, Concept Publishing Company, New Delhi
9. Chidambaram, M. (1997), A Study of Export Potentials for Gherkins (Hybrid cucumber) in Tamil Nadu. Department of Agricultural Economics, Center for Agricultural and Rural Development Studies, Tamil Nadu Agricultural University.
10. Haque, T. (1999), Contract Farming in India, National Center of Agricultural Economics and Policy Research, New Delhi (unpublished).
11. Subranmanyan, K.V. (2000), Linkages Between Farm and Non-farm Sector: Role of Processing of Horticultural Products, NABARD Occasional paper No. 16, National Bank for Agriculture and Rural Development (NABARD), Mumbai.
12. Rangi, P.S. and Sidhu, M.S., "A Study on Contract Farming to Tomato in Punjab", *Agricultural Marketing*, 42 (4), pp. 15-23.
13. Dileep, B.K., Grover, R.K. and Rai, K.N. (2002), "Contract

Farming in Tomato: An Economic Analysis, *Indian Journal of Agricultural Economics*, 57 (2).
14 op. cit. Jain R.C.A.
15. Kulkarni, S. and Grethe, H., Does Vertical integration benefit farming community? A comparative study of contract and non-contract farmers in India. www.google.com
16. Jain and Singh P. (1999), "Determinants & Resource Use-efficiency in Popular-based Agro Forestry", *Productivity*, 40 (2), July-September.
17. Sukhpal Singh (2005), *Political Economy of Contract Farming in India*, Allied Publishers Private Limited, Mumbai.
18. The HBL Bureau (19 Dec. 1997), "Reliance Agrotech into Contract Farming", *The Hindu Business Line.*
19. Datta, S.M. (June 26, 1996), "Linkages with Agriculture: The Experience of the Food Processing Industry", *The Economic Times*, Ahmedabad.
20. Kiresur, V.R., Patil, S.A. and Vijayakumar, H.S. (2002), Contract Farming – An Opportunity for Small and Marginal Farmers in the Context of Trade Liberalization, in Ramesh Chand (ed) : *Impact of WTO on Indian Agricultural*, AERA, New Delhi.
21. Agricultural information.com: an e-mail news letter, ISSUE 19,20th December 2001.
22 op. cit. Sukhpal Singh (2005).
23 Ibid.
24. Kumar, P. Mruthyanjaya and Birtnal P.S. (2007), "Changing Consumption Pattern in South Asia", In *Agricultural Diversification and Small Holders in South Asia*, P.K. Joshi, Ashok Gulati and Ralph Cummings Jr. (eds).
25. Ravi, C. and Roy, D. (2006), Consumption patterns and food demand projections: A regional analysis, Paper presented at the workshop plate to plate to plough, Agricultural Diversification and Its Implications for the Small Holders, organized by the International Food Policy Research Institute, Asia Office, New Delhi, and the Institute of Economic Growth, New Delhi at New Delhi, September 20-21.
26. Singh, S. (2005), "Role of the State in Contract Farming in Thailand: Experience and Lessons", ASEAN *Economic*

Bulletin, 22 (2), August.

27. Sarkar, A.N. (2003), Techno-Economic Feasibility Study on Contract Farming in Maharashtra, Vaikunth Mehta National Institute of Cooperative Management Pune.
28. op. cit. Rajmahohar, T.P., Kumaravel, K.S. (2006).
29. op. cit. Sarkar, A.N. (2003)
30. op. cit. Kumar, P. Mruthyanjaya and Birtnal, P.S. (2007).
31. op. cit. Ravi, C. and Roy D. (2006).
32. Government of India (2007), Agricultural Statistics at a Glance. Department of Agricultural and Cooperation, Ministry of Agriculture, Government of India, New Delhi.
33. Parthasarathy Rao P., Birthal P.S. and Joshi P.K. (2006), "Diversification Towards High-value Agricultural : Role of Urbanization and Infrastructure, *Economic and Political Weekly*, June 30, pp. 2747-2753.
34. Reardon and Gulati (2008),
35. Government of India (2005), Some aspects of farming. Report No. 496 (59/33/3). National Sample Survey Organization, Ministry of Statistics and Program Implementation, Government of India, New Delhi.
36. op. cit. Sukhpal Singh (2005).
37. op. cit. Jain, R.C.A.
38. op. cit. Deshpande, R.S. (2008).

4

SOCIO-ECONOMIC CONDITION OF SAMPLE FARMER HOUSEHOLDS

4.1 Introduction

Maharashtra is an important state of India so for as its contribution to the agricultural development is concerned. Maharashtra is the second largest state in India in terms of population and the third in respect of area. The state has the third highest per Capita State Domestic Product (SDP) among all the Indian states in the year 2000-01.[1] Though Maharashtra is one of the industrialized states in the country, agriculture and allied activities are still predominant in the state. Agriculture continues to be the major source of income as most of the population depends on agriculture for livelihood. However, contribution of agriculture and allied activities in net state domestic product (SDP) declined steeply from 36 per cent in 1961-62 to 13.0 in 2011-12. The comparable shares for all India are 47 and 28.3 percent respectively.

Thus, the contribution of agriculture to the net SDP has been less in Maharashtra as compared to the national average. Yet in terms of the proportion of labour force engaged in agriculture (55.41 percent) as mentioned earlier, Maharashtra's economy continues to be predominantly agrarian. Indeed, the share of state's rural labour force employed in agriculture was as high as 80.08 per cent even in 2001, nearabout half (38.39 per cent) of the agricultural workers being labours. Thus, the crucial dependence of its rural labour force on agriculture is quite evident and it is unlikely to diminish drastically in the future. In this context, it is important to examine critically the past performance of agricultural and based on it the future prospects of growth is needed. Keeping in view the importance of agricultural quantitative assessment of the contribution of the various factors to growth of crop output at the state or regional level is helpful in reorienting the programmers and priorities of agriculture development so as to achieve higher growth. There are so many factors, which affect the growth of crop output. Among these area, productivity and cropping pattern are the minor one.[2]

These sources of output growth have relevance in deciding programmes of agricultural development and priorities of investment in it. The growth rates as such offer no explanation for desperate performance of agriculture. Thus it becomes important to find why these growth rates differ from one another so that the bottlenecks could be removed to achieve the speedy development of agricultural sector. Decomposition of growth in agricultural output has remained of active interest to researchers and policy makers. A breakdown of growth into various components, areas, yield, cropping pattern, etc. facilitates output projection with alternative targets and policies. Thus, decomposition of agricultural growth among its constituent forces is of great importance. An analysis of the behaviour of agricultural production in the past of estimation of its growth rates can provide a basis for future projection of Agricultural output.[3]

4.2 Present Scenario of Agriculture in Maharashtra

Maharashtra is one of the progressive states in the country but it has been reported to be a deficit state for long when one considers to major pursuit of economic activity that is agriculture. Geographical area of Maharashtra state is 3.08 lakh sq. kms, out of which the net area under agriculture is about 1.77 lakh sq. kms, i.e. 57.5 per cent. This proportion at the national level is less at 43.4 per cent. However, the proportion of gross irrigated area to gross cropped area at national level is 45.3 per cent, while in Maharashtra state it is only 17.7 per cent. Thus, 83.6 percent of the area under agriculture in the state is directly dependent on monsoon. Nearly one-third area of the state falls under rain-shadow region where the rain is not only scanty, but also, erratic. The soil, topography, rainfall and climate in Maharashtra are not much favourable to agriculture. As a result, the crop per hectare yield in Maharashtra is generally lower than the national level.[4]

In 1960s, Maharashtra was not self-sufficient in food grains production. Various yield increasing methods have been tried in Maharashtra on a massive scale during the last three decades. As a result of this, the state experienced a growth in agricultural production with the food grains production increasing from 5.41 million tonnes in 1970-71 to 12.2 million tonnes in 2010-11. The area under high yielding variety seeds (HYVS) in the state increased more than twenty times while irrigated area increased from 1220 lakh ha. (1960-61) to 4,050 lakh ha. (2010-11).

The fertilizer consumption increased from 42.6 lakh M.T (2005-06) to70.3 lakh M.T (2010-11) in which per hectare consumption of fertilizer increased about two times, but is still very low as compared to Punjab. In respect of irrigation, the state (16.4 percent) is far below as compared to Punjab (95.2 percent), Haryana (75 percent), Tamil Nadu (48 percent) and the national average (39 percent). A large part of central Maharashtra and Marathwada is in rain shadow. Thus, agriculture in the state is characterized by the low rainfall and low irrigation. Maharashtra lags behind in the productivity of all the crops as compared to the national averages, which itself is behind the average of some of the other progressive countries of Europe and Asia.[5] Maharashtra state ranks first in area and production of jower, ture and cotton but lags seventh, eighth and ninth position respectively as far as productivity of these crops is concerned. The state has also gone through green revolution, but its impact is very less as compared to these states. Hence, the study requires careful analysis of contract farming in Maharashtra.[6]

4.3 Profile of Bejo Sheetal Seeds Pvt. Ltd.

Bejo Sheetal Seeds Pvt. Ltd. started operation at Jalna District of Maharashtra in India. This was the time when limited vegetable seeds knowledge was available in India. Founder of the company Suresh O. Agrawal with his great vision to fulfil the need of quality vegetable seeds started vegetable seeds research in short day onion, chili pepper, tomato, brinjal, okra, cucumber, melons, gourds and other vegetable crops with strong understanding of local climatic conditions and diverse choice with various regions of India. Suresh Agrawal had a vision for future needs of quality vegetable seeds for the farmers of India. He has identified the scope of serving Indian farmers for the betterment of the farmers' life which directly and indirectly contributes the development of the country. It was the time when there was very less known about vegetable crop breeding. Open pollinated seeds were routinely being used for vegetable cultivation and most of temperate vegetable seeds were being imported from European countries and marketed in India. Suresh Agrawal was also involved in this business of importing open pollinated seeds and selling to farmers of India. However, he realized the need of good research activities for delivering quality seeds to Indian farmers.

Bejo Zadan B.V. Nederland is very strong in temperate crops research globally, and was interested in research activities of tropical crops. Bejo was planning to do research on tropical vegetable crops for marketing at global level, keeping the need of quality and regional choice of vegetable seeds. From India Suresh Agrawal was looking for research on overall vegetable crops and from Europe Bejo Zadan was interested in tropical crop research. Hence, they joined the hands together for working on mutual interest. The joint venture vegetable seeds company Bejo Sheetal Seeds Pvt. Ltd. started research initially on short day onion. Subsequently, there entered the other tropical vegetable crops like chili pepper, tomato, brinjal, okra, cucumber, melons, gourds, etc.

Profile of Bejo Sheetal is dedicated for developing and supplying quality vegetable seeds for the farmers of India and SAARC countries using its excellence in vegetable breeding. Having strong research activities in various regions of India with the inputs of expert team developed more than 700 research hybrids of vegetables. Bejo Sheetal is the first company to develop and commercialize short day F1 Hybrid onion in India and already achieved number one position in chili pepper seed sales having good market share in India. True potato seeds and potato breeding is another innovative activity where Bejo Sheetal achieved mastery in production of true potato seeds, production facilities have spread over 6 ha area at Jalna, Maharashtra and expert team is engaged in high quality ture, potato seed production. Therefore, business extended throughout Asian and African countries.

Bejo Sheetal is keen and aware about social responsibility in order to develop expert human resource in the field of seed supply value chain and agriculture biotechnology research established "Bejo Sheetal Bioscience Foundation." Its main mandate is to conduct international training courses for developing experts.[7]

4.4 Performance of Bejo Sheetal Seeds Pvt. Ltd.

Beejo Sheetal Seed Pvt. Ltd. started operation in Jalna district of Maharashtra in India. Bejo Sheetal Seed Pvt Ltd has been involved in contract farming in all vegetable seed production. The table 4.1 shows performance of onion seed contract farming from 2006-07 to 2010-11. Through the contract farming company produces of all types of vegetable seed. Beejo Sheetal Company engaged in onion seed contract farming in Aurangabad, Jalna and Beed district contracted 300 farmers in the year 2006-07 and 350 farmers during 2010-11. They have occupied 450 acre area through onion seed contract farming in the year 2006-07. But in the year 2010-11 onion seed farming area decreased to 350 acre; because in the previous year production has been high and they have large stock. Due to this next year company contracting area was limited. The table 4.1 shows that the onion seed received in the year 2006-07, is 675 Qt and in the 2010-11 680 Qt. Researcher found that company purchased onion seed in the year 2006-07 Rs. 17000/- Qt and it continuously increased to Rs. 28000/-Qt in the year 2010-11, and the per acre yield of

Table 4.1
Performance of Bejo Sheetal Seed Pvt. Ltd.

Sr. No.	Particulars	2006-07	2007-08	2008-09	2009-10	2010-11
1	No. of Farmers	300	350	400	450	350
2	Districts	3	3	3	3	3
3	Taluka	3	3	4	5	5
4	Village	10	12	12	13	13
5	Seed Distribution (Kg/Qu)	3	3	3	3	3
6	Average Seed / Acre (in kg)	3	3	3	3	3
7	Contract Farming in Acre	450	475	500	560	400
8	Received Onion seed qts	675	700	600	700	680
9	Purchase Rate Rs. /Qu.	17000	17500	18000	23000	28000
10	Onion seed yield Qu./Acre	2.5	2.5	3	2.6	3.5

Source : Office record of Beejo Sheetal Seed Pvt. Ltd. Company.

onion seed was 2.5 Qt. /acre in 2006-07 which increased up to 3.5 Qt./ acre in 2010-2011.

4.5 Profile of Maharashtra Hybrid Seeds Company Ltd. (Mahyco)

Mahyco was founded on the foresight of a man who dared to venture beyond visible possibilities and showed immense confidence in his vision. After the independence, when India was still in the process of fortifying her weak economic strength, Badrinarayan Ramulal Barwale sowed the first seed of economic development. Breaking free from the stronghold of Nizam conservatism in the Marathwada region of Maharashtra where his family owned land, he chose to take risk and develop the immense potential that lay latent in hybrid seeds at a time when the seed industry was small. His major breakthrough came from the Pusa Sawani bhendi (lady's finger), hybrid resistant to a widely prevalent virus developed by the Indian Agricultural Research Institute (IARI). Barwale began producing and marketing this variety, which set an example of how technology can help to fulfil the promise of a bigger harvest at a lesser cost.

In 1963, Rockefeller Foundation in collaboration with the Indian Council of Agriculture Research (ICAR) chose him to help create a private sector seed industry in India. Barwale produced the first hybrid corn (maize) in 1963-64 with the seed supplied by the Rockefeller Foundation. After that, there was no turning back. The Maharashtra Hybrid Corporation (Mahyco) was founded in 1964 in Jalna as its headquarters and encouraged cultivators to grow seeds. Just two years later (in 1966), the company's first R&D centre was set up. In 1985 the first cotton hybrid MECH1 was released, in 1989 Mahyco became the first agro-based company to win the National Award for Research and Development from the Government of India. Various recognitions and awards at the National and International level followed. Recently, Mahyco Research Foundation set aside Rs. 3 crore grant to the ICAR over three years to fund the latter's research programme in rice. Today, more than 10,00,000 cultivators grow seeds for Mahyco. There are 15 production centres, 23 sales offices and about 2500 dealers located across India. The company is actively involved in the research, development, production, processing and marketing of 115 products in 30 crop species, including cereals, oilseeds, fibre crops and vegetables. It has to its credit 21 notified research varieties. The company technology is referred to as a global benchmark and is respected worldwide as a pioneer of high quality hybrid / open pollinated seeds and for its strict adherence to quality over the years. Mahyco has entered into collaborations with academia and industry to keep pace with new developments across the agri-business spectrum. Its association with Monsanto for using the Bt. technology for cotton in 1998 is one such excellent example. But all this is besides the point. The centre of this growing company still remains the same: the ability to dream high and the courage to follow those dreams. It is not surprising through a visionary like Badrinath Ramulal Barwale to emulate it cannot be anything else.

Mahyco has crossed several milestones and is well on its path to redefine the seed industry in India. The most significant milestone would be the one which eventually ignited the forming of a full-fledged seed company. Rockefeller Foundation, in their endeavour to help create a private seed-sector in India approached a barely 30 year old Barwale who then successfully produced his first hybrid maize seed in Rabi, in 1962. 11th November 1964, the day Mahyco formally came into existence, after the phenomenal success of the Pusa Sawani okra. The year 1988 opened floodgates for research by the private sector in agriculture, which laid the foundation for Mahyco's state-of-the art R&D centre. While Mahyco has also been applauded with several national and International recognitions, these milestones proved to be turning points for Mahyco.[8]

Mahyco's affiliated companies are given below:

1. Sungro Seeds Limited.
2. John Fowler Ocular Lenses.
3. Fowler Westrup (India) Pvt. Ltd.
4. Westrup A/s Denmark, Dickinson Fowler Pvt. Ltd.

4.6 Performance of Mahyco Seeds Company

Table 4.2 shows the performance of five years of contract farming in cotton seed production. According to Mahyco's their motto is that provide pure and genetically certified seed to the farmers. Since its inception Mahyco has been providing

Table 4.2

Performance of Maharashtra Hybrid Seeds Company Ltd.

Sr. No.	Particulars	2006-07	2007-08	2008-09	2009-10	2010-11
1	No. of Farmers	4000	3700	1700	1600	3200
2	Districts	2	2	2	2	4
3	Taluka	3	3	3	3	6
4	Village	147	170	245	250	236
5	Seed Distribution (Kg/Qu)	female 120 gm male-40 gm	female 120 gm male-40 gm	female 120 gm male-40 gm	female 120 gm male-40 gm	female 120 gm male-40 gm
6	Average Seed / Acre	female 480 gm male 160 gm	female 480 gm male 160 gm	female 480 gm male 160 gm	female 480 gm male 160 gm	female 480 gm male 160 gm
7	Contract Farming in Acre	4000	3700	1700	1600	3200
8	Received cotton qts	3080	3000	1500	1200	2400
9	Purchase Rate Rs. /Qt	25000	27000	32000	41000	55000
10	Cotton yield Kg/Acre	165	170	225	145	100

Source : Office record of Mahyco Seed Pvt. Ltd., Company.

their services to the nation. Mahyco has been involved in contract farming. Through the contract farming Mahyco company increased seed production and provided farmers sustainable income. Mahyco isengaged in cotton contract farming in 4 districts of Maharashtra particularly Marathwada region.

It is observed that 4000 farmers contracted with Mahyco for cotton seed only in the year 2006-07 and 3,200 farmer, contracted with company in 2010-11. Mahyco occupied 4000 acre area through cotton seed contract farming in the year 2006-2007. But in the year 2010-2011 cotton seed contract farming area decreased to 3200 acre; reason behind it may be climate, water and labour, etc. It is found that in the year 2006-2007 cotton seed yield was 165 kg per acre and it was decreased upto 100 kg per acre in 2010-11. Company helps cotton farmer to get the sustainable income through the contract farming. Company purchased cotton seeds at Rs. 25,000 per quintal in the year 2006-2007 the purchasing amount has been increased upto Rs. 55,000 per Qt. in the year 2010-2011.

4.7 Profile of PepsiCo India Holdings Pvt. Ltd.

The company is a subsidiary of the US multinational PepsiCo which has a large network of operations in India. PepsiCo supplies its products to 3.5 lakh outlets in the country, and adds 80-100 thousand outlets every year with 5000-7000 being new and are for the company's products line alone. It owns 19 factories, and 22 franchise factories are owned by bottlers of its soft drinks in India. Its annual exports from India are of the order of Rs. 200 crore. Besides soft drinks, which is their main business in India? Pepsi also operates in rice, potato chips, traditional Indian snacks (bhujia), chilli paste, and other products like paper boxes, molded grade resin, PET bottles, and plastics crates. It also procures items like trucks, paper cups and cardboard boxes from India for its Pepsi system worldwide.[9]

The company started its operations in India in 1989 by setting up plants for processing of tomatoes, potato respectively in Houshiarpur district and Sangrur district of Punjab.

PepsiCo has food processing operations in 150 countries and practices global sourcing of various raw materials for export production across the world. It has an annual turnover (revenue) of $ 22.3 billion and profits of the order of $ 2.58 billion in 1998 and employs 1.51 lakh people. If franchisees are included, the turnover is $ 35 billion and employment reaches 4.7 lakh people. It controls one-fourth of the US and 15 per cent of the world soft drink market. It runs three fast food chains – Kentucky Fried Chicken (KFC). Pizza Hut and Taco Bells-is with operations across the world. The KFC alone has 9400 outlets is 78 countries. Pizza Hut has 1000 outlets in 50 countries. It has its KFC and Pizza Hut outlets in major metro cities of India as well.[10]

PepsiCo India Holdings Pvt. Ltd. operates through its subsidiaries including Pepsi Foods Ltd, Frito - Lay India, and Tropicana Beverages Company. The firm, through its subsidiaries manufactures, bottles, and exports fruit juices and carbonated beverages and packaged snacks such as Lays, Ruffles, Fritos, and Cheetos. The company is based in Gurgaon, India. PepsiCo India Holdings Pvt. Ltd. operates as a subsidiary of 'PepsiCo India' has grown phenomenally in the recent years and now is the largest salty snacks company in the world, accounting for two-third of its revenue, and 50 percent of the US market for salty snacks. It has the experience of contract farming and potato processing countries of Mexico, Egypt and China. In fact, its successful entry into Mexico is a classic example of a company beating the stringent local laws wherein it used the routes of nonprofit organization (NPO) to import and of partnership with farmers to produce seed of potato and improve the raw material for its chips plants in Mexico.[11]

The company has its potato chips units at Ranjangaon in Ahamad Nagar district of Maharashtra state. The chips are produced by a subsidiary of Pepsi Foods Limited, Colled Frito–Lay India. The company has four types of chips: salted classic, pudina, tomato, and massala all sold under the brand name of Lays. In the initial years, most of the produce was procured from the states of Madhya Pradesh, Himachal Pradesh, Uttar Pradesh and even as far as Karnataka, and Maharashtra, as the potatoes produced in Punjab were not fit for processing due to high reducible sugar and moisture content and low dry matter content which led to browning of chips.[12]

4.8 Performance of PepsiCo India Holding Private Ltd.

The table 4.3 shows the performance of PepsiCo India Holding Pvt. Ltd. The company is engaged in potato contract farming in Maharashtra in 4 districts. The table shows that 1000 farmers contracted with company in the year 2006-07 and the number of contracted farmers increased and stood at 2450 farmers in 2010-11. PepsiCo India Holding occupied 3100 acre land through potato contract farming in the year 2006-07 and in the year 2010-11 contract farming area increased to 5600 acre. It is also observed that yield of potato increased from 4 tunne to 7.5 tunne during 2006-07 to 2010-11.

The working area of PepsiCo company was 2 districts, 4 taluka and 30 villages in 2006-07, which increased 4 district, 6 taluka and 50 villages in 2010-11. PepsiCo Company purchased the potato fixed rate of Rs.7 per kg. in 2006-07 and Rs. 10 per kg. in 2010-11. PepsiCo company purchased 15000 Qts. ootato in 2006-07 and its purchase increased up to 43000 Qts. in 2010-11.

4.9 Profile of Jain Irrigation System Pvt. Ltd.

Jain Irrigation System Ltd's journey began in 1887 when his forefathers left the deserts of Rajasthan, their home state, in search of water and food and reached Waked, at the foothills of the famous Ajanta Caves. They started farming as a means of livelihood. In 1963 selling kerosene in pushcart, the young

Table 4.3
Performance of PepsiCo India Holding Pvt. Ltd

Sr. No.	Particulars	2006-07	2007-08	2008-09	2009-10	2010-11
1	No. of Farmers	1000	1200	1400	1500	1450
2	Districts	2	2	3	4	4
3	Taluka	4	4	5	6	6
4	Village	30	35	40	45	50
5	Seed Distribution (Kg/Qt)	800	800	800	800	800
6	Average Seed / Acre Qts.	3.1	3.12	3.07	3.33	3.86
7	Contract Farming in Acre	3100	3750	4300	5000	5600
8	Received Potato Qts.	15000	20000	27000	25000	43000
9	Purchase Rate Rs. /Kg.	7	8.3	9.30	9.30	10
10	Potato yield Tunne /Acre	4	7	7	7	7.5

Source : Office record of PepsiCo India Holding Pvt. Ltd.

law graduate, Bhavarlal Jain, founded the family business in trading. The family partnership with a meager Rs.7,000, accumulated savings of three generations, as capital. Soon, agencies for two wheelers, auto vehicles and automobile accessories were established in quick succession.

Inspired by a quote, "Agriculture: a profession with future" young Jain added dealership of tractors, sprinkler systems, PVC pipes and other farm equipment. In order to broaden the base of agri-business, agencies for farm inputs such as fertilizers, seeds, pesticides were also added. Sales grew from Rs. 1 million in 1963 to Rs. 110 millions in 1978, a phenomenal increase of 110 times. These formative years helped them build a unique and lasting enterprise. This was achieved through consistent high standards of performance and personal behaviour on the one hand and a strong sense of commitment for meeting targeted volumes and for payment of debts in time, on the other. Dealing with national and international principles was a contributing factor towards building these attitudes. In time, they came to be recognized as a reputable, trustworthy and prestigious house. This background augured well for an entry into industrial ventures. JISL took over a 14 year-old sick banana powder plant in April 1978 at a high auction price of Rs. 3 million while they only had Rs. 0.2 million as inevitable surpluses. The plant was quickly modified for the production of Papain from Papaya latex. In December 1978, the founder traveled to New York in search of customers for Jain Papain. The competition for purchase of raw materials at home and for sale of Papain abroad was stiff and stifling. However, Jain developed purified Papain through ceaseless in-house R&D and emerged as the `Number One' supplier of the highest purity refined Papain. Thus Papain put Jains on the international map.

In 1980, manufacturing of PVC pipes commenced with a small annual capacity of 300 MTs which was increased to over 35,600 MTs per annum by 1997, making Jains the largest single producer of PVC pipes in the country. A close-knit dealer distribution network in the rural areas coupled with continuous automation and upgradation of product facilities and in-house R&D for maximum capacity utilization has kept Jain at the forefront. This further helped Jain to expand the range to casing & screen piping systems thereby continuing to contribute to the growing export volumes. Beginning in 1989, Jain toiled and struggled to pioneer water-management through micro irrigation in India. Jain have successfully introduced some hi-tech concepts to Indian agriculture such as 'Integrated System Approach', 'One-Stop-Shop for Farmer,'

'Infrastructure Status to Micro Irrigation and Farm as Industry.' Jain has come a long way.

In 1994 Jain set-up world class food processing facilities for dehydration of onion, vegetable and production of fruit purees concentrates and pulp. These plants are ISO 9001 and HACCP certified and meet international FDA statute requirements. Combining the modern technologies of the west with the vast, mostly untapped agriculture resources of India, using the local human resources and inculcating the culture of excellence in quality and total customer service they have set their goal to become a major and reliable global supplier of food ingredients of finest quality. Today with over 7,000 committed employees strength worldwide, Jain have established his leadership in diverse products like micro and sprinkler irrigation, agricultural inputs, agro-processed products, plastic pipes and sheets.

Jains at Jalgaon manufacture dehydrated onion and vegetable products and Aseptic fruit purees, concentrates clarified juices, IQF, and frozen products of finest quality. Jain markets these under their brand name Farm Fresh. For centuries, India has been the premier supplier of spices and tea to the world. It is also the second largest producer of fruits and vegetables in the world. Fertile soils, a dry climate, clean water and abundant sunlight help the hard working farmers to produce a bountiful harvest. Though vast, these resources have so far remained mostly untapped. Jain's have the most controlled modern, world class fruit processing facility setup at Jalgaon. Selected varieties of banana, guava, mango, pomegranate, anoles, papaya and tomato puree are grown in the farms and processed in the plant.

Jain have dedicated themselves to the development of agriculture and agroprocessing and have evolved an integrated approach. Jains help the Indian farmers to produce more and better quality products by providing genetically superior planting materials, efficient water and fertilizer management system and agronomical guidance. This is the largest supplier of these products and services to the Indian growers. Jains buy the fruits and vegetables from the growers and process them. Jains produce the finest quality dehydrated onion and vegetable products aseptic fruit purees, pulps. They concentrate and export these to customers throughout the world. Jains commitment to quality and R&D product innovation is deep rooted. GMP, QA, SPC, strict sanitation, hygiene, HACCP food safety and ISO 9001:2000, quality management systems are applied throughout the manufacturing. Jain have evolved and implemented very elaborate quality management system starting from raw material to delivering finished products to their quality conscious customers throughout the world. Dry climate, fertile soils and sanitary plant design enables production of FARMFRESH products of finest quality and consistency. The Food Divisions are accredited by Food Cert, Netherlands; for ISO 22000:2005 FSMS, the latest International Food Safety Standard. In addition, the 'Onion and Vegetable Dehydration' Division is accredited by Food Cert, Netherlands; to 'BRC' [British Retail Consortium] Global Standard – Food. Jain have established modern laboratories (including microbiology, pesticide residues and heavy metal analysis and sensory evaluation) for analysis and testing, backed by the team of highly qualified and experienced scientists and staff. Jains have also established R&D centres, both at the laboratory and in the field.

Jains have established sales and service network to service the customers throughout the world. FarmFresh products are readily available from their regional sales centers and warehouses, strategically located in different parts of the world. Jain's dedicated sales teams are available to discuss individual customer requirements and will make every possible effort to provide the finest quality FarmFresh food products and services. Jains are committed to their total customer's satisfaction. Combining the modern technologies of the west with the east, largely untapped agriculture resources of India, using the local human resources and including in them the culture of excellence in quality and total customer service, Jain have set their goal to become a major and reliable global supplier of food ingredients of finest quality.[13]

Jain Irrigation Systems Ltd. (JISL) has state-of-the-art world-class and scale, integrated dehydration facilities. Jain Irrigation has commissioned its first onion dehydration plant 10 years back, a 100 percent export oriented unit. JISL is the largest processor of onion in the country (10,000 tonnes of DHO). The company entered into contract farming way back in 2001-02 with the principal objective of ensuring assured and consistent supply of onion bulbs, to enhance productivity and uniformity with better agronomical practices and also to improve the quality of onion bulbs. During milling, the products undergo metal-detection, colour sorting at the last stage and are then packed in bag-in-box. These are then stored under lower temperature and humidity and are supplied to the customers throughout the world.

In contract farming of onion undertaken by JISL, the seeds of high-yielding onion varieties are distributed to the registered growers and the seeds are sown and transplanted in the farmers' field by the farmers using their own resources. Company's R&D, extension wing and the contract farming team help the cultivators from time to time through frequent field-visits, guidance and input supplies. Contract farming scheme not only offers guaranteed buy-back price to farmers but also provides a complete package of practices for improved productivity and quality. The package of practices that the company offers to farmers for obtaining quality bulbs with high yield, contains information on drip and sprinkler irrigation, fertigation and fertilizer doses, weeds management, pest and disease control, harvesting practices etc are noteworthy.[14]

4.10 Performance of Jain Irrigation System Pvt. Ltd.

Table 4.4 shows the Jain Irrigation System Pvt. Ltd. (JISL) performance of five years during 2006-07 to 2010-11 of contract farming in white onion production. Jain Irrigation System Pvt. Ltd. engaged in white onion production in Maharashtra through 8 districts in 2006-2007 and same district in 2010-2011. It is observed that, 1780 farmers contracted with company in 2006-07, it increased and stood at 2385 farmers in 2010-11. The working area of Jain Irrigation Company was 8 district, 25 taluka and 198 villages. In 2006-07, it was 8 district, 25 taluka and 400 village in 2010-11 in 2006-07 company

Table 4.4
Performance of Jain Irrigation System Pvt. Ltd.

Sr. No.	Particulars	2006-07	2007-08	2008-09	2009-10	2010-11
1	No. of Farmers	1780	1616	2051	2260	2385
2	Districts	8	8	8	8	8
3	Taluka	25	25	28	28	25
4	Village	198	287	340	404	400
5	Seed Distribution (Kg/Qu)	11839	14158	15014	16342	18320
6	Average Seed / Acre in kg.	4.5	4.1	4.2	6.3	6.3
7	Contract Farming in Acre	2639	3470	3565	2613	2897
8	Purchase of White Onion mts.	23315	34324	26995	20600	24946
9	Purchase Rate Rs. /Kg.	6.71	3.5	5.25	5	5
10	Onion yield Tunne /Acre	8.8	9.9	7.6	7.9	8.6

Source : Office Record of the Jain Irrigation System Ltd.

distributed 11839 kg seeds, while in 2010-11 distributed 18320 kg seeds to farmers. The average seeds per acre was 4.5 kg which goes upto 6.3 kg. per acre in 2010-11. Jain Company occupied 2639 acre area through onion contract farming in the year 2006-2007, after in the five year contract fluctuation but in 2010-2011 onion contract farming area was increased to 2897 acre. The company purchased 23315 Mts. white onion in 2006-07 and the purchasing of white onion was 24946 Mts. in 2010-11. The researcher has found in the year 2006-07 company purchased white onion at Rs. 6.71 per kg in 2006-07, but the purchase rate was Rs. 5 per kg. in 2010-11. It is observed that the per acre yield of onion decreased from 8.8 tunne per acre of 2006-07 to 8.6 tunnes per acre in 2010-11.

4.11 Educational Level of Sample Farmers

The following discussion is focused on identifying and comparing factors that can be used to explain differences in participation in contract farming. Results for participants of contract farming are compared with non-participant farmers. Table 4.5 shows educational level of sample farmers engaged in contract farming. It is found that maximum 45 percent farmer's educational level is secondary followed by 32 percent contract farmers education level is higher secondary and only

Table 4.5

Educational Situation of Sample Farmer Households

Sr. No.	Particular	Contract Farming	Non -contract Farming
1	Illiterate	00	08
2	Primary	11	11
3	Secondary	45	39
4	Higher secondary	32	37
5	Graduate	10	05
6	P.G.	02	00
	Total	**100**	**100**

Source : Field Survey.

12 percent contract farmers are graduate and PG level educated No farmer is illiterate among selected contract farmers. Among non-contract farmers 8 percent are illiterate, having PG zero percent to and 5 percent farmers have obtained graduation level education.

It means contract farmer are more educated than non-contract farmers. The respondent's education helps them present their right against the contracting companies.

4.12 Distribution of Sample farmers by Social Group

Table 4.6 shows the distribution of sample farmers by social groups. It is found that 4 percent contract farmers belonged to SC category and 1 percent belonged to non-contract segment and 15 percent farmers belonged to OBC category. On the other hand 19 percent farmers belonged from non-contract segments. 8 percent contract farmers belonged to N.T. category while 4 percent belonged to non-contract segment. It is observed that 73 percent contract farmers belonged to General category, whereas, 76 percent farmers belonged from non contract segment. It means there is awareness developed about contract farming in general categories. In comparison with other categories their low percentage showns that there is low awareness about contract farming.

Table 4.6

Distribution of Sample Farmers by Social Group

Sr. No.	Particular	Contract Farming	Non-contract Farming
1	SC	04	01
2	ST	-	-
3	OBC	15	19
4	NT	08	04
5	General	73	76
	Total	**100**	**100**

Source : Field Survey.

4.13 Family Size and Family Workers

The family size, family workers are shown in table 4.7. Family size of farmers distribution of cropwise and contract farmer and non-contract farmerwise is also given in the table 4.7. It is found that average family size among contract farmer was 4.91 and 5.77 among non-contract farmers. According to family workers 3.06 workers per family in contract farming and 2.61 workers per family in non-contract farming. It is found that as high as 5.5 family size among the onion seed contract farmers and it was 3.20 among onion seed non-contract farmers. It was lowest 4.4 in onion seed contract farmers and only 2 among potato non-contract farmers during study period. Above discussion concludes the average of family was big of non-contract farmer and family work was large in contract farming means that contract farming used high labour.

Table 4.7
Distribution of Sample Farmer's Households Size of Family and Family Workers.

Sr. No.	Particular	Total no. of H.H. Average size of Family				Family work per H.H.	
		C.F.	Non-C.F.	C.F.	Non-C.F.	C.F.	Non-C.F.
1	Onion Seed	25	25	4.4	5.8	3.32	3.20
2	Cotton Seed	25	25	5.24	5.56	3.44	2.52
3	Potato	25	25	4.5	5.25	2.5	2
4	Onion	25	25	5.5	6.5	3	2.75
	Total	**100**	**100**	**4.91**	**5.77**	**3.06**	**2.61**

Source : Field survey

4.14 Distribution of Farmers Involved in the Other Business

In the modern farming there is big importance of subsidiary business as many farmers were found involved in subsidiary business. Table 4.8 shows subsidiary business of farmers may be stationery, livestock, dairy business and a host of other. In today's concern farmer needs subsidiary business to help increasing income. Among 100 selected farmers 16 percent contract farmers involved dairy business which provides additional income. On the other side out of 100 non-contracted farmers only 4 percent farmers have been engaged in dairy business. And only 1 percent contract farmer engaged in livestock business. Not even a single percent found in stationery business in contract farming and non-contract farming segment. The 10 percent farmers are engaged in other business in contract segment, and on other side only, 4 percent engaged in other business in non-contract segment. But there is a huge percentage i.e. 73 percent farmers do not have any other business in contract segment and also 92 percent farmer does not have in subsidiary business in non contract. It means contract farmers are more aware about subsidiary business than non-contract farmers. But it shows that there is a lack of awareness among both segments.

Table 4.8

Farmers involved in other business

Sr.No.	Particulars	C.F.	Non-CF
1	Dairy business	16	04
2	Livestock business	01	-
3	Stationery	-	-
4	Other	10	04
5	No	73	92
	Total	**100**	**100**

Source : Field Survey

4.15 Agewise Classification of Sample Farmers

Agewise distribution has been given in table 4.9. In the age group 25 to 40 there were 54 percent contract farmers and 49 percent non-contract farmers. In the age group 40 to 50 there were 32 percent contract farmers and in case of non-contract farmers it is 34 percent. While in the age 50 to 60 or above only 9 percent. are contract farmer and 15 percent in non-contract farmers. It means that young farmers have been found moving towards contract farming which is helping them in stable income source in comparison with non-contract farming.

Table 4.9

Age of Sample Farmers

Sr.No.	Age Group	C.F.	Non-CF
1	18-25	05	02
2	25-40	54	49
3	40-50	32	34
4	50-60	07	08
5	Above 60	02	07
	Total	**100**	**100**

Source : Field Survey

4.16 Pattern of Land Holdings of the Sample Farmers

The pattern of land holdings of sample farmers is indicated in table 4.10. The average size of the land holdings of contract growers were 3.13 hectare and non-contract growers was 3.1 hectare of which contract farming growers average rainfed area was 1.40 hectare (44.72 percent) and irrigated area was 1.73 hectare (55.27 percent). On the contrary, their counterparts among non-contract growers rainfed area was 1.8 hectare (58.06 percent) and irrigated area was 1.3 hectare (41.93 percent). The average area under contract farming crops of onion seed 0.76 hectare (22.28 percent), cotton seed 0.58 hectare (18.53 percent), Potato 2 hectare (63.89 percent) and white onion 0.90 hectare (28.75 percent). On the contrary, their counterparts non contract crops area of onion seed 0.60 hectare (19.35 percent), Cotton Seed 0.50 hectare (16.12 percent), Potato 1.75 hectare (56.45 percent) and onion 0.80 hectare (35.80 percent). It means in contract farming contracting company gives preference to developed and

Table 4.10

Pattern of Land Holding of the Sample Farmers

Sr. No.	Particulars	Unit	Contract Farming	Non-contract Farming
1	Average size of holding	ha	3.13	3.1
(a)	Rainfed area	ha	1.40 (44.72)	1.8 (58.06)
(b)	Irrigated area	ha	1.73 (55.27)	1.3 (41.93
2	Area under crop Production	ha		
(a)	Onion Seed		0.76 (24.28)	0.60 (19.35)
(b)	Cotton Seed		0.58 (18.53)	0.50 (16.12)
(c)	Potato		2 (63.89)	1.75 (56.45)
(d)	Onion		0.90 (28.75)	0.80 (25.80)
3	Experience with contract	Year	4.82	-

Note : Bracketed figures show percentage to total average size of holding.

Source : Field Survey

irrigated land. Therefore, in contract farming the percentage of irrigation land is higher than non contract farming.

4.17 Modern Irrigation Facilities Used by Sample Farmers

Table 4.11 shows modern irrigation system adopted by sample farmers. Modern irrigation facilities are quite helpful to the farming. It is helpful in increasing the production and irrigation area. When we compared contract farming and non contract farming segment, we found some truth. In the contract farming 38 percent farmers used drip irrigation at the same time 25 percent non-contract farmer used dripped irrigation. The sprinkler irrigation system is used by 17 percent contract farmer household and by 6 percent non-contract farmer household. According to both irrigation system 23

Table 4.11
Farmer using Modern Irrigation Facility

Sr.No.	Particulars	C.F.	Non-CF
1	Drip	38	25
2	Sprinkler	17	06
3	Both	23	02
4	None	22	67
	Total	**100**	**100**

Source : Field Survey.

percent contract farmers are using both system, while only 2 percent non-contract farmer used both irrigation systems. Further it is found that 22 percent contract farmers have not using any irrigation system to the irrigation. On the other hand 67 percent non-contract farmers do not use any irrigation facility. It means contract farmers are more aware about irrigation facility use than non-contract farmers.

4.18 Cost Structure in Onion Seed Production

The cost of cultivating onion seed crop per acre under contract and non-contract farming are presented in Table 4.12. Among the input cost expenditure fertilizers' Rs. 3672 per acre was the major cost i.e. 24.67 percent of total cost of cultivation followed by pesticides 21.80 percent, seeds 9.81 percent and cost on management 6.02 percent. The labour costs included expenditure on ploughing 4.73 percent, sowing 7.83 percent and marketing cost 15.14 percent. On the contrary, their counterpart non-contract farmers spend the input cost expenditure on marketing cost Rs. 5116 per acre was the major cost i.e. 36.12 percent of the total cost of cultivation followed by fertilizer 16.38 percent, pesticides 13.92 percent, management 4.01 percent, the labour cost expenditure being ploughing 4.63 percent, sowing 5.76 percent, weeding 5.19 percent, pesticides 3.16 percent.

The total cost of onion seed production worked out to be in contract farming Rs. 14880 per acre, out of which input

Table 4.12
Cost of Cultivation of Contracting Crop and Non-contracting Crop (onion seed)

Sr. No.	Particulars	Contract Farming	Non- contract Farming
A	**Input Cost**		
1	Seeds	1460 (9.81)	1528 (10.79)
2	Fertilizers	3672 (24.67)	2320 (16.38)
3	Pesticides	3244 (21.80)	1972 (13.92)
4	Management	896 (6.02)	568 (4.09)
	Sub Total	7272 (63.31)	6388 (45.11)
B	**Labour Cost**		
i	Ploughing	704 (4.73)	656 (4.63)
ii	Sowing	1166 (7.83)	816 (5.76)
iii	Weeding	872 (5.86)	736 (5.19)
iv	Pesticides	532 (3.57)	448 (3.16)
	Sub Total	3354 (22.54)	2626 (18.75)
C	**Marketing cost**	2254 (15.14)	5116 (36.12)
	A+B+C Total	**14880 (37.05)**	**14160 (43.79)**
	Gross Return	**40160**	**32480**
	Net Returns	**25280 (62.94)**	**18320 (56.40)**

Note : Bracketed figures show percentage to total.
Source : Field Survey.

cost Rs. 9272/ acre which accounted 63.31 percent and labour cost Rs. 3354/ acre which accounted 22.54 percent, marketing cost Rs. 2254/ acre which accounted 15.14 percent. On the contrary, in their counterpart non-contract farming the total cost of onion seed production worked out to be Rs. 14160 / acre out of which input cost Rs. 6388/ acre which accounted 45.11 percent, labour cost Rs. 2656/ acre which accounted 18.75 percent and marketing cost Rs. 5116/ acre which accounted 36.12 percent. It is found that marketing cost in non-contract farming is 2.27 times more than contract farming.

Per acre gross returns under contract farming were Rs. 40160 and Rs. 32840 in non-contract farmings. The net returns were Rs.25280 in case of contract farmers compared to that of

Rs.18320 of non-contract farming. Though the per rupee returns over total cultivation costs were much higher in the case of contract farmers, the returns over total cost were slightly lesser than those of the non-contract farmers. It may be attributed to exorbitant marketing charges.

4.19 Cost Structure in Cotton Seed Production

The cost of cultivating cotton seed crop per acre under contract and non-contract farming is presented in table No. 4.13. Among the input cost, expenditure on pesticides Rs. 4780/- acre was the major cost acconting 24.43 percent of total cost of cultivation followed by fertilizer 21.88 percent, and cost on management 4.94 percent and seeds cost 4.04 percent. In case of labour costs the highest expenditure was on weeding which was 10.49 percent, sowing 4.94 percent, ploughing 4.45 percent and pesticides 2.61 percent in contract farming. The marketing cost was Rs. 4336/ acre accounting 22.16 percent. It can be observed that in contract farming the highest production cost of cotton seeds was input cost 55.31 percent, then lebour cost 22.51 percent and marketing cost 22.16 percent. On the contrary, their counterpart non-contract farmers' input cost expenditure on fertilizer was Rs.2740/ acre which is accounting 16.19 percent of the total cost of cotton seed cultivation followed by pesticides 15.41 percent, seed 6.19 percent and management 5.43 percent. The highest labour cost expenditure was on weeding 5.34 percent, sowing 5.08 percent, ploughing 4.58 percent, pesticides 2.90 percent and the cost of marketing is also very high in the non-contract farming i.e. Rs. 6580/- acre which is amount to 38.88 percent of the total cost of cultivation.

Per acre gross returns under cotton seed contract farming was 40.26 percent with compare to non-contract farming. The net return was 66.34 percent in case of contract farming with compare to the net return of 51.26 percent of non-contract farming. Though the per rupee return over total cultivation cost was much higher in the case of contract farmers, the

Table 4.13
Cost of Cultivation of Contracting Crop and Non-Contracting Crop (Cotton seed)

Sr. No.	Particulars	Contract Farming	Non- contract Farming
A	Input Cost		
1	Seeds	792 (4.04)	1048 (6.19)
2	Fertilizers	4280 (21.88)	2740 (16.19)
3	Pesticides	4780 (24.43)	2608 (15.41)
4	Management	968 (4.94)	920 (5.43)
	Sub Total	10820 (55.31)	7308 (43.19)
B	Labour Cost		
I	Ploughing	872 (4.45)	776 (4.58)
II	Sowing	968 (4.94)	860 (5.08)
III	Weeding	2052 (10.49)	904 (5.34)
IV	Pesticides	512 (2.61)	492 (2.90)
	Sub Total	4404 (22.51)	3032 (17.91)
C	Marketing cost	4336 (22.16)	6580 (38.88)
	A+B+C Total	19560 (33.65)	16920 (48.73)
	Gross Returns	58120	34720
	Net Return	38560 (66.34)	17800 (51.26)

Note : Bracketed figures show percentage to total.
Source : Field Survey.

returns over total cost were slightly lesser than those of non-contract farmers which may be attributed to exorbitant marketing charges.

4.20 Cost Structure in Potato Production

The costs of cultivating potato crop per acre under contract and non-contract farming is presented in table 4.14. Among the input cost, the expenditure on seeds was Rs. 19432/ acre which was the major cost accounting 56.95 per cent of total cost of cultivation followed by fertilizer 8.79 per cent, pesticides 8.44 per cent and management 2.67 per cent. In case of labour costs the highest expenditure was on ploughing which was 6.84 per cent, followed by weeding 4.45 per cent, sowing 4.06 per cent and pesticides 1.47 per cent in contract farming. The marketing cost was Rs. 2148 / acre accounting 6.29 per cent. It can be observed that in contract farming the highest production cost of potato was input cost 76.85 percent than labour cost 16.84 percent and marketing cost 6.29 percent. On the contrary their counterpart non-contract farmers, input cost expenditure on seeds was Rs. 18640 / acre which is accounting 58.79 percent of the total cost of potato cultivation followed by fertilizer 8.98 percent, pesticides 6.52 percent and management cost was 0.82 percent. The higher labour

Table 4.14
Cost of Cultivation of Potato Crop in Contract and Non-contract Farming

Sr. No.	Particulars	Contract Farming	Non- contract Farming
A	**Input Cost**		
1	Seeds	19432 (56.95)	18640 (58.79)
2	Fertilizers	3000 (8.79)	2448 (8.98)
3	Pesticides	2880 (8.44)	2068 (6.52)
4	Management	912 (2.67)	260 (0.82)
	Sub Total	26224 (76.85)	23816 (75.11)
B	**Labour Cost**		
i	Ploughing	2336 (6.84)	2088 (6.58)
ii	Sowing	1388 (4.06)	1020 (3.21)
iii	Weeding	1520 (4.45)	988 (3.11)
iv	Pesticides	504 (1.47)	292 (0.92)
	Sub Total	5748 (16.84)	4388 (13.84)
C	**Marketing cost**	2148 (6.29)	3302 (10.41)
	A+B+C Total	**34120 (62.90)**	**31704 (72.25)**
	Gross Return	**54240**	**43880**
	Net Return	**20120 (37.09)**	**12176 (27.74)**

Note : Bracketed figures show percentage to total.
Source : Field Survey.

expenditure was on ploughing 6.58 percent followed by sowing 3.21 percent, weeding 3.11 percent and pesticides 0.92 percent. The marketing cost is also very high in the non-contract farming Rs. 3302 / acre which is accounting 10.41 percent of the total cost of cultivation.

Per acre gross returns under potato contract farming was 19.10 percent with compared to non-contract farming. The net return was 37.09 percent in case of contract farming with compared to net return of 27.74 percent of non-contract farming though in the contract farming and non-contract farming seed cost is very high.

4.21 Cost Structure in White Onion Production

The cost of cultivation of white onion crops per acre under contract and non-contract farming are presented in table 4.15. Out of total cultivation cost the cost on fertilizer was Rs. 4868/ acre was the major cost accounting 25.81 percent of total cost of cultivation followed by pesticides 18.78 percent, seeds 10.41 percent and cost on management 3.01 percent. In case of labour costs the highest expenditure on sowing accounted 12.69 percent followed by weeding 9.83 percent, ploughing 6.13 percent and pesticides 1.84 percent in contract farming. The marketing cost was Rs. 2138 / acre accounting 11.34 percent. It can be observed that in contract farming the highest production cost of onion was input cost 58.03 percent followed by labour cost 30.61 percent and marketing cost 11.34 percent. On the contrary their counterpart non-contract farmers, input cost expenditure on fertilizer was Rs. 2740/ acre which is accounting 19.24 percent of the total cost onion cultivation followed by pesticides 11.51 percent, seed 11.43 percent and management 3.57 percent. The highest labour expenditure was on sowing 10.56 percent, weeding 9.24 percent, ploughing 8.59 percent and the cost of marketing is also very high in the non-contract farming Rs. 3664/ acre which is accounting 25.73 percent of the total cost of cultivation.

Per acre gross returns of white onion under onion

Table 4.15
Cost of Cultivation of Contracting Crop and Non-contracting Crop (onion)

Sr. No.	Particulars	Contract Farming	Non- contract Farming
A	**Input Cost**		
1	Seeds	1962 (10.41)	1628 (11.43)
2	Fertilizers	4864 (25.81)	2740 (19.24)
3	Pesticides	3540 (18.78)	1640 (11.51)
4	Management	568 (3.01)	524 (3.67)
	Sub Total	10934 (58.03)	6532 (45.87)
B	**Labour Cost**		
i	Ploughing	1156 (6.13)	1224 (8.59)
ii	Sowing	2392 (12.69)	1504 (10.56)
iii	Weeding	1852 (9.83)	1316 (9.24)
iv	Pesticides	3.48 (1.84)	-
	Sub Total	5768 (30.61)	4044 (28.39)
C	**Marketing cost**	2138 (11.34)	3664 (25.73)
	A+B+C Total	**18840 (26.59)**	**14240 (54.85)**
	Gross Return	**70840**	**25960**
	Net Return	**52000 (73.40)**	**11720 (45.14)**

Note : Bracketed figures show percentage to total.
Source : Primary Survey.

contract farming was higher than non-contract farming. The net return was 73.40 percent in case of contract farming with compared to 45.14 percent net return of 45.14 percent of non-contract farming.

4.22 Average Annual Income of Sample Farmer Before and After Contract Farming

The average annual income of sample farmers before and after contract farming is shown in table 4.16. It is observed that the cash flow has increased having a direct bearing on farmers income. Table 4.16 indicates that before the contract farming the average income of 50 percent sample farmers was

Table 4.16
Average Annual Income of Sample Farmers Before and after Contract Farming

Sr. No.	Particular	Before		After	
		Frequency	**Percent**	**Frequency**	**Percent**
1	Below Rs. 20,000	50	50	1	1
2	Rs. 20,001-40,000	50	50	29	29
3	Rs.40,001-60,000	00	00	39	39
4	Above 60,000	00	00	31	31
	Total	**100**	**100**	**100**	**100**

Source : Field Survey.

below Rs. 20,000 and remaining 50 percent sample farmer average annual income was upto Rs. 40,000. It is found that after involving in contract farming the average income of only one percent farmer was below Rs. 20000, 29 percent farmers average annual income was upto Rs. 40000 while in group Rs. 40,001 to 60,000 in was 39 percent and 31 percent sample farmers average annual income was above Rs. 60,000. It means after contract farming the income of sample farmers increased.

4.23 Per acre Output of Sample Farmers

Contract farming has been used to promote new high value crop, which are more input intensive, risky, and market dependent for profitability, to lower costs either by yield improvement or cutting input costs through better extension services, and to raise returns by value addition to primary produce. In order to examine impact of contract farming in yields, we compared productivity levels of selected crops such as, onion seed, cotton seed, potato and onion and compared before contract farming productivity and after contract farming productivity. Table 4.17 shows that yield of onion seed before contract farming was 2.70 quintal per acre and it was 3.52 quintal per acre after contract farming. The cotton

Table 4.17

Per Acre Output of Sample Farmers

(in quintals)

Sr. No.	Particular	Before C.F.	After C.F.	Increased/ Decreased	Percentage
1	Onion Seed	2.70	3.52	0.82	23.29
2	Cotton Seed	1.60	2.5	0.9	36
3	Potato	45	80	35	43.75
4	Onion	60	98.10	38.1	38.43

Source : Field Survey.

seed crop yield before contract farming was 1.60 quintal per acre and after contract farming it was 2.5 quintal per acre. The production of potato before contract farming was 45 quintal per acre and after contract farming 80 quintal per acre. In case of onion production the yield was 60 quintal per acre before contract farming and it was 98.10 quintal per acre after contract farming. It is found that due to contract farming the per acre yield of onion seed increased by 23.39 percent, cotton seed by 36 percent, potato by 43.75 percent and onion by 38.43 percent with compared to non-contract farming.

It means farmers believe that better quality seeds supplied by the companies along with better extension services, appropriate crop management practices have been responsible for increased crop yields in the area.

4.24 Comments of Sample Farmers According to Suitable Income

Table 4.18 shows the statements of sample farmers regarding sustainable income. It is observed that 32 percent sample contract farmers agreed that they are getting sustainability of income, while only 9 percent non-contract sample farmer agreed that they have sustainability of income. In case of income sustainability 68 percent contracted farmers

Table 4.18
Sustainable Income

Sr. No.	Particular	Contract Farmers	Non- contract Farmers
1	Yes	32	09
2	No.	68	91
	Total	**100**	**100**

Source : Field Survey.

and 91 percent non-contracted farmers stated that they do not have sustainable income.

4.25 Availability of Transport Facility

Table No. 4.19 indicates the transport situation, transport facility provided by contract companies to the farmers under the contract. This facility helps farmers to save the cost of transportation and minimize the production cost. Transport facility is of the key importance. The farmers said that as the process is driven mostly by forces, a fluctuation in market will shatter the whole economy. They also argued that no coping mechanism is in place to face. In the study area it is found that contracting company provided transport facility and nearly 95 percent of the farmers confirmed the statement and said that there is adequate transport facility in the area. This is a major reason of product fetching higher price in the

Table 4.19
Availability of Transport Facility for Sample Farmers

Sr. No.	Particulars	Contract Farmers	Non- contract Farmers
1	Yes	95	24
2	No.	05	76
	Total	100	100

Source : Primary survey.

market. But in the non-contract farming 91 percent farmers said there is adequate transport facility in the area or transport facility is not given by the trader to the non contract farmers. Therefore, transport cost is borne by the farmers. This is a major reason of product not fetching higher price in the market and not getting higher returns.

4.26 Loan for Crop Production to Sample Farmers

Table No. 4.20 shows the position of credit facilities of selected sample farmers in Maharashtra. Some time company provided direct loan facility to the farmer. But few companies make some arrangement for farmers to get the loans through the banks. 72 percent farmers agreed that they have got the loan facility from the company and 28 percent farmer denied. Non-contracted farmers got loan from the banks but the percentage is low i.e. only 33 percent. Therefore the process is leaving many of the farmers in debt trap.

Table 4.20

Credit for Crop Production to Sample Farmers

Sr. No.	Particulars	Contract Farmers	Non- contract Farmers
1	Yes	72	33
2	No.	28	67
	Total	**100**	**100**

Source : Field Survey.

4.27 Possibility of Increase in Crop Production

Table No. 4.21 presents the possibility of increasing in yield. The question asked to farmers was whether there is possibility of increase the yield in their land or not ? It revealed an interesting picture that nearly 62 percent farmers are still hopeful for an enhanced production. The contract farmers were very much affirmative but in the non-contract farming farmers were very negative because 78 percent farmers said that there is not any increase in the yield as they do not have

Table 4.21

Possibility of Increase in Yield

Sr. No.	Particulars	Contract Farmers	Non- contract Farmers
1	Yes	62	22
2	No.	38	78
	Total	**100**	**100**

Source : Field Survey.

the quality input and scientific advice. It means contract farmers are more hopeful because contract company provides gainful and quality inputs.

4.28 Absolute Average Income of Sample Farmers

Table 4.22 shows companywise average income of selected farmers compared before contract farming income and after contract farming income. The income of farmers of Bejo Sheetal Seeds Pvt. Ltd. before contract farming was Rs. 26,640 and it was Rs. 40,160 after contract farming. The average income of Mahyco's cotton seed farmers was Rs. 33,000 before contract farming and it was Rs. 58,120 after contract farming. The income of the PepsiCo's potato farmers before contract farming

Table 4.22

Farmers Average income Before and After Contract farming

Sr.No.	Company	Before C.F.	After C.F.	Increase/ decrease	Percentage
1	B.S.S. Pvt. Ltd.	26640	40160	13520	33.66
2	Mahyco Pvt. Ltd.	33000	58120	25120	43.22
3	PIH Pvt. Ltd.	19560	54240	34680	63.93
4	JIS Pvt. Ltd.	24960	70840	45880	64.76

Source : Field Survey.

average income was Rs. 19,560 before contract farming and after contract farmers average income increased to Rs. 54,240. In case of Jain irrigation system onion farmers average income was Rs. 25,960 before contract farming and it was Rs. 70,840 after contract farming. It is found that after contract farming average farmers income of Bejo Sheetal Seed Pvt. Ltd. increased by 33.66 percent, Mahyco's farmers average income increased by 43.22 percent, PepsiCo's farmers average income increased by 63.93 percent and Jain Irrigation system Ltd. farmers average income increased by 64.76 percent.

It means after contract farming selected companie's farmers average income has increased. In the selected companies Jain's contracted farmers income average increased as high as 64.76 percent.

4.29 Cropping Pattern of Sample Farmers

The present era of globalization and liberalization has witnessed significant changes in agriculture. These changes include cropping technology as well as cropping patterns. Export oriented products and processed food items occupy a vital position in the market. Table 4.23 shows that 74 percent farmer expressed that there has been a change in the cropping pattern. Traditional patterns have been changed after the induction of contract farming, because farmer cultivated new cash crop and got more benefit. Due to contract farming traditional crop ratio has decreased and cash crop ratio increased. It has been affecting on food grain and food grain prices.

Table 4.23
Change in Cropping Pattern

Sr. No.	Particular	Frequency	Percentage
1	Yes	74	74
2	No.	26	26
	Total	**100**	**100**

Source : Field Survey.

4.30 Structure of Cropping Pattern of Sample Farmer

In the study area farmers grew different crops in their land. Table 4.24 shows the farmers cropping pattern before contract farming and after contract farming. Before contract farming farmers used their land for food grain crop, 48.5 percent land was used for only jawar crop, 13.5 percent land use for bajara, 10.5 percent used for tur, 4.5 percent land used for cotton and 7 percent land used for potato. But after contract farming the cropping pattern of farmers changed. In contract farming farmers used 33 percent land for jawar, 9.25 percent land for Bajara, 14.5 percent land for Wheat, 7.5 percent land for Tur, 7.5 percent land for Cotton and 9.5 percent land for potato crop. The above discussion indicates that after contract farming cropping pattern has been changed. The area

Table 4.24
Structure of Cropping Pattern of Selected Farmers in Maharashtra

Sr. No.	Crop	Before contract Farming	After contract Farming
1	Jawar	48.5	33
2	Bajara	13.5	9.25
3	Wheat	5	14.5
4	Tur	10.5	7.5
5	Chana	2	-
6	Sugarcane	-	5
7	Cotton	4.5	7.5
8	Soyabean	1.	1
9	Groundnuts	2.	1
10	Potato	7	9.5
11	Onion	2.5	5
12	Onion seed	2	4
13	Banana	2.5	2.5
	Total	**100**	**100**

Source : Field Survey.

under jawar crops land is decreased from 48.5 percent to 33 percent bajara 13.5 to 9.25, and Tur 10.5 to 7.5 percent. Whereas the area under wheat, Sugarcan, Cotton, Potato, Onion, Onion seed crops increased in the contract farming. It Means contracted farmers moved towards the cash crops in comparison with non-contracted farmers. The highest percentage of increase in cultivation area was 100 percent in case of sugarcane crop follows by wheat 65.51 percent.

4.31 Impact of Contract Farming on Water Level

Table 4.25 shows the impact of contract farming on water table level. In the contract farming 30 percent farmers agree that there is an effect on water table and 70 percent farmers has not agreed with effect on water level. Because farmers use new irrigation equipment like drip, sprinkler and it is provided by contract company through instalment and marginal rate.

Table 4.25

Impact of Contract Farming on Water Table

Sr. No.	Particulars	Frequency	Percentage
1	Yes	30	30
2	No.	70	70
	Total	**100**	**100**

Source : Field Survey.

4.32 Farmer Suggestive Mitigation Measures in Contract Farming

Table 4.26 records the suggestions given by the farmers in order to improve the production and sustainability of soil fertility to improve the production in quality of soil. There are number of ways to be used like applying varmi compost, regular soil testing, control water flow, minimum level of chemical fertilizer and rotation crop pattern etc. For the question asked by the researcher to the farmers about the mitigation of productivity 82 percent farmers suggested to

Table 4.26

Suggestive Mitigation Measures by Sample Farmers

Sr. No.	Particulars	Frequency	Percentage
1	Applying vermi compost	82	83
2	Minimum chemical fertilizer	83	83
3	Regular testing soil	49	49
4	Regular testing of water table	20	20
5	Rotation cropping pattern	53	53
	Total	**100**	**100**

Source : Field Survey.

use varmi compost, 83 percent farmer suggested to use minimum level of chemical fertilizer for the better productivity, 49 percent farmer suggested to supportive opinion to use the regular soil testing in order to improve production. 20 percent farmers suggested to testing water level and 53 percent farmers suggested to use the rotation cropping pattern. It means farmers for the best yield and production apply some suggestive navigation.

4.33 Benefits of Contract Farming

Table 4.27 shows the benefits of contract farming stated by sample farmers. 72 percent contract farmers replied that their income has been increased, 75 percent farmers replied that they have got appropriate price through contract farming and are satisfied by given prices, 80 percent contract farmers replied that in the contract farming, transport service was provided by the contract company. They are having minimum transport cost. 71 percent contract farmers said that total input is provided by contract companies to contract farmers. According to their feedback 65 percent farmer are satisfied with the guidance provided by contracted company.

Table 4.27
Benefits of Contract Farming by sample farmers

Sr. No.	Particular	Contract Farming	Percentage
1	Increased Income	72	72
2	Correct Price	75	75
3	Minimum Transport Cost	80	80
4	Inputs	71	71
5	Guidance	65	65
	Total	**100**	**100**

Source : Field Survey

4.34 Reasons for Adopting Contract Farming

Table 4.28 indicates the reasons given by sample farmers for adopting contract farming. Selected farmers were asked to list reasons for adopting contract farming and the results are presented in table. Although, producers participate in contract farming for many reasons, access to assured market was the

Table 4.28
Reasons for Adopting Contract Farming by Sample Farmers

Sr.No.	Reasons	Frequency	Percentage
1	Assess to assured market	86	86
2	Assured price	74	74
3	Assess to better seed	72	72
4	Assess to better extension services	71	71
5	Higher returns than competing crops	71	71
6	Inspired by other contract farmers	20	20
7	Personal relation	15	15
	Total	**100**	**100**

Source : Field Survey.

most opted reason with 86 percent farmers. Assured price was another reason for adopting contract farming in the case of 74 percent farmers, company provided quality seeds and due to this 72 percent farmers have adopted contract farming. This is also one reason for adopting contract farming, 71 percent farmer adopted contract farming for access to better extension services and another reason is higher returns than competing crops, and inspired by other contract farmers, personal relations etc.

4.35 Contract Farming Arrangements Provided to Sample Farmer Household by Bejo Sheetal Pvt. Ltd.

Table 4.29 shows that productivity and price is very important factor in contracted farming where the farmer get the proper counselling from contract company. There will be change in the improvement of productivity and also minimum supporting price help increase the productivity. Company appointed field officer for field visit. It helped to improve the productivity. About 40 per cent farmers said that field officer visited twice in a week and 60 percent farmer said that field officer visited once a weak. Out of 100 sample farmers 80 per cent farmer said that they are fully satisfied by the field officer's visit. Whereas 80 percent respondent said that they need financial loan. When the contract has been done 100 percent respondent expected the higher price for their production as it delivers mitigation to the farmer for improving the productivity. Out of selected sample household cent per cent respondents said that regular field visits conducted by the field officer would be helpful.

4.36 Contract Farming Arrangements Provided to Sample Farmer Household by Mahyco Seeds Pvt. Ltd.

Table 4.30 shows the contract farming arrangement provided to sample farmer households by Mahyco. About information of contract farming, 40 per cent field staff of processor delivered information to the farmer, 20 per cent information comes from fellow farmers. Fellow farmer promoted to farmer to make the contract with contracting company in cotton crop. 40 percent sample farmers got the information about the contract farming from their friends and relatives. Mahyco has contracted with farmers in the written

Table 4.29
Contract Farming Arrangements Provided by Bejo Sheetal Seed Pvt. Ltd.

	Particulars	Frequency	%
1	Total Sample	25	100
2	Introduction to onion seed crop by (%)		
i	Field staff of processor	10	40
ii	Fellow farmers	10	40
iii	Friends and relatives	05	20
iv	Others	-	-
3	Type of Agreement (written)	25	100
4	Frequency of fields visits by field officers %		
i	Daily		-
ii	Once in 2 days	10	40
iii	Twice a week	15	60
iv	Once in a week	-	-
v	Once in 15 days	-	-
5	Satisfaction with processor and field staff (%)	20	80
6	Willingness to grow again (%)	20	80
7	Growers expectation from processor (%)		
i	Cash advance	20	80
ii	Loan for other crop	-	-
iii	Higher price for produce	25	100
iv	Prizes and a word	25	100
v	Regular field visit by filed staff superior	25	100
8	Problem areas between grower and processors (%)		
i	Grading of Produce	20	80
ii	Delay in input Supply	-	-
iii	Insufficient supply	10	40
iv	Transport of produce	-	-
v	Delay in payment	07	28

Source : Company Office Record

Table 4.30
Contract farming Arrangements Provided by Mahyco

Sr. No.	Particulars	Frequency	%
1	Total Sample	25	100
2	Introduction to cotton seed crop by (%)		
(i)	Field staff of processor	10	40
(ii)	Fellow farmers	05	20
(iii)	Friends and relatives	10	40
(iv)	Others	-	
3	Type of Agreement (written)	25	100
4	Frequency of fields visits by field officers %		
(i)	Daily		
(ii)	Once in 2 days		
(iii)	Twice a week	5	20
(iv)	Once in a week	20	80
(v)	Once in 15 days	-	-
5	Satisfaction with processor and field staff (%)	22	88
6	Willingness to grow again (%)	18	72
7	Growers expectation from processor (%)		
(i)	Cash advance	22	88
(ii)	Loan for other crop		-
(iii)	Higher price for produce	25	100
(iv)	Prizes and a word	25	100
(v)	Regular field visit by filed staff superior	25	100
8	Problem areas between grower and processors %		
(i)	Grading of Produce	7	28
(ii)	Delay in input Supply	-	-
(iii)	Insufficient supply	5	20
(iv)	Transport of produce	-	-
(v)	Delay in payment	5	20

Source : Office Record of Mahyco.

mode. Mahyco appointed various field officers any they visited the field. They delivered the information about crop disease, production, fertilizer, irrigation, pesticides, etc. About 20 per cent farmers said that field officer visited them twice a week and 80 per cent farmers replied that field officers visited to their farm. 88 percent sample farmers said that they are satisfied with field staff and their councelling. Out of 25 sample farmer 88 per cent are willing to continue with Mahyco in cotton crop seed production. It is found that 88 per cent farmers have cash advances from the company, 100 per cent farmers expected the company loan, higher price for product, regular field visit by the field officers. In case of grading 28 percent sample farmer said that they had problem when the company decides grading of product. While in case of inputs 20 per cent farmers said that they have had problem with company, when company provides insufficient inputs. Payment matter is the major problem between the company and farmers, 20 per cent sample farmers said that company delayed the payments.

4.37 Contract Farming Arrangements Provided to Sample Farmer Household by PepsiCo India Holding Pvt. Ltd.

Table 4.31 shows the contract farming arrangements provided promotion of potato cultivation is carried out to a large extent by 40 per cent field staff of contracting company and to certain extent by fellow growers and friends (40 per cent) and relatives 20 per cent. The contract arrangement is signed by both the contracting parties. The field staff visited the farmers regularly and provided technical assistance. Field staff visited once a week 40 per cent farmers said and one in 15 days said 60 per cent farmers. The 80 per cent farmers are satisfied with the services provided by field staff. Loyalty of farmers towards processor is the key for successful contract and it is evident from the present study. The processor met the input requirement of farmer in a majority of the cases. However there are certain expectations from 92 percent farmers like cash advance and preference for specific potato cultivation, which are yet to be met by the processor. Whereas, 60 per cent farmers experienced difficulties in terms of grading of products and 20 per cent farmers complained delayed insufficient input supplies and 40 per cent farmers complained delay in payment. Most of the selected sample farmers (72 per

Table 4.31
Contract Farming Arrangements Provided by PepsiCo India Holding Pvt. Ltd.

S. N.	Particular	Frequency	%
1	Total Sample	25	100
2	Introduction to potato crop by (%)		
(i)	Field staff of processor	10	40
(ii)	Fellow farmers	10	40
(iii)	Friends and relatives	05	20
(iv)	Others	-	-
3	Type of Agreement (written)	25	100
4	Frequency of fields visits by field officers %		
(i)	Daily		
(ii)	Once in 2 days		
(iii)	Twice a week		
(iv)	Once in a week	10	40
(v)	Once in 15 days	15	60
5	Satisfaction with processor and field staff (%)	20	80
6	Willingness to grow again (%)	18	72
7	Growers expectation from processor (%)		
(i)	Cash advance	23	92
(ii)	Loan for other crop	-	-
(iii)	Higher price for produce	25	100
(iv)	Prizes and a word	25	100
(v)	Regular field visit by filed staff superior	25	100
8	Problem areas between grower and processors %		
(i)	Grading of Produce	15	60
(ii)	Delay in input Supply	05	20
(iii)	Insufficient supply	-	-
(iv)	Transport of produce	-	-
(v)	Delay in payment	10	40

Source : Office Record of PepsiCo India Holding Pvt. Ltd.

cent) potato growers are willing to continue the contract with the same processor.

4.38 Contract Farming Arrangements Provided to Sample Farmer Household by Jain Irrigation System Pvt. Ltd.

Table 4.32 shows the contract farming arrangement provided by Jain Irrigation System Pvt. Ltd. The promotion of white onion cultivation is carried out to a large extent (48 per cent) by field staff of contracting company and 40 per cent by fellow growers and 12 per cent by friends and relatives. The contract arrangement is signed by both contracting parties. The field staff visited farmers regularly and provided the technical assistance. Field staff visits once a week. The 80 per cent farmers are satisfied with the services provided by field staff. Loyalty of farmers towards processor is the key for successful contract and it is evident from the present study. The processor met the input requirement of farmer in a majority of the cases. However, there are certain expectations from 80 per cent farmers like cash advance and preference for specific white onion cultivation, which are to be met by the processor. Out of 25 selected sample farmers 40 per cent farmers experienced difficulties in terms of grading of produce and 20 per cent farmers said, that there is delayed insufficient input supplies, 40 per cent farmers said delay of payments. Most of the 80 per cent white onion growers are willing to continue the contract with the same processor.

4.39 The Comparative Study of Selected Companies

A comparative study of four selected companies is shown in table 4.33. These four selected companies have been working in four different district. Bejo Sheetal Seed Ltd., Mahyco and Jain Irrigation System Pvt. Ltd. do the direct contract with farmers. Whereas PepsiCo contracts through hundekari with farmers. All the companies have dual prices formula. They have fixed price and open market linked price. Bejo Sheetal

Table 4.32
Contract Farming Arrangements Provided by Jain Irrigation System Pvt. Ltd.

Sr. No.	Particulars	Frequ -ency	%
1	Total Sample	25	100
2	Introduction to onion seed crop by (%)		
i	Field staff of processor	12	48
ii	Fellow farmers	10	40
iii	Friends and relatives	3	12
iv	Others	-	
3	Type of Agreement (written)	25	100
4	Frequency of fields visits by field officers %		
i	Daily	-	
ii	Once in 2 days	-	
iii	Twice a week	-	
iv	Once in a week	25	100
v	Once in 15 days		
5	Satisfaction with processor and field staff (%)	20	80
6	Willingness to grow again (%)	20	80
7	Growers expectation from processor (%)		
i	Cash advance	20	80
ii	Loan for other crop	-	-
iii	Higher price for produce	25	100
iv	Prizes and a word	25	100
v	Regular field visit by filed staff superior	25	100
8	Problem areas between grower and processors %		
i	Grading of Produce	10	40
ii	Delay in input Supply	5	20
iii	Insufficient supply	5	20
iv	Transport of produce	-	-
v	Delay in payment	10	40

Source : Office Record of Jain Irrigation System Pvt. Ltd.

Table 4.33
A Comparative Picture of the Contracts of Selected Companies

Sr. No.	Company Parameter	B.S.S.L. Onion Seed	Mahyco Cotton Seed	PIH (PepsiCo) Potato	JISL White Onion
1	Area (District)	Aurangabad	Jalna	Pune	Jalgaon
2	Nature of Contract	direct	direct	contract growers thru hundekari	direct
3	Pricing Formula	fixed price and open market linked price	fixed price and open market linked price	fixed price and open market linked price	fixed price and open market linked price
4	Delivery point	Company	Company	Collection centre	Company
5	Time of Payment	After 15 days	After 15 days	Within 15 days	Within a week
6	Major Market	Domestic	Domestic	Domestic and Export	Domestic and Export
7	Company Benefited	1 raw material 2 quality product 3 production guarantee 4 suitable price	--	--	--
8	Payment mode	by cheque	by cheque	Through account	by cheque
9	Technical guidance	provides	provides	provides	provides
10	Training and assistance	given	given	given	given
11	Crop Insurance	No	No	No	No
12	Life Insurance	Yes	No	No	No
13	crop failure	No liability of company	--	--	--
14	Input supply	Seed, pesticide fertilizer	seed pesticide	seed, pesticide fertilizer	seed irrigation equipment
15	Technical instrument	Thresher	-	irrigation equipment pesticide spray thresher	irrigation equipment thresher

Source : Field Survey.

Seed Ltd., Mahyco and Jain Irrigation System Pvt. Ltd. collect product at company itself whereas PepsiCo as its hundekari collection centre. It collects the products through these cantres. After the collection of products Bejo Sheetal Seed Ltd., Mahyco and PepsiCo pay after fifteen day to the farmers whereas Jain Irrigation System Pvt. Ltd. pays within a week. Bejo Sheetal Seed Ltd. and Mahyco have domestic selling market whereas PepsiCo and Jain Irrigation System Pvt. Ltd. have domestic as well as international market. All the companies have been benefited from contract farming. The benefits of these companies are raw material, quality product, production guarantee, suitable price etc. Bejo Sheetal Seed Ltd., Mahyco, Jain Irrigation System Pvt. Ltd. pay the payments to the farmers by cheque whereas PepsiCo pays through account. All the companies provide technical guidance and they also provide training and assistance during the crop cultivation period. These companies do not provide any crop insurance. Only Bejo Sheetal Seed Ltd. provide life insurance. In case of crop failure these companies do not provide any facilities. During the crop cultivation Bejo Sheetal Seed Ltd. provides seed, pesticides, fertilizer etc.; Mahyco provides only seed and pesticides, PepsiCo provides seed pesticides fertilizer; whereas Jain Irrigation System Pvt. Ltd. provides seed, irrigation equipment etc. Regarding the technical equipment Bejo Sheetal Seed Ltd. provides only thresher; Mahyco provides no technical instrument, PepsiCo provide thresher, pesticides spray, irrigation instrument whereas Jain Irrigation System Pvt. Ltd. provides irrigation equipment and thresher.

4.40 Loan Facility Provided by Contracting Companies to Farmers

Loans provided by selected contracting companies to sample farmers are shown in table 4.34. It is found that Bejo Sheetal Seed Ltd. company provided cash loans, while PepsiCo and Jain Irrigation System Pvt. Ltd. provide loan through different banks. Mahyco does not provide loan facility to the

Table 4.34

Loan Facility Provided by Contracting Companies to Farmers

Sr.No.	Companies	Loan (Rs.)	Interest rate
1	B.S.S.L.	25,000 per acre	7 %
2	Mahyco	-	-
3	PepsiCo	25,000 per acre	7 %
4	JISL	25,000 per acre	7 %

Source : Field Survey.

farmers. Every selected company provides Rs. 25,000 per acre at the interest rate of 7 percent per year to the selected farmers.

Conclusion

Maharashtra is an important state of India so for as its contribution to the agricultural development is concerned. Maharashtra is the second largest state in India in terms of population and the third in respect of area. The state has the third highest per Capita State Domestic Product (SDP) among all the Indian states in the year 2000-01. Though Maharashtra is one of the industrialized states in the country, agriculture and allied activities are still predominant in the state. Agriculture continues to be the major source of income as most of the population depends on agriculture for livelihood. However, contribution of agriculture and allied activities in net state domestic product (SDP) declined steeply from 36 per cent in 1961-62 to 13 per cent in 2011-12. The comparable shares for all India are 47 and 28.3 percent respectively.

Based on the foregoing discussion of the results of this study, the following conclusions could be drawn. There is a need to assist farmers to have better education, access to timely and quality inputs such as extension services, institutional credit, and better opportunities of off-term income to improve financial status. The cost incurred, yield and gross return obtained by the contract farmers were almost double that of the non-contract farmers. The functional analysis revealed that there existed a substantial scope to increase the production of crops through making judicious use of critical inputs, particularly chemicals. The price received by direct selling to the consumers was the highest, followed by retailers and wholesalers in the case of non-contract farmers. Transportation charges formed the major component of marketing cost, which was severely felt by the farmers.

The education level of sample farmers engaged in contract farming shows that maximum 45 percent farmers education level is secondary, 8 percent non-contract farmers are found to be illiterate and highest 39 percent farmers educational level was secondary. Contracted farmer are found to be more educated than non-contracted farmers.

It is observed that in the study area 73 percent sample contract farmers belonged to general category whereas 76 percent sample farmers belonged to non-contract segment. There is awareness developed about contract farming in general categories. Average family size among contracted farmer was 4.91 and 5.77 among non-contract farmers. According to family workers 3.06 workers per family in contracted farming and 2.61 workers per family in non-contracted farming. The contracted farmers average family size is small than non-contracted farmers. Total 27 percent contracted farmer worked in various subsidiary business and only 8 percent non-contracted farmers involve subsidiary business. The contracted farmers aware about subsidiary business than non-contract farmers. But there is a lack of awareness found in both segments.

The total cost of cultivation for crops grown by contract farmers was reported to be higher as compared to non-contract farmers due to excess expenditure incurred on costly variable inputs by contract farmers compared to non-contract farmers. This was because of modern farming adopted and more focused and efficient management practices by the contract farmers. Assured price realization, supply chain with improved market outlets, increased cash flow, access to irrigation were the most influencing factors for adopting the contract farming by the sample farmers.

Notes:

1. Government of Maharashtra (2010-11), Economy Survey Report.
2. Tasi, Kaye (2006), *Role of Regional Rural Bank in Economic Development*, Abhijeet Publications, New Delhi.
3. Kalamkar, S.S. (2002), Agricultural Development and Sources of Output Growth in Maharashtra State, Gokhale Institute of Politics and Economics.
4. Government of Maharashtra (2002), Economic Survey.
5. Dastane R. (2002), Maharashtra
6. op.cit, Shrikant Kalamkar S.
7. Profile of Bejo Sheetal Seed Pvt. Ltd. www.bejoseeds.com
8. Profile of Mahyco, www.mahyco.com
9. Singh, S. (1997), "Multinational Enterprises and Agribusiness Sector in Developing Economic: A Case Study of Pepsi in India", in K.J. Azam (Ed.), *Economic Liberalization in India, Implications for Indo-US Relations*, Hydrabad, Delta.
10. Ibid
11. Ibid
12. Singh, S. (2005), *Political Economy of Contract Farming in India*, Allied Publishers Private Limited, Mumbai.
13. Profile of Jain Irrigation System Ltd. www.jisl.com
14. Jain R.C.A., *Regulation and Dispute Settlement in Contract Farming in India*, www.ncap.res.in

5

FINDINGS AND SUGGESTIONS

Summary

The importance of the agricultural sector in the economic development of India is clearly indicated by its contribution to the national gross domestic product (GDP). In 2011-12, agricultural contributed 13.9 percent to GDP (at current prices), industry 27.0 percent and services 59.0 percent. The agricultural sector is also important to the socio-economic development as about 68 percent of the population live in rural areas and most of them depend on agriculture.

While the economy has been growing at about 8 percent yearly, agricultural growth has been dismal at nearly 2 percent during the last ten years. This is in sharp contrast to the average annual growth rate of more than 4 percent during the 1980s and early 90s. It is this sharp decline in agricultural growth that is causing distress in rural areas. The present era of globalization and liberalization has witnessed significant changes in agricultural the mainstay of Indian economy. These changes include cropping technology as well as cropping patterns. Export oriented products and processed food items occupy a vital position in the market these days. Such value added agricultural product needs heavy dose of costly inputs, improved crop varieties, and advanced technology to comply with the quality standards set by international organizations like WTO.

The new market realities due to focus on liberalization, privatization and globalization of the post WTO regime are here to stay, bringing in its wake new opportunities and challenges as well. The agriculture sector, like any other sector of the economy, has got to put its act together to evolve a response mechanism to face this ineluctable reality. This may call for a paradigm shift in its focus and approach. Introduction of reforms in agricultural marketing is the need of the hour to bring the requisite changes in its structure and to push the sector to take off from its low growth rate of 2-3 percent to at least a respectable 4.5 percent. Contract farming proves to be beneficial to and fulfils the desired demand of both farmers and companies. In India most of the farmers belong to small and marginal categories, and are found resource poor. Against this backdrop, contract farming is billed to be a variable instrument to address many of the traditional ills affecting the agriculture sector and the farmers, such as fragmentation of holdings, long chain of market intermediaries, ignorance about the requirements of the buyers, low farm mechanization, inadequacy of capital and distress sale and consequent heavy losses to farmers etc. Contract farming is an exciting way of giving the power of scale to the small farmers, of marrying the small farmer efficiency to the scale economy, transferring corporate management skill to the agriculture field, providing assured markets for the produce, reducing the transaction costs involved in the value chain of the commodities and of ensuring vertical integration through forward and backward linkages. At the same time the agroprocessing firms are lacking in possession of land for cultivation of high valued crops. That is why these companies come forward with contracts in providing such costly inputs, improved crop varieties and advanced technology to the resource poor farmers. Hence, contract farming his attained a greater place in today's agriculture and it continues to play a major role in commercializing it.

Contract farming system has old historical resonances, such as the infamous contracts enforced by indigo planters in eastern India during the early colonial period. But recent pattern of contract farming has been developed especially in the United States where corporate penetration of agriculture is probably the most advanced. Agricultural trade globally is dominated by transnational corporations like Cargill, Archer Daniels Midland and Monsanto, which are increasingly involved at each stage of the agriculture system. These corporations achieve domination over the market through a combination of horizontal and vertical integration. This has increased the margins for the procuring and processing firms while at the same time reducing farm incomes and increasing the prices for the consumers. This explains the rising spread between retail prices and the prices received by farmers. The farmers really gain from agribusinesses which provide them huge and increased profits.

Contract farming arrangements of different types have existed in various parts of the country for centuries for both subsistence and commercial crops. The commercial crops like sugarcane, cotton, tea, coffee, etc. have always involved some forms of contract farming or the other. Even in the case of some fruit crops and fisheries, contract farming arrangement, involving mainly the forward trading of commodities have been observed. However, in the wake of economic liberalization, the concept of contract farming in which national or multinational companies enter into contracts for marketing of the horticultural produce and also provide technologies and capital to contract farmers has gained importance. Contract farming is generally defined as farming under an agreement between farmers and sponsor (processing and / or marketing firm) for the production and supply of agricultural products under forward agreements, frequently at predetermined prices. Within this broad framework, there are different variants of contracts depending on the intensity of contractual arrangements. The basis of such arrangements is a commitment on the part of the farmer to provide a specific commodity in quantities and at quality standards determined by the purchaser and a commitment on the part of the sponsor to support the farmer's production and to purchase the commodity. Thus, under contract farming, the farmers grow selected crops under a buy back agreement with an agency called sponsor engaged in trading or processing and the latter contributes directly to the management of the farm through input supply including planting materials as well as technical guidance through intermittent crop supervision and also markets for the produce. Thus farmer assumes the production related risks, and the price risk is transferred to the company. In some cases, the company also bears the production risk, depending on the stage of crop growth at which the contract is made. If the contract is made at flowering or fruiting stage the company bears the production risk also. It is this variant of contract farming which is said to be one of the ways by which small farmers can participate in the production of high value crops like fruits, vegetables, flowers etc. and benefit from market-led growth.

Small farmers in India are generally capital starved and cannot make major investment in land improvement and modern inputs. Contract farming can fil up this gap by providing the farmers with quality inputs, technical guidance and managements skills. Although the company deals only with the contract crop, the farmers overall management skill may improve, thereby helping him to raise the yields of contract crops.

From the standpoint of corporate bodies farming reduces the supply risk, while the farmers enter into contractual arrangements with companies in order to minimize price risks. The company and the farmers enter into contracts to supply or purchase a specified quantum of the commodity at agreed prices. The agreed contract may be either formal or informal and may cover supply of inputs and marketing of output. By entering into contract, the company reduces the risk of non-availability of raw material and the farmer reduces the risk of market demand and prices of his produce. The input and services supplied by firms may include seeds, fertilizers, pesticides, credit, farm machinery, technical advice, extension etc. or may involve only the supply of hybrid seeds and marketing of produce.

Contract farming is becoming an increasingly important aspect of agribusiness, whether products are purchased by multinationals or by smaller companies. There are a few success stories on contract farming such as PepsiCo India in respect of potato, tomato, groundnut and chili in Punjab, safflower in Madhya Pradesh, oil palm in Andhra Pradesh, white onion, cotton fruit in Maharashtra seed production contracts for hybrids seed companies etc. which helped the growers in realization of better returns for their produce. Other success stories of contract farming are Amul and NDDB for milk procurement, sugarcane cooperative in Maharashtra and prawn-aquaculture in Andhra Pradesh. In our country this approach has considerable potential where small and marginal farmers can no longer be competitive without access to modern technology and support. The contractual agreement with the farmer provides access to production services and credit as well as knowledge of new technology. Pricing arrangements can significantly reduce the risk and uncertainty of market place.

Most of the studies reviewed above have indicated that the results of contracting are very promising in the early year. Farmers benefits from improved technology and higher productivity, quality and production. Some study indicated that contract farming helped farmers for the better, gave more reliable income, generated employment especially for women, provided new skills. In the review also indicate in contract farming has several disadvantages too: poor extension services, low prices to farmer due to haphazard pricing of the produce, inherent higher risk to cultivators, frequent delays in payment, week bargaining power of farmer, sole dependence on companies for inputs as credit, over exploitation of ground water and the threat of the environmental. Some study indicates generally the contracts are not written and the legal enforcement system is too tedious for both growers and firms. Today in India new national agriculture policy (NAP) favours such types of private sector participation through contract farming and land leasing to accelerate technology transfer, accumulate capital flow and organize assured market for crop production, especially of oil seeds cotton, horticultural crops, food grains crops and fruits, all types Agribusiness companies need an assured and regular inflow of supplies to operate their processing facilities efficiently and often, they require the commodities to be processed to satisfy certain quality standards. The conditions that favour contracting are an opportunity for reducing price and sales volume uncertainties, the need for the standardized farm market to provide such produce, etc. The review of study indicate that the way contract contributes to farm income varies between commodities, contract growers receive higher prices yields presumably due to better quality. In the reviewed studies also stated that contract farming has a positive impact on crop production and farm income. The socio-economic factors that influenced participation in contract farming has education, age farm size, access to institutional credit, source of off-farm income and membership to an organization.

Most of the studies reviewed above have indicated that changing agrarian production structure under contract farming, especially issues associated with transfer of skills, choise of technology organization of labour, working conditions and terms of work. Some studies stated that several state governments, including Andhra Pradesh, Gujarat, Karnataka, Punjab and Tamil Nadu have already started promoting contract farming with desired changes in the policy and the market front. They have started changing laws to enable and support such contractual relationship and providing companies interested in it which a variety of incentives, subsidies and tax rebates including lifting of land ceiling. There is a need for developed agriculture sector and increasing production and income by using optimum utilization of resources for the development of agriculture sector in the various state. No study has so for been conducted for studding contract farming in Maharashtra therefore, the present study is a sincere effort to study contract farming in India.

It is observed that the process of contract farming in India involves, engaging rural Indian farmers for the cultivation of agricultural produce under strict government policies. The role of contract farming in Indian rural economy involves government and private participation along with the rural workers. Further, it engages a good number of farmers and other rural workers to discharged other agriculture related activities. Contract farming is providing technology, extension services, credit, etc. to the farmers. A number of agribusiness firms have entered into contract farming agreements for a number of agricultural and horticultural crops, such as tomatoes, potatoes, chili, gherkin, baby corn, rose, onions, wheat, basmati, cotton, groundnuts flowers, medical plants, etc. produced in some from of contractual arrangements with the farmers in India. The state like Maharashtra, Andhra, Pradesh, Karnataka, Punjab, Haryana, Madhya Pradesh, Chattisgarh, Rajasthan, Tamil Nadu, Uttarkhand and Uttar Pradesh provide favourable conditions for contract farming and success of contract farming in these states owes to lower total land under marginal fields, better irrigation facilities, soil productivity and yield per hectare.

Contract farming in Maharashtra will get the much needed impetus, following the passage of the bill to amend the Maharashtra Agricultural Produce Marketing (Development and Regulation) Act which has passed in the

State Assembly on Thursday 20 April 2006. The government claimed that contract farming would boost food processing and export of agricultural produce. The contract farming act is designed to encourage the investment in the food processing industry of Maharashtra, which would ensure farmers get the best prices for their produce. The government further said, "food processing industry and exporters of farm produce have always wanted assured supply of quality farm produce. The act will not only assure this would happen, but also iron out vagaries in prices that plague farmers every year." As the new law allows buyers of farm produce to enter into direct agreement with the farmers, the farmers will also be saved from paying commission and other charges to agriculture market produce committees. Food processing units are topically located in areas that are far removed from the place of production and the act will go a long way in creating new employment opportunities in rural areas.

Findings

Some important findings of the present study are as under:

1. In global world liberalization, corporatization has been playing an active role in all sectors of economy. Agricultural sector has also taken a different shape with latest developments.
2. Corporate mediation in agriculture through contract farming arrangements is taking a vital role in linking the corporate firms and the farmer.
3. Contract farming was expected to modernize the pleasant farmers by providing new technology, credit, inputs and technical advice besides linking them to the international market.
4. In India, after pronouncement of national agricultural policy, contract farming gained prominence. Many crops in different parts of the country are produced under contract arrangements.
5. The terms and conditions of the contract are

determined by the processor. The growers have little say in deciding contractual obligations.

6. The NGOs also play a role in information provisions and in monitoring and regulating the working of contracts.
7. Contract farming is not a panacea to solve all related problems of agricultural production and marketing system. But contract farming could be evaluated as a way of providing easier access credit, input, information and technology and product markets for the small scale farming structure.
8. Contract farming might also be seen as a way or as a part of rural development and promoted to improve agricultural performance especially in backward area.
9. Farming to both sides, there are some problems for successful implementation of contract farming having co-ordination and collaboration consciousness and acting in an organized manner are advisable for both sides.
10. In India modern contract farming was started by PepsiCo in 1980 and in the year 2000 variants of contract farming were introduced for various crops like wheat, basmati rice, tomato, fruits, horticultural all crops, vegetables etc. In the year 2003 Government of India accepted new policy framework for contract farming.
11. Contract farming has been successful in effecting crop diversification in many states. It was observed that different commodities covered under contract farming in different states are both traditional ones like basmati rice, wheat, maize, red gram, bengal gram, groundnut, sesame, cashew nut, coconut, onion, potato all seed etc. and non-traditional ones like medicinal plants (Ashwagandha, Dhavana, Coleus, Safed Musli) and gherkins. In the various state corporate involve in different crops in contract farming in India. The

contract farming spread across crops, regions and agencies (public, private and multinational) in India.

12. The changes in 1980 in the National Agricultural Policy allowed private companies to operate in the seeds production sector. They were also allowed to import commercial seed and germplasm for vegetables. The first large scale activity of seed production started under the aegis of Mahyco in the early 1980 mainly in the Marathwada region of Maharashtra. It spread to neighbouring areas of Andhra Pradesh, Vidarbha and Karnataka. These state / areas dominate the seed business.
13. In India Ministry of Agriculture has taken several policy steps and had formulated a law, to promote contract farming and to allow accelerated technology transfer, credit flow and assured market for crop production. Agriculture Produce Marketing Act (APMC) has been amended in accordance with the emerging trends. So far 15 states and 5 union territories have amended their APMC act to derive the benefits of market reforms.
14. The Government of Maharashtra had decided in June 2005 to modify the 1963 APMC act (Distribution) in which contract farming has been included and rename it as Model Act 7. Early implementation of this act would encourage farmers, because despite the present constraint, success with strong linkages between farmers and processors marketing agencies has been achieved. Such partnership is essential so that the objective is fulfilled for a sustainable business relationship and marketing performance.
15. In Maharashtra 12 companies were working in 10 district in 2008-09 and area under contract farming was 34,880.53 hectare and 14004 farmers involved. During 2010-11 7 contracting companies in 5 district were involved and it has covered 60,207.8 hectare of

land and nearly 19,154 farmers. In 2011-12 only one company was working in three district. It has covered 1200 hectare land and near about 499 farmers for potato production.

16. Bejo Shetal company engaged in onion seed contract farming in Aurangabad, Jalna and Beed in 2006-07 had 300 farmers contract in 2006-07 and 350 farmers contract during 2010-11 Bejo Shetal Seed Pvt. Ltd. accupied 5 talukas and 13 villages during 5 year. The purchase rate of onion in the year 2006-07 was Rs. 17,000 / Qt. which increased up to Rs. 28,000/Qt. in 2010-11. The Mahyco purchase rate of cotton seeds in the year 2006-07 was Rs. 25,000/Qt. it increased continuously and readed upto Rs. 55,000/Qt. during 2010-11. Mahyco increased purchasing rate of cotton seeds by 54.54 percent in five year.
17. The PepsiCo contracting company purchases potato crop for processing. The purchase rate of potato in 2006-07 was 700/Qt. which continuously increased upto 1000/Qt. in 2010-11. This company increased potato price by 30 percent in five years.
18. The Jain Irrigation System Ltd. contracting company purchases white onion crop for processing. During 2006-07 purchase rate of white onion was Rs. 671/Qt. This rate decreased upto Rs. 500/Qt. in 2010-11.
19. Average family size was 4.91 among contracted farmer and 5.77 among non-contracted farmers.
20. The education level of sample farmers in contract farming maximum 45 percent farmers education level was secondary and in non-contract farmers' 39 percents farmers education level was secondary. Study found that contracted farmers were more educated than non-contracted farmer.
21. In contracted farmers family worker was 3.06 workers per family and in non-contracted farmer it was 2.61 workers per family. In the contract farming average

family size is small and familly worker involve is large and employment generation is also high.

22. Out of 100 selected sample farmers 27 percent contract farmers were working in various subsidiary business and only 8 percent non-contract farmers working in subsidiary business. Contract farmers are more awared about subsidiary business than non-contract farmers.
23. The sample contracted farmers average farm size is 3.13 hectare and non-contracted farmer farm size is 3.1 hectare. 1.40 hectare which calculate 44.72 percent has contracted farmers average rain fed area was 1.40 hectares and non-contracted farmers average rainfed area was 1.8 hectares. Contracted farmers irrigated area was 55.7 percent and it was 41.93 percent in case of non-contract farmers during study period. It is observed that in contract farming contracting company gives preference to develop irrigated land and provide irrigation instrument so that in contract farming the percentage irrigated land was highest than non-contract farming.
24. In the age group 25 to 40 there were 54 percent contract farmers and 49 percent non-contract farmers. It means youth farmers have been found moving towards contract farming which is helping to him stable income source in comparison with non-contract farming.
25. In contract farming 38 percent farmers used drip irrigation at the same time 25 percent non-contract farmers used dripped irrigation. The sprinkler irrigation system is used by 17 percent contracted farmer households and only 6 percent by non-contract farmers. Contract farmers are using more irrigation facility than non-contracted farmers.
26. Per acre gross returns of onion seeds under contract farming was Rs. 40,160 which is 1.24 time more than the per acre gross returns of non-contract farming.

The net returns of onion seeds was 62.94 percent in case of contract farming with compared to 56.40 percent of non-contract farming.

27. Per acre gross returns of cotton seeds under contract farming was Rs. 58,120 which is 1.67 times more than per acre gross returns of non contract farming. The net returns of cotton seeds was 66.34 percent in case of contract farming with compared to 51.26 percent of non-contract farming.
28. Per acre gross returns of potato under contract farming was Rs. 54,240 which is 1.24 times more than per acre gross returns of non contract farming. The net returns of potato was 37.09 percent in case of contract farming with compared to 27.74 percent of non-contract farming.
29. Per acre gross returns of white onion under contract farming was Rs. 70,840 which is 2.73 times more than per acre gross returns of non contract farming. The net returns of onion was 73.40 percent in case of contract farming with compared to 45.14 percent of non-contract farming.
30. It is observed that before contract farming 50 percent contracted farmers annual income was bellow Rs. 20,000. After involvement in contract farming one percent farmers average annual income was bellow Rs. 20,000 during study period.
31. Due to contract farming per acre yield of onion seed increased by 23.39 percent, cotton seeds by 36 percent, potato by 43.75 percent and onion by 38.43 percent.
32. In the contract farming 72 percent farmer agreed that they have got the loan facility from the company on the contrary in non-contract farming only 33 percent farmers have got bank loans.
33. In the study area 62 percent contracted farmers are still hopeful for an enhanced production but in non-contract farming 78 percent farmer said that there is

not increase in the yield as they do not have the quality input and scientific advice.

34. After contract farming the income of sample farmers of Bejo Sheetal Seed Pvt. Ltd. increased by 33.66 percent, Mahyco's contracted farmers average income increased by 43.22 percent, PepsiCo's contracted farmers average income increased by 63.93 percent and Jain Irrigation System Ltd. farmers average income increased by 64.76 percent. After contract farming selected contracted farmers average income was increased.
35. After contract farming the cropping pattern has been changed. After contract farming the area under jawar crop decreased from 48.5 percent to 33 percent, Bajara 13.5 to 9.25 percent, tur 10.5 to 7.5 percent whereas, the area under wheat, sugarcane, cotton, onion, onion seed crop increased due to contract farming. It means contract farmers moved towards the cash crops in comparison with non-contract farmers.
36. In the contract farming farmer use new irrigation equipment like drip, sprinkler provided by contracting company.
37. Selected farmers participate in contract farming for many reasons like assess to assured market, assured price, assess to better seeds, assess to better extension services, higher returns inspired by other contract farmers and contracting companies personal relation etc.
38. The contract farming gives benefits to farmers like increasing income, higher contract price, minimum transport cost, quality inputs and technical guidance etc.

Suggestions

In the light of findings and conclusions of this study, the following suggestions are important to improve the present situation.

1. The contract farmers said that there are no adequate infrastructure facilities. So it is necessary to contract farming to increase infrastructure facilities like roads, public transport, telephones, postal services, stable electric power and water supply, cold storage facilities, etc.
2. The government needs to ensure that contract farming, which is generally commodity specific and tends to promote monoculture, does not grow beyond proportion to destroy bio-diversity and agricultural ecology. It may be necessary to provide necessary guidelines for land use planning in each region in order to prevent such eventualities.
3. The central and state governments are already considering Value Added Tax throughout the country. The other barriers particularly, the high level of public intervention in the market need to be completely stopped or greatly liberalized in order to allow free flow of trade in agricultural commodity.
4. Generally, most of the agreements of contract companies are found in English. So, it is suggested that companies should write their agreements in regional languages. So that the local farmers can understand the terms of contracts. At least it should be made bilingual, standard formats for farmer-friendly agreement should be designed and mandated by the government.
5. In the contract farming agreement record is not available. Therefore, it has been suggested that record of contract farmers, along with other relevant details such as the area and crops under contract, contracting agency and contract farmers, etc. should be maintained at a state level, country level and should be made available to the public through the website.
6. On a larger scale, the sponsors themselves should be honest. Therefore, the contract should be managed in

a more transparent and participatory manner. So that there is greater social consensus in handling contract violation from either side without getting involved in costly as well as lengthy process of litigation.

7. In the study area main crops were jawar, bajara, pulses, cotton, etc. After the contract farming, farmers diverted to cash crops which give more income to farmers but at the same time due to this profit food grain crops have been neglected. Even major food producing areas now are gradually moving towards non-food crops under contract cultivation. So it is suggested that in the contract farming farmers should also cultivate food grains and government should give some intensive for improving production of food grains.
8. It is observed from the study of selected four contract farming company the average annual income of farmers increased by on an average 51.39 percent. But in India contracting companies are limited. So it is necessary to involve more companies in contract farming.
9. In the study area 27 percent contracted farmers are working in other commercial business. It is necessary to provide agro-based business to contracted farmers.
10. It is found that only 38 percent farmers used modern irrigation facilities. So it is suggested that government and contracted company should provide modern irrigation facilities to farmers.
11. Net returns of potato under contract farming was 37.09 percent which is much lower than onion seeds (62.94 percent), cotton seeds (66.34 percent) and white onion (74.40 percent). So it is suggested that PepsiCo contracted company should take effects to minimize production cost of potato and increases per acre yield of potato by using modern production techniques.
12. The purchase rate of white onion of Jain Irrigation

Company was Rs. 671 / Qt. in 2006-07, which reduced upto 500 per quintal in 2010-11. So it is suggested that Jain company should increases per acre yield of white onion by using modern production methods and paid maximum purchase cost to farmers.

13. It is observed that on an average per acre yield of selected contracted crops increased by 35.39 percent. So for increase in the agricultural production government should give some intensives to contract farming like providing irrigation facilities, fertilizers and other agricultural subsidies.
14. Only 33 percent selected sample non-contracted farmers have banking facilities. So it is necessary to provide more loans to farmers through banking and free them from cultehes of moneylenders.
15. The positive feature of model agreement in protecting the interests of farmers is that the loans and advances facility increased by sponsors due to contract farmers to cover higher cost of variable inputs.
16. Under unfavourable climatic conditions, the quality of farm produce cannot be maintained or the whole crop may fail. So it is suggested that the government should provide crop insurance scheme effectively to farmers on cheap rates.

BIBLIOGRAPY

BOOKS AND REPORTS

1. Burch, D., Rickson, R.E. and Lawrence, G. (1996), Globalization and Agri-Food Restructuring Perspective from the Australasia Region, Avebury, Brookfield (USA).
2. Clapp and Roger A., (1994), "The Moral Economy of the Contract in Living Under Contract", eds Peter D. Little and Micheal J Watts, The University of Wisconsin Press, Wisconsin.
3. Chandy, K.T. and Tyagi, O.S. (1998), *Future of Farming in India: Contract or Cooperative Farming,* Indian Social Institute, New Delhi.
4. Datt and Mahajan(2012) *Indian Economy.* S. Chand and Company Ltd., New Delhi.
5. Davis (1979), "Property without Power: A Study of the Development of Contract Farming in the US", Ph.D Dissertation Cornel University in Little D Peter and Micheal J Watts (ed) *Living Under Contract: Contract Farming and Agrarian Transformation in sub Saharan Africa,* The University of Wisconsin Press, Wisconsin, 1994.
6. Deepika, M.G. and Fasahat, A. Khan (2005), *Corporate Contract Farming in India: A Review of Concepts and Issues,* Reference book on Corporate Agribusiness-Concepts and cases, The ICFAI University Press.

7. Deodhar, S.Y. (2001), WTO *Agreements and Indian Agriculture Retrospection and Prospects in Implications of WTO Agreements and Indian Agriculture,* Oxford and IBH, New Delhi.
8. Deshpande, C.S. (2005), Contracting Farming As Means of Value-added Agriculture, Department of Economic Analysis and Research, National Bank for Agriculture and Rural Development, Mumbai.
9. Deshpande, R.S. (2008), *Contract Farming and Tenancy Reforms Entangled without Tether,* Concept Publication Company, New Delhi.
10. Dhaka, J.M. (2009), *Economics of Agricultural Production and Farm Management,* Aavishkar Publishers and Distributors, Jaipur.
11. Dunham, D. (1995), Contract Farming and Export Horticulture: Can Agribusiness Revitalize the Peasant Sector in Sri Lanka? IPS Agricultural Policy Series No. 3, Institute of Policy Studies, Colombo.
12. Eaton and Shepherd (2001), "Contract Farming, Partnership for Growth, FAO Agricultural Services", Bulletin 145, Rome.
13. FAO (1999), "Law and Markets – Improving the Legal Environment for Agricultural Marketing", Agricultural Services Bulletin No. 139, Rome.
14. Government of India (2005), Some Aspects of Farming. National Sample Survey Organization, Ministry of Statistics and Program Implementation, Government of India, New Delhi, Report No 496 (59/33/3).
15. Government of India (2007), Agricultural Statistics at a Glance. Department of Agricultural and Cooperation, Ministry of Agriculture, Government of India, New Delhi.
16. Government of Maharashtra (2002), Economic Survey Report.
17. Government of Maharashtra (2010-11), Economic Survey Report.
18. Grossman, L.S. (1998), *The Political Ecology of Bananas: Contract Farming, Peasants and Agrarian Change in the Eastern Caribbean,* Chaperl Hill and London, University of North Carolina Press.
19. Glover, D. and Kusterer K. (eds) (1990), *Small Farmers, Big Business-Contract Farming and Rural Development,* Macmillan, London.

20. Dhaliwal, H.S., Kaur, M. and Singh J. (2003), Evaluation of Contract Farming Scheme in the Punjab State, Department of Economic, PAU.
21. ITCOT: (2004) Report on Contract Farming, Industrial and Technical Consultancy Organization of Tamil Nadu.
22. Jorger, M. F. Win (2000), "Food Supply Chains from Productivity toward Quality in Fruit and Vegetables Quality: An Integrated View" (ed) Shewfelt L Robert and Bernhard Brucker Technomic Publishing Company Inc. Lancaster.
23. Joy, H. et al. (1999), Managing Risk in Farming: Concepts, Research, and Analysis, Agricultural Economic Report No. 774, USDA.
24. Kiresur, V.R., Patil, S.A. and Vijayakumar, H.S. (2002), "Contract Farming – An Opportunity for Small and Marginal Farmers in the Context of Trade Liberalization", in Ramesh Chand (ed) : *Impact of WTO on Indian Agricultural,* AERA, New Delhi.
25. Mathur, K. and Vinayagam, S.S.(2011), Training Programme on Agricultural Marketing Management for Officials of Maharashtra Agriculture Competitiveness Project (MACP), Government of Maharashtra, CCS National Institute of Agricultural Marketing, Jaipur,.
26. Little P.D. and Watts M.J. (1994), *Living Under Contract, Contract Farming and Agrarian Transformation in Sub Saharan Africa,* The University of Wisconsin Press Modison.
27. Nagraj, N., Chandrakanth, M.G. and Gacy, C.P. (2008), Contract Farming and Related Issues. Department of Agricultural Economics University of Agricultural Sciences Bangalore.
28. Rajmanohar, T.P. and Kumaravel, K.S. (2006), *Contract Farming In India An Introduction,* ICFAI Books, ICFAI University Press, Agartala, Tripura.
29. Roy and Poul E. (1963), *Contract Farming,* The Interstate Printers and Publishers Inc., Denville, Illinois.
30. Sadhu and Sing (2007), *Fundamentals of Agricultural Economics,* Himalaya Publication House, Mumbai.

31. Sahay, B.S. (2000), *Supply Chain Management in the 21st Century*, Macmillan India Ltd., Delhi.
32. Sarkar, A.N.(2003), Techno-Economic Feasibility Study on Contract Farming in Maharashtra, Vaikunth Mehta National Institute of Cooperative Management Pune.
33. Shiva, V. (1991), *The Violence of the Green Revolution: Third World Agriculture Ecology and Politics*, Zed Books, London.
34. Sharma, Premjit (2007), *Contract Farming*, Gene-Tech Books, New Delhi.
35. Shrikant, S. K. (2002), Agricultural Development and sources of output Growth in Maharashtra State, Gokhale Institute of Politics and Economics.
36. Singh G. (2003), *Contract Farming in India: Text and Cases*, Oxford & IBH Publishing Co. Pvt. Ltd., New Delhi.
37. Singh S. (1997), Multinational Enterprises and Agribusiness Sector in Developing Economic: A Case Study of Pepsi in India, in K.J. Azam (Ed.), *Economic Liberalization in India*, Implications for Indo-US Relations, Hydrabad, Delta.
38. Singh (2006), Organic Produce Supply Chains in India, A Research Report, CMA, IIM, Ahmedabad.
39. Singh, G. and Asokan, S.R. (2005), "Contract Farming in Ramesh Chand" (Ed) *India's Agricultural Challenges: Reflections on Policy Technology and Other Issues*, Centrad.
40. Sukhpal, Singh (2005), *Contract Farming for Agricultural Development. Review of Theory and Practice with Special Reference to India*, New Concept Information Systems Pvt. Ltd., New Delhi.
41. Sukhpal, Singh (2005), *Political Economy of Contract Farming in India*, Allied Publishers Pvt. Ltd., Mumbai.
42. Singh, S. (2006), Contract Farming for Agricultural Development-Review of Theory and Practice with Special Reference to India,
43. Tasi, Kaye (2006), *Role of Regional Rural Bank in Economic Development*, Abhijeet Publications, New Delhi.
44. Williams, S. and Karen, R. (1985), *Agribusiness and the Small-scale Farmer: A Dynamic Partnership for Development*, West View Press, London.

JOURNALS

1. A Study of Export Potentials for Gherkins (Hybrid cucumber) in Tamil Nadu, Department of Agricultural Economics, Center for Agricultural and Rural Development Studies, Tamil Nadu Agricultural University, 1999.
2. "A Study on Contract Farming to Tomato in Punjab", *Agricultural Marketing,* 42 (4).
3. "Agricultural Contracting. Trading: Autonomy for Risk Reduction", *Amber Waves,* February,2006.
4. "Changing Consumption Pattern in South Asia", In *Agricultural Diversification and Small Holders in South Asia,* P.K. Joshi, Ashok Gulati and Ralph Cummings Jr., (eds.), 2007.
5. Consumption Patterns and Food Demand Projections: A Regional Analysis, Paper presented at the workshop plate to plate to plough, Agricultural Diversification and Its Implications for the small holders, organized by the International Food Policy Research Institute, Asia Office, New Delhi, and the Institute of Economic Growth, New Delhi at New Delhi, September 20-21, 2006.
6. "Contract Farming and Agricultural Diversification in the Indian Punjab: A Study of Performance and Problems", *Indian Journal of Agricultural Economics,* 55 (3), July-September, 2000.
7. "Contract Farming and Contractual Arrangement A Descriptive Analysis", *Southern Economist,* June-2011.
8. "Contract Farming for Agricultural Diversification in the Indian Punjab: A Study of Performance and Problems", *Indian Journal of Agricultural Economics,* 56 (3), July-Sept, 2000.
9. "Contract Farming for Organic Crop Production in India", *Current Science,* Nagpur, Vol.93, No.12, 2007.
10. "Contract Farming in India: Progress and Potential", *Agricultural Marketing,* Vol. XLVIII, No.1, 2005.
11. "Contract Farming in India, Impact on Women and Child Workers", Gatekeeper Series no. 111 IIED London WCIN ODD, U.K.
12. Contract Farming in India, National Center of Agricultural

Economics and Policy Research, New Delhi (unpublished), 1999.

13. "Contract Farming in India: Impact on Women and Child Workers", Gatekeepat Series No. 111 IIED3 London, 2003.
14. "Contract Farming in Potato Production : An Alternative for Managing Risk and Uncertainty", *Agricultural Economics Research Review*, Vol. 18, 2005.
15. "Contract Farming System, Punjab State Policy Issues", *Productivity*, October-December, Vol.44, No. 3, 2003 .
16. Contract Farming, Smallholders and Rural Development in Latin America : The Organization of Agro Processing Firms the Scale of Out Grower Production, World Development, 27(2) 1999.
17. "Contract Farming", News Letter, *IMAGE*, Chennai, AISSUE-17, 2004.
18. "Contract Farming: An Opportunity for Small and Marginal Farmers in the Context of Trade Liberalization", PII, *Agricultural Economics Research Review*, 2002.
19. "Corporate Initiatives in Indian Agriculture", *Indian Management*, February, 2004.
20. "Determinants & Resource Use-efficiency in Popular-based Agro Forestry", *Productivity*, 40 (2), July-September, 1999.
21. "Development of Market Infrastructure for Globalization in India", *Indian Journal of Agricuture Marketing*, Vol. 18(3),2004.
22. "Diversification towards high-value agricultural : Role of Urbanization and Infrastructure", *Economic and Political Weekly*, June 30, 2006.
23. "Food Processing and Contract Farming in Andhra Pradesh: A Small Farmer Perspective", *Economic and Political Weekly*, June 25, 2005.
24. Global Partnership in Poverty Reduction: Contract Farming and Regional Cooperation, ADB Institute Discussion Paper No. 89, 2008.
25. Grower Heterogeneity and the Gains from Contract Farming: The Case of India Poultry. Indian Statistical Institute, New Delhi, June- 2007.

26. Impact of Contract Farming on Income International Food Policy. Research Institute, Discussion paper 00742, 2007.
27. "Increasing the Benefits to Smallholders from Contract Farming, Problems for Farmers, Organizations and Policy Makers", *World Development*, 15 (4), 1987.
28. "India's Agrarian Crisis and Corporate-led Contract Farming: Socio-economic Implications for Smallholder Producers", *International Food and Agribusiness Management Review*, Volume 11, Issue 4, 2008.
29. India's Agrarian Crisis and Small holders Producers Participation in New from Supply Chain Initiatives: A Case Study of Contract Farming, Indian Institute of Management, Ahmadabad, 2007.
30. *Indian Journal of Agricultural Economics*, April-June, Vol. 57, No.2, 2002.
31. Linkages Between Farm and Non-farm sector: Role of Processing of Horticultural Products, NABARD Occasional paper no. 16, National Bank for Agriculture and Rural Development (NABARD), Mumbai, 2000.
32. Linkages with Agriculture-The Experience of the Food Processing Industry, *The Economic Times*, Ahmedabad, 1996.
33. "Multi-National Corporations and Agricultural Development: A Study of Contract Farming in the India Punjab", *Journal of International Development* 14, 2002.
34. "Mode of Operation and Performance of Contract Farming of Cotton Seed in Haryana", *Agricultural Economics Research Review*, Vol. 20 Jan.-Jun, 2007.
35. "National Bank for Agriculture and Rural Development (NABARD)", *News Review*, Jan-March Volume 15, No. 1:56, 1999.
36. "On the Class Location of Contract Farmers in the Kenyan Economy", *Economy and Society*, 15 (4), 1999.
37. "Opportunity for Contract Farming in Banana: A Case Study at Tamil Nadu State", *Agricultural Situation in India*, 2006.
38. "PepsiCo Partnership with Farmers", *Span*, 37 (6) Oct.-Nov. 1996.
39. "Prevailing Practices and Dimensions of Contract Wheat Seed

Farming in Haryana State", *Agricultural Economics Research Review,* Vol. 17 July –Dec., 2004

40. "Reliance Agrotech into Contract Farming", *The Hindu Business Line,* 1997 .
41. "Role and Constraints of Contract Farming in Agro-Processing Industry", *Indian Journal of Agricultural Economics,* 58 (3), 2003.
42. "Role of the State in Contract Farming in Thailand: Experience and Lessons", *ASEAN Economic Bulletin,* 22 (2), August, 2005.
43. Scope of Contract Farming in India, read at a seminar on contractual and cooperative farming held at GAU, Anand, 2004.
44. *Small Farmer, Big Business; Contract farming and Rural Development,* London, Macmillan, 1990.
45. "Small Farmers;An Enlarlaged Species", *Political Economy Journal of India,* 10(142), 2006.
46. "Success and Failure of Contract Farming in Himachal Pradesh: A Case Study of Cauliflower Seed Production", *Indian Journal of Agricultural Marketing,* (19 (2), 2005.
47. "The Private Sector and Rural Development: can Agribusiness Help the Small Farmers?" *World Development*-13, 1985.
48. "Theory and Practice of Contract Farming: A Review", *Journal of Social and Economic Development,* 2(1),2000.
49. "Value addition to organically produced naturally coloured cotton under contract farming", *Agricultural Economics Research Review,* Vol.20, 2007.

WEBSITE:

Agricultural information.com: an e-mail news letter, ISSUE 19,20th December 2001.

Braja, Bandhu Swain, An Evaluation of Constraints of Contract farming System: A Case study of Orissa, www.google.com.

Jain, R.C.A., Regulation and dispute settlement in contract farming in India, www.ncap.res.in

Kulkarni, S. and Grethe, H., Does vertical integration benefit farming community? A comparative study of contract and non-contract farmers in India. www.google.com

Pratap, B., Birtnal, Marketing contract farming work in small holder agricultural www.ncap.res.in/contract-%20 farming/ …. /5.1% 20 pratap %205%20 Brithal, pdf.
Profile of Bejo Sheetal Seed Pvt. Ltd. www.bejoseeds.com
Profile of Jain Irrigation System Ltd. www.jisl.com
Profile of Mahyco, www.mahyco.com
Parmod Kumar, Resources provision, productivity and contract farming : A Case study of Punjab. www.google.com
Phil Simmons, Overview of small holder contract farming in developing countries. www.google.com
Shoja Rani B. N., Globalization and Contract Farming in India Advantages and Problems, www.dspace.iimk.ac.in./bitstream/520/1/6337-647pdf
Sukhpal Singh, Understanding Practice contract farming in India: A small producer perspective. www.google.com